Timpani Tone
and the Interpretation of Baroque and Classical Music

In Memoriam

Cloyd Duff

Whose musicianship, love of his instruments, kindness, teaching, and integrity continue to inspire those who had the rare chance to study with him.

TIMPANI TONE

and the Interpretation of Baroque and Classical Music

Steven L. Schweizer

2010

OXFORD
UNIVERSITY PRESS

Oxford University Press, Inc., publishes works that further
Oxford University's objective of excellence
in research, scholarship, and education.

Oxford   New York
Auckland   Cape Town   Dar es Salaam   Hong Kong   Karachi
Kuala Lumpur   Madrid   Melbourne   Mexico City   Nairobi
New Delhi   Shanghai   Taipei   Toronto

With offices in
Argentina   Austria   Brazil   Chile   Czech Republic   France   Greece
Guatemala   Hungary   Italy   Japan   Poland   Portugal   Singapore
South Korea   Switzerland   Thailand   Turkey   Ukraine   Vietnam

Copyright © 2010 by Oxford University Press, Inc.

Published by Oxford University Press, Inc.
198 Madison Avenue, New York, New York 10016

www.oup.com

Oxford is a registered trademark of Oxford University Press

All rights reserved. No part of this publication may be reproduced,
stored in a retrieval system, or transmitted, in any form or by any means,
electronic, mechanical, photocopying, recording, or otherwise,
without the prior permission of Oxford University Press.

Recorded audio tracks (marked in text with ) and supplemental timpani
parts are available online at www.oup.com/us/timpanitone. Access with username
Music3 and password Book3234. For more information on Oxfordwebmusic.com, visit
www.oxfordwebmusic.com

Library of Congress Cataloging-in-Publication Data
Schweizer, Steven L. (Steven Laurence), 1948–
Timpani tone and the interpretation of baroque and classical music /
Steven L. Schweizer.
   p. cm.
Discography: p.
Includes bibliographical references and index.
ISBN 978-0-19-539555-6; 978-0-19-539556-3 (pbk.)
 1. Timpani—Acoustics. 2. Timpani—Construction. 3. Timpani music—
17th century—Interpretation (Phrasing, dynamics, etc.) 4. Timpani music—
18th century—Interpretation (Phrasing, dynamics, etc.)   I. Title.
ML1036.S39 2010
786.9'3—dc22   2009029968

9 8 7 6 5 4 3 2 1

Printed in the United States of America
on acid-free paper

Preface

The purpose of this book is to provide timpanists with a text exploring the theory and practice of timpani tone production and the interpretation of timpani parts in the symphonic repertoire. More specifically, the book examines the acoustics of timpani tone production and explains how to produce a variety of tones to effectively convey the musical meaning of Baroque and Classical music. In the process, the author argues that the timpani were capable of greater tone production than is commonly supposed and that timpanists need to be much more aware of the tonal capabilities of the timpani in Classical music after 1725. Finally, the author provides the reader with his thoughts on how to interpret Baroque and Classical timpani parts. In so doing, the author pays particular attention to the role that period performance practices, timpani playing style, stick selection, timpani size, articulation, and tone production techniques contribute to interpreting timpani parts during these two musical periods.

This book fills a niche in the timpani repertoire because there is no book or tutor devoted solely to production of tone color and interpretation of timpani parts. In fact, most method books on the market today insufficiently address the production of tone color. These tutors usually discuss the playing fundamentals: legato and staccato strokes, rolling, tuning, articulating passages, ear training, muffling, cross sticking, dynamic contrasts, and negotiating two or more drums. While these skills are necessary to successfully play the timpani, it is equally important to understand how timpanists can use their skills and imaginations to produce the kind of tone that best expresses what he or she feels the music and orchestral context requires. Thus, while timpanists are called upon to rhythmically articulate a passage and play a melodic or harmonic line, the production of tone is equally a part of the timpanist's art. I hope this book will provide the reader one way of looking at how the tonal capabilities of the timpani can be fully exploited. There are few books or tutors that address the interpretation of timpani parts. Fred Hinger's composers' series, *The Timpani Play-*

er's *Orchestral Repertoire* (1982–1986), Gerald Carlyss's *Symphonic Repertoire for Timpani* (2005–2006), Roland Kohloff's *Timpani Master Class with Roland Kohloff* (2007), Jacques Remy's *Symphonies* series (n.d.), and John Tafoya's *The Working Timpanist's Survival Guide* (2004), come to mind. Nevertheless, no book looks carefully at (1) the stylistic context in which composers wrote for timpani; (2) the dynamic relation between the evolution of timpani, sticks, heads, and playing style, on the one hand, and the tonal and rhythmic use of timpani in instrumental settings, on the other; and (3) the impact that playing style has on the interpretation of timpani parts. This book will address these concerns.

While little need be said about the importance of mastering the fundamentals of timpani technique (rolls, the placement of the stroke, muffling, and tuning for example), it is equally important to develop the techniques that will permit timpanists to create the tonal shading they desire—like developing a legato stroke. Creating the appropriate tone requires the development of specific techniques. On the one hand, these techniques often exploit the rudiments of timpani playing that timpanists develop in beginning and intermediate study. For example, timpanists often speak of a legato sound as a broad sound that brings out the darkness or richness of the fundamental, and to get this sound, timpanists talk about using a large, softer stick. On the other hand, when we focus on producing a particular tone, we ask ourselves another kind of question: what technique can I use or develop that will allow me to produce the tone that best expresses what the music demands? In asking this question, timpanists think beyond the fundamentals of timpani playing and stretch their imaginations to develop other techniques that will allow them to elicit the appropriate tone. Thus, tone production requires us to reorient our thinking about playing the timpani: we become concerned with finding the techniques that will allow us to shade a passage in the way we desire.

As most compositions are spiritual creations intending to convey a feeling, an emotional state, or an idea, timpanists are constantly challenged with (1) coming to terms with the fundamental meaning of that music, (2) identifying what tonal shading and articulation is needed to express that idea, and (3) using the techniques that allow the timpanist to convey that musical concept. Music that is mechanically played in expert fashion often sounds stale and meaningless, and more often than not, the sterility of the performance typically comes from three sources. First, the musician doesn't understand the spirit or the meaning of the music. Absent that understanding, it is virtually impossible to play an inspired performance—after all, the meaning is in the music. Second, musicians who are unable to commune with the music—to feel in their hearts what the music is saying, even if they understand what the composer intends to convey—will find it difficult to give a convincing performance. Third, timpanists may understand and feel what the composer intends, but without the proper means to express the spiritual dimension of the music, the timpanist will inevitably fall short of a committed performance. It is the primary task of this book to address this last concern and suggest techniques timpanists can use to express what they understand to be the spiritual dimension of music.

Yet our focus on developing a technique often diverts us from seriously thinking about tone. Developing the techniques to "get around the drums," play staccato and legato, execute effective rolls, play at different dynamic levels, dampen notes at the proper time, and play rhythms accurately are fundamental goals of the timpanist's art. However, to emphasize technique to achieve these goals, without giving due weight to the quality of tone color, is to produce mechanistic timpanists. Given modern technology, one could, with little difficulty, create a robot to play the timpani: it would play rhythms precisely, legatos would sound broad and sonorous, staccatos would be articulate, and crescendos and decrescendos would ebb and flow. Yet we would all agree that the passage would sound mechanical: ruthlessly precise and spiritually meaningless. Our mechanical timpanist would sacrifice the nuances of tone and musical meaning for technique. To emphasize technique to the virtual exclusion of tone production creates a false, technique/tone dichotomy: technique as an end or goal in itself with little attention paid to a deeper understanding of tone production (Duff 1968). We can avoid the tech/tone dichotomy by thinking about tone-technique; that is to say, by developing those playing methods that will permit us to draw the desired tone from the timpani. This reorientation in thinking about our art requires us to be keenly aware of the tone we wish to produce and to develop the techniques to coax that tone from the drum. Further, it requires us to learn the rudimental techniques that will allow us to execute the passages effectively. With this new approach to timpani, the end or goal of the timpanist's art is creating the proper tone and the means to that end is developing the techniques to produce that tone.

While technique is put in service to tone production and rhythmic articulation, so tone production should serve or support the meaning of the music. Meaningful playing requires the timpanist to emotionally understand the music and to convey its meaning to the listener. They do this by shaping their parts (tonally and rhythmically) to support the meaning of the music. Yet interpreting the meaning of music is no easy task. Having an understanding of the musical period, the composer's style, the sound and articulation that the composer wants the timpanist to produce, the purpose or program of the music, and the dynamic synergism of timpanist and music during a performance are all ingredients in understanding the music. Music of the Romantic era places different demands on the timpanists than music of the Classical era. Hector Berlioz expects more tone color and dynamic shading than does Wolfgang Mozart. Jean Sibelius's *Finlandia* might be considered a programmatic piece: music reflecting the oppression, struggle, liberation, and final triumph of Finnish people over tyranny. This mental preconception of the meaning of *Finlandia* is important in defining the kind of sound the timpanist must produce to support the underlying musical meaning. Regardless of the mental preconceptions of the music, how the music makes us feel is the final ingredient in interpreting music. Some music is essentially joyful, like Ludwig van Beethoven's "Ode to Joy" in Symphony No. 9. Other music is fundamentally sad or forlorn as we encounter in the final movement of Tchaikovsky's Symphony No. 6, the "Pathétique." Timpanists are called to marry their interpretation of the music to tone-technique so that the timpanist's part can be played with sensitivity, meaning, and conviction.

This book will be divided into four chapters. The first will discuss the theory of tone color production. It will examine the nature of tone color and the techniques that can be employed to create the color appropriate to the musical passage. The second chapter will examine approaches to interpreting and creating musical emotion. The third and final chapters will explore the interpretation of Baroque and Classical timpani parts, respectively. In these chapters, the author will explore how period style; the evolution of timpani, mallets, and drumheads; the timpanist's playing style; and the application of articulation and tone-techniques to the standard repertoire can be used in effectively conveying the meaning of the music.

I would like to acknowledge the contributions that my spouse, teachers, friends, and students have made to this book. I thank my spouse, Denise Elmore Schweizer (MMM in Organ Performance, Indiana University), for her insights into interpreting J. S. Bach and for her willingness to share her summers with this book. For research support, I am particularly appreciative of Larry Ellis (Director), Sandy Smith, and Cathy Snediker of the Newberry College Library; Joe Henderson, percussionist and Director of Circulation at the University of South Carolina Music Library; and Director Alexa Bartel and staff at the Coker College Library-Information Technology Center. All have been helpful in gaining access to manuscripts, articles, and books used in this text. I thank Sally Beggs, Associate Professor of Music at Newberry College, for advice regarding Bach's performance practice issues. I appreciate Warren Moore's (Ph.D. and percussionist) review and critique of an earlier draft of this manuscript. He provided insightful comments on content and style. I thank John Tafoya (Professor of Percussion and Chair of the Department of Percussion, Indiana University) for his comments on an earlier draft of this manuscript and his encouragement to complete the project. I also thank the anonymous readers at Oxford University Press for their comments and constructive criticism, which strengthened the text and encouraged my efforts to bring my thoughts to a wider audience. I am particularly indebted to the staff at Oxford University Press, Music Books. Norman Hirschy, associate editor, was helpful in the early stages of manuscript evaluation and provided guidance on the companion Web site. I owe a debt of gratitude to him and his staff. I thank Suzanne Ryan, senior editor, for helping me fulfill my dream of making this book available to a wider audience than is possible through my studio and classroom. Madelyn Sutton, editorial assistant, provided professional, thoughtful, and timely advice on negotiating the manuscript preparation, submission, and publication process. I extend my grateful appreciation to her. To Gwen Colvin, production editor, and Julianne Eriksen, copyeditor, I express my deep appreciation for the professional manner in which she and her office handled the copyediting. I remember and thank the timpanists and percussionists with whom I have studied: Cloyd Duff and Paul Yancich of the Cleveland Orchestra, Mark Yancich of the Atlanta Symphony Orchestra, and George Boberg, Professor of Percussion, Emeritus, University of Kansas Department of Music and Dance. I have drawn strength, wisdom, and insight from their instruction and advice. I acknowledge my deep debt to them, but I am ultimately responsible for how I have twisted and turned their ideas about style, interpretation, and timpani tone! I extend my special thanks to Michael Kenyon, Hillary Henry, and Lynna Mills of the Percussive Arts Society; they provided Cloyd Duff's picture used in this book. Finally, I thank fellow percussionists and students who have challenged me to become not only a better teacher, but also a more sensitive, nuanced timpanist.

Contents

Symbols and Markings   xiii
About the Companion Web Site   xv

1 Theory and Practice of Timpani Tone Production   3
2 Musical Interpretation and the Timpanist   35
3 Interpretation of Baroque Music   61
4 Interpretation of Classical Music   95

Appendix: Discography   169
Notes   173
References and Resources   179
Index   189

Symbols and Markings

The symbols and markings used in this text and on the companion Web site are cited above. For a fuller description of bounce strokes and intensifying notes and rolls, see chapter 1 ("Theory and Practice of Tone Production").

About the Companion Web Site

www.oup.com/us/timpanitone

Oxford has created a password-protected Web site to accompany *Timpani Tone and the Interpretation of Baroque and Classical Music*, and the reader is encouraged to take full advantage of it. With the author at the timpani, he demonstrates and describes the fundamentals of timpani tone discussed in the book. Hearing what the author describes in the book will deepen the reader's understanding of timpani tone and the text. Audio examples available online are found throughout the text and are signaled with Oxford's symbol ⊙. Equally helpful are thirty PDFs of timpani parts extensively analyzed in the text. Fully marked by the author, the timpani parts apply the principles of timpani tone, articulation, and interpretation discussed in the text. Timpani parts available online are found throughout the text. Readers may find the requisite username and password on the copyright page.

Timpani Tone
and the Interpretation of Baroque and Classical Music

1

Theory and Practice of Timpani Tone Production

Every instrument has its own tone color or timbre. The tone color of the trumpet is so much different from the clarinet that we are able to easily tell the difference between them. Like the trumpet and clarinet, the timpani have their own tone color. Acoustically, the fundamental and the distribution of partials above the fundamental determine not only the pitch, but also the timpani's tone color. All brands of timpani on the market today share a common physical construction that permits them to sound like timpani. However, variations in bowl construction, hammering, bowl composition, weight, and physical support produce timpani with different acoustical characteristics, hence, different tone color. Some timpani, such as Walter Light timpani with semiflat bottom bowls, tend to emphasize the upper partials or frequencies relative to the audible fundamental (the octave above the true fundamental). Walter Light timpani tend to blend with the ensemble, that is, they do not have a compact, dark fundamental that drives its way through the orchestra (see figure 1). Adams, Schnellar, and Ringer timpani emphasize the lower partials over the upper partials. Thus, they have a very strong, dark fundamental and lack the acoustic translucency of Light drums. Clevelander timpani have a strong fundamental and an extended ring that gives them a strong presence in the ensemble. There is much speculation over why various brands of drums sound different. This timpanist suspects that quality of construction, materials, weight, bowl size, and most important, bowl shape account for the variations in tone color between different brands of timpani.[1]

The Timpani

Differences in the tone production of various brands of timpani are very important to timpanists: careers and "schools" are built upon these differ-

Figure 1. Walter Light Dresden Timpani.
These Mark XI timpani have an apple-
or semiflat-shaped bowl.

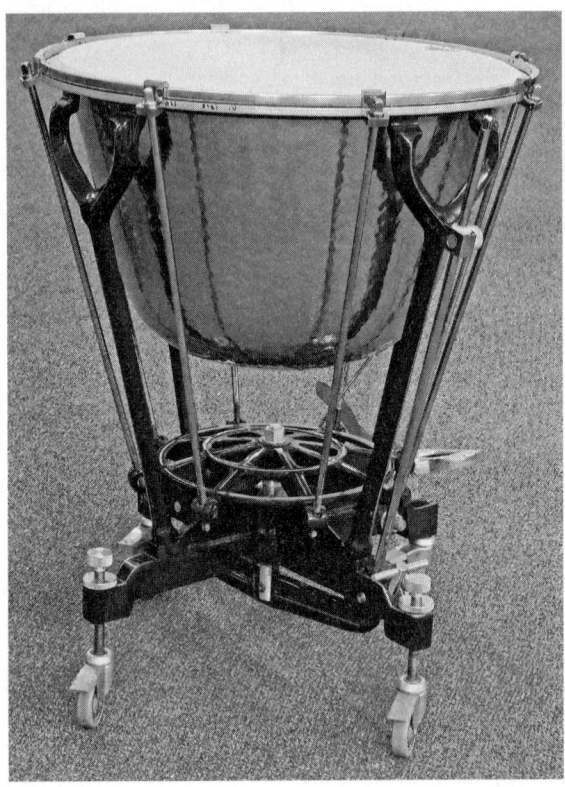

ences. When considering the sound the timpanist wishes to project, the most important decision concerns the brand of timpani to play. Perhaps it is an oversimplification, but the sound of the timpani range between those that tend to be more translucent and those that have a darker, core sound. Light timpani with semiflat bottom bowls blend with the orchestra. The sound is more transparent and brighter in color, it has a general presence, and it is less articulate or percussive. Ringer timpani produce a tone that has a much stronger fundamental, the tone tends to be darker in color, and single strokes sound more articulate or percussive. Other timpani (Clevelander, Adams, Goodman, Ludwig, Hinger, and Yamaha, for example) have acoustical characteristics that range between these two extremes. The choice of timpani is determined by the extent to which the timpanist wishes to play a darker or translucent sound—whether the timpanist wants to blend more with the orchestra or to project a darker, even soloistic, sound. Several factors condition the selection of drums: orchestral repertoire, the orchestra's size, the conductor's preference, ensemble, and auditorium acoustics. For example, in orchestras playing more Classical era music, a timpano producing greater acoustic transparency fits the music supporting norms of instrumental balance and clarity. Timpanist Cloyd Duff, principal timpanist of the Cleveland Orchestra under George Szell, once told the author a story of how Szell pulled him aside early in Duff's career and asked him to play his drums with a variety of sticks, in a variety of ways. After Duff's demonstration, Szell told Duff what sound he preferred. While not all conductors have the penetrating, orchestral vision of Szell, this case demonstrates how factors external to timpanist preference can affect the choice of timpani, playing style, and stick construction.

The choice of timpani both frees and challenges the timpanist. On the one hand, the timpani liberate timpanists to create the sticks and to develop the tone-technique that help them play the part in a meaningful way. As described below, each brand of timpani has an inherent, natural color. That color is brought out by the proper sticks and playing technique. Through experimentation and critical listening, the timpanist quickly learns what type of stick best elicits the color and articulation of their timpani. Some sticks stifle the tone, restrict the projection of sound, or produce a poorly focused fundamental: in short, the mallets don't sound good! Adopting the appropriate sticks liberates the natural sound of the timpani and frees the timpanist to explore the tone-techniques needed to meet the demands of the music. On the other hand, a particular brand of timpani provides some challenges. Drums that have a translucent sound do not lend themselves easily to playing particularly dark passages requiring awe-inspiring presence. Therefore, the timpanist must finesse the part by using darker sticks or by playing in a heavier manner. The opposite is true for drums that have a fundamentally dark color: additional effort must be exercised in "lightening up" the color of a dark sound when a brighter sound is demanded. But generally speaking, a naturally darker drum will produce a darker tone than is possible with a drum that has a brighter and transparent sound, and conversely, a brighter drum will produce a brighter sound than is possible with a naturally darker drum. Timpanists are challenged to build sticks that will (1) bring out the natural color of the timpani, (2) give them a palette of tone color that they can draw upon in shading their parts, and (3) provide the needed articulation.

Acoustics of the Timpani

In the last quarter of the twentieth century, considerable advances have been made in understanding the acoustics of the timpani. Thomas Rossing and his associates' analysis of musical acoustics of the timpani build on the scholarship of Robert Lundin in his *Objective Psychology of Music* (1953) and Lord Rayleigh's *The Theory of Sound* (1929). Rossing and his associates map the harmonics of the timpani and in so doing give timpanists a greater understanding of timpani acoustics (Rossing 1982). While his studies do not specifically address the impact that different size and weights of mallets have on timpani tone color, Rossing demonstrates that the location on a head where a stroke is placed shapes the harmonic structure and color of the corresponding sound (Rossing 1982, 178). Experience confirms that the playing spot; the weight of the mallet; the outer and inner mallet covering; and the size of the mallet head affect tone color.

What are the acoustical characteristics of the timpani? The timpani have a discernible pitch and a unique tone color because a stroke placed on the drumhead produces a fundamental or principle pitch and a distinctive series of harmonic overtones or partials. The overtones are *typically* a fifth, sixth, octave, and tenth, and twelfth above the principle tone (Rossing 1982, 174–176; 2000, 8; 1998, 595–598). Because a circular membrane does not produce a definable pitch, why do the timpani do so? Rossing and others confirm that the bowl, head stiffness, and the surrounding air mass coaxes certain inharmonic frequencies into an ordered set of partials (typically the fifth, sixth, octave, tenth, and twelfth), making the timpani a pitched percussion instrument. The mass of air inside and outside of the bowl accentuates the lower partials. The tension on the drumhead emphasizes the upper partials (the fifth and above). The bowl separates the upper and lower parts of the head, decreases the decay of the partials, and accentuates the principle frequency (Rossing 174–175; 2000, 6–12; 1998, 584–599). For an explanation of timpani tone, visit the companion Web site. ◓

Donald Sullivan provides scientific evidence that the decay of timpani sound impacts timpani tone. After placing a stroke on the drum, the principle tone decays quickly, but the fifth, octave, and tenth remain stronger. This results in the impression that the tone of the timpani becomes brighter. For example, Sullivan strikes an F on a 32-inch Ludwig timpani with a medium stick. At the moment it is struck, the fundamental tone (approximately 100 Hz), fifth (150 Hz), and octave (200 Hz) are strong. However, after 2.5 seconds, the strength of the fundamental is much weaker relative to the other overtones. Thus, at 2.5 seconds the tone is not as dark as it was when it was first struck. Rossing independently discovers that the principle and the fifth decay faster than the other partials (Rossing, 2000, 12).

Does the shape of the bowl influence timpani tone? Timpanists and scientists dispute this. Most timpanists I know say that the shape of the bowl affects timpani tone. Henry Taylor concludes that hemispherical bowls are not particularly resonant and shallow hemispherical bowls produce a "short" note. Hemispherical bowls with straight sides near the bearing edge and apple-shaped bowls produce a satisfactory pitch and tone (Taylor 1964, 20–22). Similarly, the American Drum Company, manufacturer of Walter Light Dresden Timpani, describes semiflat or apple-bottom bowls as slightly dark with excellent resonance, flat-bottomed bowls as quite dark, and parabolic bowls as very bright (American Drum, 2009). In his scientific studies, Rossing claims that the shape of the bowl has no effect on timpani sound. However, experience trumps science in this case.

In the following analysis, the author used AudioXplorer software and a Sound Professionals SPSM-13 microphone (20–20,000 Hz) to map timpani acoustics. The microphone was placed two feet from the drum. The drum was struck (normally in the playing spot) and the sound recorded for ten seconds. The sound was analyzed at one second after striking the drum. Using AudioXplorer software, the author analyzed the sound and created a spectrograph. The Y-axis measures the strength of the partial relative to other partials, and the X-axis displays the frequency in hertz.

Mallet construction affects timpani tone and articulation. Mallets that are heavier with larger and softer mallet heads are more colorful than timpani mallets that are lighter with smaller and harder mallet heads. This is graphically depicted in the following two spectrographs. Examine the spectrograph of a c played with a heavier, softer legato mallet (see figure 2). Notice the strength of the principle and the ordered set of harmonic overtones. In the next spectrograph, a c is played with a lighter, harder staccato mallet (see figure 3). Notice the similarities and differences. In each case, the principle and harmonic partials are clearly present and this gives the timpani their distinct pitch and tone color. However, the staccato stick differs in two ways. First, there are more nonharmonic partials present (between 138 and 200 hertz and throughout the frequency spectrum). These frequencies are also stronger relative to the harmonic partials. Together, these acoustical characteristics give the staccato stick a brighter color and a more articulate sound. It is brighter because of the presence of the upper partials (a fifth, an added sixth, and higher partials). The sound is more articulate due to the presence of nonharmonic partials that give the sound a slight thud.

Timpanists are also concerned about the sound produced by a loose (slack) and tight head. Many timpanists prefer to play in the upper register of a timpano—roughly the upper third of the head. They believe this gives a more focused sound. Acoustical analysis bears this out. The next two spectrographs represent the acoustical characteristics of two sounds: a c and a G played on a 29-inch Walter Light Dresden timpano with a medium mallet. In the first spectrograph, the c has a strong principle tone

Figure 2.   Spectrograph of a legato mallet

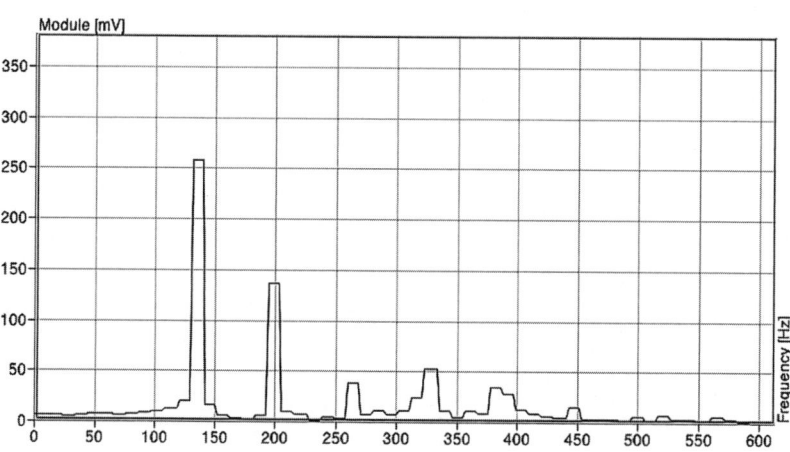

Figure 3. Spectrograph of a staccato mallet

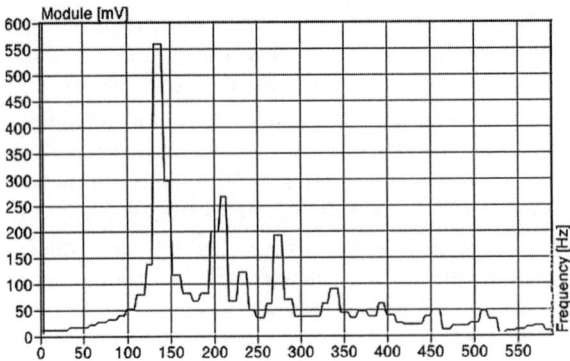

and an ordered set of harmonic partials with a minimum nonharmonic partials (see figure 4). This gives the c a sharp focused pitch and a resonant sound. However, the G is less defined (see figure 5). The harmonic partials above the fifth are less well defined and as a result, it loses tonal clarity. Clearly, playing on a tighter head brings with it greater pitch definition and more color.

Timpanists know that muffling the timpani with a mute produces a more staccato sound. In conducting an acoustical analysis, a 29-inch Walter Light Dresden timpano was dampened with a leather mute placed in the center of the drum. The strokes on the dampened and unmuffled timpani were placed in a legato fashion using staccato mallets. The acoustical characteristics of the muted and muffled drum are displayed in figures 6 and 7. The spectrograph of the unmuted drum (see figure 6) demonstrates the characteristics of a typical brighter stick: a principle tone with a well-ordered but brighter set of harmonic partials. The muffled drum provides

Figure 4. Spectrograph of a note played in a tight head

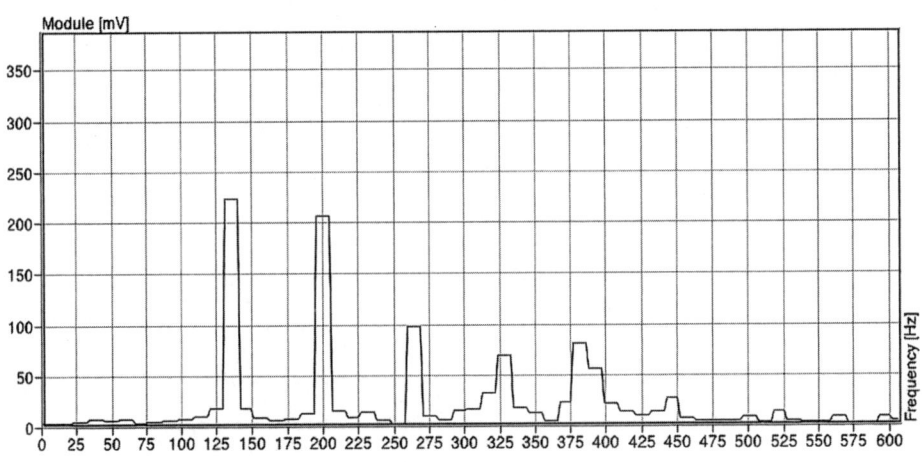

8   *Timpani Tone and the Interpretation of Baroque and Classical Music*

Figure 5. Spectrograph of a note played on a loose head

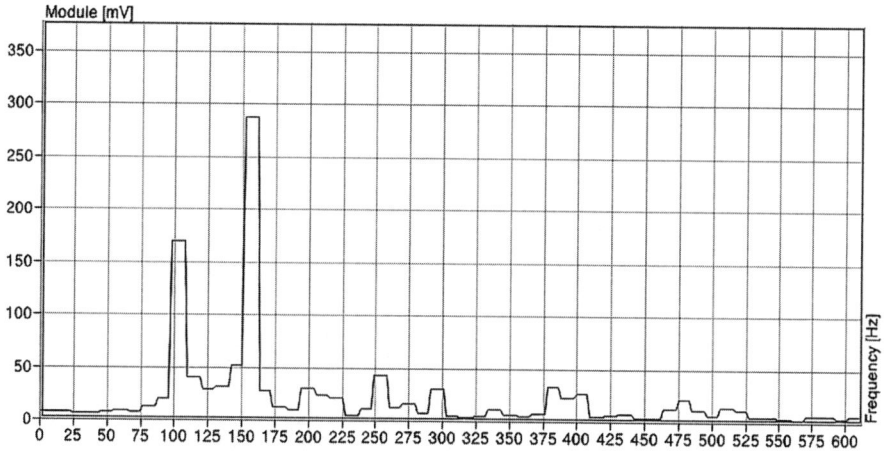

a much different picture (see figure 7). First, there are many nonharmonic frequencies that give a darker and percussive sound. Particularly noticeable are those frequencies below 132 hertz. Second, the upper partials (the first octave and above) are almost entirely muffled. This has the effect of destroying the sense of pitch and the brightness of the sound. The overall effect of muffling a drum is to produce a sound that is darker and that has less pitch clarity. It simply sounds more articulate or pointed.

Timpani Mallets

Timpani mallets are critical in bringing out the natural tone of the timpani and in expanding the tonal capabilities of the timpani. Not all sticks bring out the natural, tonal characteristics of a timpano. One general purpose mallet may sound very good on one brand of timpani but not on another

Figure 6. Spectrograph of an unmuted drum

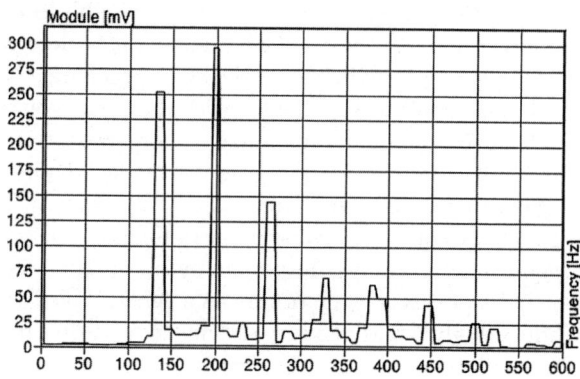

Figure 7. Spectrograph of a muted drum

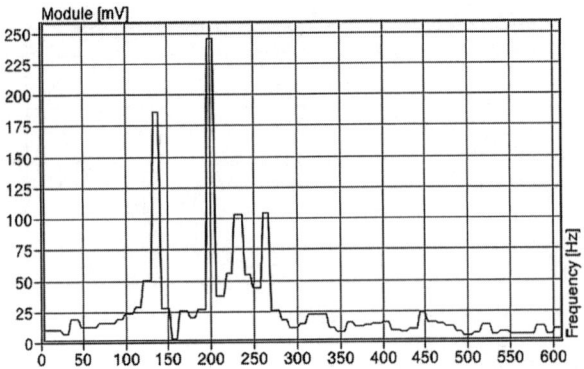

brand. It may bring out the fundamental tone very well on one drum, but it might produce a tone that is too weak or lacking conviction on another drum. A legato mallet might bring out the dark richness of the timpani on one brand of drum but stifle the sound on another brand. Therefore, it is critical that timpanists choose (or preferably build) timpani sticks that bring out the tonal characteristics of their drums. The critical elements in selecting or building timpani sticks include the weight of the sticks, the size of the mallet head, the composition of the core, and the mallet covering. See figure 8 for a picture of the mallets discussed in this book.

In building sticks, there are two principles to keep in mind. First, drums that naturally produce darker tones should be played with sticks that produce a darker color and drums that naturally produce a brighter sound should be played with sticks that produce brighter colors. As different brands and bowl shapes produce different sounds, match the mallet to the drum. Second, a variety of sticks should be made to bring out a variety of tone and articulation (from bright to dark and from legato to staccato). Thus, one builds sticks that elicit the tone quality of the instrument; within the tonal parameters of the stick, one constructs a variety of sticks that give the needed articulation and tone color. Stick weight is important in producing the articulation and tone color one needs. Lighter sticks (sticks that weigh less) produce a brighter color with fewer audible lower partials, and heavier sticks tend to emphasize the fundamental, with fewer audible upper partials. For example, to bring out the blending character of Walter Light drums, timpanists can use a lighter stick than one would use on a Ringer drum. However, in building sticks that will give progressively darker sounds, the timpanist should develop a variety of mallets that become progressively heavier. In so doing, timpanists create a variety of sticks that give them the ability to produce a wide range of tones.

Stick weight is not the only determinant of tone quality; the diameter of the mallet head (core) is also important. As a general rule, smaller mallet heads produce higher partials, less resonance, and diminished principle tone. The result is that these mallet heads sound more percussive and

Figure 8. Timpani Mallets. The author's mallets discussed in this text. B. Hard. Y. Medium Hard. R. General Purpose or Medium. W. General Purpose Warm. G. Legato. P. Large Legato. 5. Mozart Mallet. 7. Large Articulate.

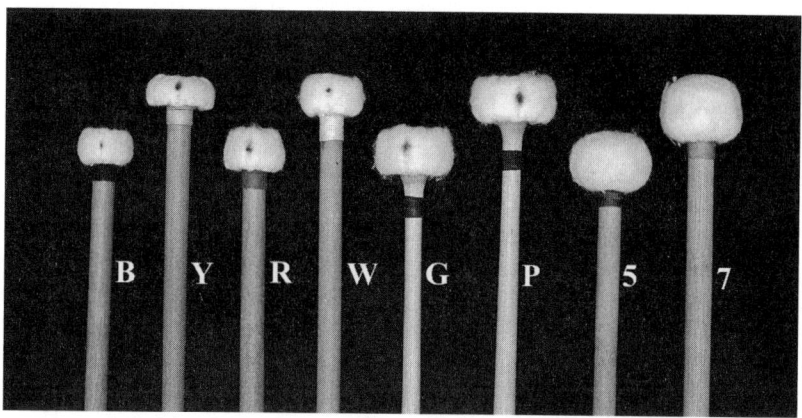

bright. The converse is true with larger mallet heads: they produce a stronger fundamental, are more resonant, and create fewer audible upper partials. To produce a variety of tones and articulations, it is wise to craft sticks with different-sized heads. In many sets of sticks on the market today, the diameter of mallet core becomes progressively larger, permitting each successive stick to produce a somewhat darker sound. As the weight *and* the diameter of the core increases, the sticks progressively get darker. These two physical characteristics of the timpani stick mutually reinforce each other.

The composition of the stick has an important impact on the color of the mallet. Today sticks are made of many materials. The most common shafts are made from maple (or other hard wood) and bamboo. However, Fred Hinger produced an aluminum mallet. On the whole, wood sticks are heavier than bamboo and aluminum. This makes wood sticks more useful for players who want to produce a darker tone, because (as noted above) heavier sticks strengthen the lower partials and produce a darker tone. For those who wish a translucent blending sound, bamboo (or aluminum) sticks might be the mallets of choice. Bamboo sticks tend to produce more upper partials—making the stick sound brighter. There may be very good reason to mix and match wood and bamboo sticks. On the one hand, a staccato sound typically emphasizes upper and nonharmonic partials; thus, a bamboo stick—that elicits upper partials—could be the stick of choice. On the other hand, a legato stick—that brings out the fundamental and lower partials—could be made from a wood stick. Thus, a timpanist could have a number of sticks with more staccato or brighter sticks made of bamboo or aluminum, and legato or darker sticks constructed from wood. But there is no reason why bamboo or wood sticks could not be made in differing weights; and some manufacturers make no significant distinctions between the weights of the sticks. They rely on other principles of stick construction (for example, core size, core weight, core composition, and covering) to shape the tone produced by the stick.

Closely tied to stick composition is stick balance. Broadly speaking, sticks can be head-heavy, evenly balanced, or butt-heavy. Head-heavy mallets have the weight or balance point projected forward. The effect of this is to allow the mallet heads to penetrate the drumhead and to produce a deeper fundamental, a point discussed in greater detail below. At the other extreme, butt-heavy mallets project weight more toward the rear of the stick. This stick has a tendency to limit the ability of the mallet head to penetrate the drumhead; this stick tends to produce more upper partials and greater articulation. Balanced sticks represent a golden mean between the color and articulation: they give the timpanist somewhat greater control over the variety of tones this stick is capable of producing. The attentive reader will note that stick balance can be added to stick weight and core diameter to further shape the relative dark or bright character of a stick's sound.

The core material of the mallet is also important in shaping the tone. Examples of materials used for cores include wood, felt, cork, and tape. Wood is the most common core; it elicits the fundamental and a full range of harmonic partials. It is particularly effective with staccato mallets and it gives good articulation. Many general mallets (as opposed to staccato or legato mallets) using wood cores cover it with a very thin strip of felt that warms the sound of the stick. Felt cores are not as hard as wood cores and, on the whole, they produce a warmer sound. Cork and tape mallets ordinarily weigh less than wood and felt. Cork cores elicit more middle and upper partials. This means they do not elicit the darker character of the audible fundamental. The shape, size, and weight of the cores differ. Most cores are either cartwheel or ball (spherical); however, these cores vary in size. Smaller cores tend to be used on staccato sticks and they get progressively larger in order to bring out progressively darker tones. In general, heavier cores produce more tone color than lighter cores; thus, heavier cores (whether wood or felt) can be used effectively in legato mallets where a broad, resonant, and colorful tone is needed.

The type of mallet covering is also very important in shaping mallet tone. Today, the common coverings include German (soft) felt, American (hard) felt, linen, and chamois. As we have seen above, the materials used in building mallets help determine a stick's ability to draw a particular tone from the timpano. The same holds true for the kind of material that covers the core. The history of stick making, in no large part, reflects the desire of timpanists to craft sticks that produce different articulations and a variety of tone color. The history of timpani mallet construction suggests that the earliest sticks were made from wood and ivory. Chamois, wool, and leather was added in the eighteenth century to soften the impact of a wood or ivory stick on the timpani head. Berlioz pioneered the sponge stick that later led to the use of piano felt: a material lending itself to a greater variety of tone color and articulation. Today, felt and linen covers many sticks. Linen-covered sticks tend to produce much more articulate sounds with an emphasis on higher partials. This covering fitted on cartwheel sticks tends to be used on thicker or sluggish timpani heads. When compared to felt mallets, these sticks do not produce a colorful tone.

Today, the most common covering is felt (piano felt). Felt is often termed American and German. American felt is woven tighter, is comparatively harder than German felt, and is used to make general and staccato mallets. Because of its tighter weave, it tends to enhance the middle and upper partials; thus, it tends to produce a brighter tone than German felt. Because German felt is less tightly woven, it is softer and is particularly good in producing legato, darker tones. Therefore, German felt is good for producing legato and rolling sticks. In addition to the type of felt, the depth of felt shapes timpani tone. The thicker the felt, the more it dampens the upper partials produced by the core and the more it produces lower partials. Thus, thicker felt (especially German felt) gives a darker sound. Felt that is too thick has a tendency to dampen the tone and should generally be avoided. Conversely, the thinner the felt, the more it enhances the color of the core and the more it produces upper partials. Thus, thinner felt (particularly American felt) is effective in producing staccato sticks or sticks that blend better with the orchestra. Between the core and outer covering, a thin layer of felt can be used to further darken the color of the mallet. In stick construction, thought should be given to the relative advantages of using American felt, German felt, or even linen in shaping the tone and articulation of a particular stick. Obviously, linen or American felt can be used on lighter sticks to produce a more articulate and brighter stick, and German felt can be used on a heavier stick with a larger core to produce a darker, more legato tone.

Once sticks have been made, they can be voiced to further shape the color of the mallet. Voicing is a process of "fluffing up" or "picking" the felt with a piano felt pick or a sewing needle. Felt is picked for three reasons. First, cartwheel sticks have a seam which, when it strikes the timpani head, produces a sharp slap. To eliminate this sound, the seam is fluffed up. This has little effect on the stick's tone color and it eliminates the slapping sound. Second, voicing the felt allows the timpanist to voice the stick relative to other sticks in the set. For example, if a legato mallet needs to be slightly darker than a general stick, additional fluffing will achieve this result. Finally, picking allows the timpanist to match the tones of similar sticks. In the mallet recovering process, sticks often do not sound the same—one sounds more articulate or brighter than the other. Fluffing the brighter stick is one way of matching its tone to the darker mallet. As a general rule, voicing a mallet head makes it sound somewhat darker, more tonal, and less articulate.

Making sticks is an art. Stick building requires an understanding of how weight, mallet head shape, mallet head covering, and the mallet core synergistically work together to produce the kind of tone and articulation that is needed from that stick. For example, a very articulate stick might have a light bamboo handle, a small wooden head, and a very thin American felt covering. A legato mallet might have a heavier maple handle, a larger felt core, and a thicker German felt covering. A general purpose stick might have a medium-weight bamboo or maple handle, a moderately sized wood core, and an American felt cover that would be thicker than the staccato stick(and perhaps thinner than the felt on the legato mallet. In this way mallets can be shaped to elicit the sound the timpanist desires.

In summary, the brand of timpani, the manner in which the mallet is built, and the style of playing and type of timpani head (discussed later) combine to produce the sound that the timpanist wishes to elicit from the drum. The selection of timpani provides the timpanist with a general sound. The sound of the timpani is enhanced by the creation of mallets that bring out the fundamental sound of the timpani, and a variety of thoughtfully crafted mallets give the timpanist the sticks to produce various tones and types of articulation. Stick making is a true art, and making a good mallet requires knowledge of the stick, core, mallet head shape, balance, covering, and weight.

Playing Style

Much attention is given to style of playing. By common agreement, the two fundamental styles are the French and the German, and timpanists use variations on these styles to create the sound they desire (see figures 9 and 10). The American style is commonly described as a hybrid French and German grip (see figure 11). Within the German school, variations include the Viennese and Amsterdam schools (Kruse 2003). Each style has impor-

Figure 9.   French grip variation (side view)

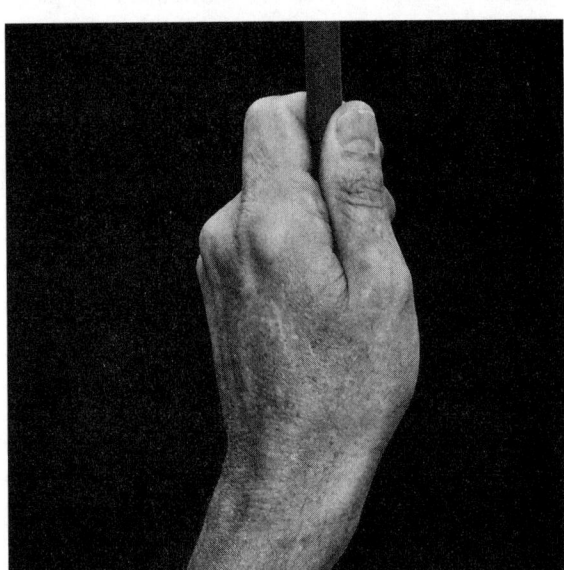

Figure 10. German variation (side view)

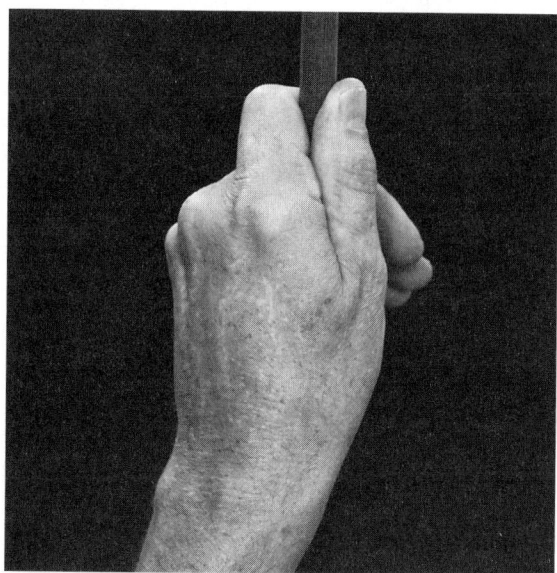

Figure 11. American, "Duff style" variation (top view)

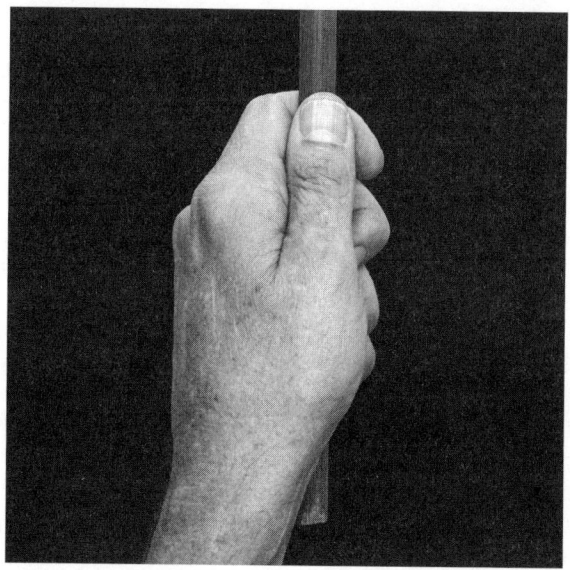

tant implications for the production of tone. In the French style, the stick is commonly gripped between the first joint of the index finger and the pad of the thumb. The remaining fingers lightly ride the mallet shaft or are cupped to let the stick freely traverse the cupped hand. Strokes are made thumbs up, permitting the timpanist to draw the greatest amount of tone from the head. Historically, timpanists playing the French style stand while playing. Practitioners of this approach argue that the French style produces better tone than the German style. In the German style, the shaft of the mallet is gripped between the first joint of the thumb and somewhere along the index finger. The remaining fingers are wrapped lightly around the stick. Strokes are made palms down, which tends to drive the mallet head into the timpano head creating a darker, more articulate sound. That said, some European timpanists choose to play *forte* or *piano* passages with differing grips.[2] Historically, timpanists playing the German style sit while playing. Of course, there are variations to these two styles. Some timpanists, like Paul Yancich of the Cleveland Orchestra, use the French grip, rotating their thumbs inward one-eighth of a turn when playing. And others timpanists use the German grip but they take extra effort to bring the mallet off the head as quickly as possible. This produces a darker, but tonal sound.

In many ways, the selection of style is dependent on the general sound the timpanist wants to project. Timpanists who wish to blend more with the orchestra would want to play on brighter drums, with comparatively lighter sticks, and with a French style. Timpanists who wish a darker sound want to play on darker drums, with comparatively heavier sticks, and with their palms down. In other words, a timpanist's style (combined with the sticks) should help bring out the natural color of the drum. This is not to say that a timpanist playing in the French manner should exclusively play that way. Since turning the thumb over as little as one-eighth of a turn darkens the sound somewhat and playing palms down darkens the sound even more so, there may be times when playing palms down helps timpanists elicit the tone color they need.

Timpani Heads

Timpani heads are important in determining the character of the sound.[3] Calfskin heads have served and continue to serve timpanists well. On the whole, calfskin heads tend to produce a warmer tone than do Mylar or plastic heads. For those wishing a warmer sound, calfskin is clearly preferable to plastic heads. But the skins must not be too thick or too thin. In either direction, they produce a less resonant tone. Of course, calfskin heads are more expensive and more susceptible to fluctuations in humidity and temperature. This practically limits their use to climate-controlled concert halls. Goatskin heads are similar to calfskin; however, they produce a darker sound and are a bit less resonant. At *fortissimo*, Gerald Fromme of the Vienna Radio Symphony Orchestra argues that the goatskin maintains a better tone than plastic heads (Kruse 2003, 17). However, composite heads, now being produced by Remo (Renaissance) and Evans (Strata), approach the warmness of calfskin heads without the trouble. The composite head addressed some problems with the simple Mylar head: thin and brittle sound, poor harmonic overtone definition, and limited resonance (Taylor 1964, 38). What follows represents the experience of the author with Remo and Evans composite heads. The Renaissance head tends to be very warm and produces a sound similar to calfskin. Herbie May, Director of Engineering and Research and Development at Remo, provided me with a spectrograph of the Renaissance head. It visually confirms what a timpanist hears: the Renaissance head emphasizes the lower partials and, therefore, sounds warm. However, the life span of the Renaissance head is shorter than the Evans Strata timpani head; although, recent improvements in the manufacturing process have increased head life and made them nearly equivalent to the Strata head. The Evans Strata is not as warm as the Renaissance head and on Walter Light drums, it produces a strong fifth above the principle. With what appears to be very solid construction, the life of these heads is slightly greater than Remo's Renaissance head. The textured composite covering of the Strata head rubs off much easier than the Remo Renaissance head. The timpanist can "sand" the playing spot of a Renaissance head to smoothen the texture of the playing spot and limit mallet head wear but this is not an option with the Strata head. "Sanding" the Strata's playing spot removes all the composite covering. For those wishing a thinner sound with plenty of upper partials, a regular Remo plastic head will serve the purpose. Finally, Remo and Evans place steel insert rings on their high-end heads. Originally, high-profile insert rings introduced by Remo replicated the tuck of a calfskin-mounted head. This would place the plastic head's flesh hoop further beneath the lip of the bowl than is possible without insert rings. Many timpanists believe that the replicated tuck on plastic heads helps focus the head's pitch and project the sound better. Remo and Evans also offer a low-profile steel insert ring on premium heads. As of this writing, the jury is still out on whether or not the height of the insert ring will materially affect the sound of the head; although, both companies believe that the insert ring (whether steel or aluminum) helps prevent the head from breaking away from the flesh hoop.

Timpanists Cloyd Duff and Vic Firth claim that Remo plastic heads, like calfskin, have definite playing spots—a point that applies to Remo Renaissance heads, too (Duff, n.d.a and n.d.b). As we know, calfskin heads have a backbone that runs down the center of the head and divides the head into roughly two equal halves. Playing directly on the backbone or at the two spots at right angles to the center of the backbone (and near the flesh hoop) produces less tone and resonance; the sound is more percussive. To get the most resonant sound—one blossoming upward and outward when it is played—it is best to play on either the four playing spots (one on each side of the backbone and near the flesh hoop). These acoustical properties seem to be incorporated, unknowingly, in the production of plastic and composite heads. Thus, there appears to be four playing spots on either side of an imaginary backbone. (Remo marks this backbone with a line down the center of the TI series head; however, this is absent on the Renaissance head.) These playing spots tend to sound more resonant and less percussive. Not every one of these four playing spots has the same acoustical properties: one might project better, one might be more tonal, and one might ring better. In replacing drumheads, timpanists should find the one playing spot that best brings out the kind of sound they want. Therefore, selection of the playing spot is important in determining the amount of tone or articulation that is produced in normal playing. For a discussion of finding the playing spot, visit the companion Web site.

The Evans Strata head mimics the tonal architecture of calfskin timpani heads. However, there is no discernable backbone with playing spots on either side of that backbone. While there might be one part of the head that produces better tone color and ring, other parts of the head produce a very fine sound.

Playing the Head

There is consensus among timpanists that the playing spot is normally about three or four inches from the counterhoop—depending on the diameter of the head. This produces the best tone with a centered pitch, rich in partials. As one moves toward the counterhoop or the center of the timpano, the color changes. Playing toward the middle of the drum produces several changes in tone. The tone becomes noticeably darker; it becomes less resonant, loses its pitch definition, and becomes more articulate. The tone brightens as one plays progressively closer to the counterhoop. It also becomes less resonant, loses its pitch definition, and produces a much thinner tone. The timpanist may play on different parts of the head to achieve the articulation or tone color most appropriate to the music.

Timpanists make use of the tonal qualities of the head. Under the most delicate circumstances when a crescendo roll must emerge from virtual silence, some timpanists find it helpful to begin rolling very quietly near the flesh hoop, and as one crescendos, move slowly toward the playing spot. But the timpanist rarely plays near the counterhoop. There are times when it makes sense to move out of the playing spot and play more toward the center of the drum. When a more staccato sound is needed—especially if the timpanist is unable to change to a more staccato mallet—playing more toward the center can give the note a shorter, more percussive sound. Articulate *piano* or *pianissimo* passages can be effectively played by moving toward the center of the drum by about an inch or so—depending on the level of articulation the timpanist wants to produce. For an explanation of how to articulate staccato notes in quiet passages, visit the companion Web site.

The quality of the sound can be crafted by varying the depth of penetration of the mallet into the drumhead. It is possible to play on the top of the head, the bottom of the head, and in between. The purpose of playing different depths is to bring out contrasting tones. Playing on the top of the head produces a tone that creates a strong fundamental pitch and rich partials. But when one plays the bottom of the head, the fundamental and lower partials are emphasized at the expense of the upper partials. Some timpanists object to progressively playing deeper into the head. They believe this technique changes the pitch of the note. In the author's opinion, if the pitch changes, the change is due to a poorly tuned head and not to the penetration of the mallet into the head.

Why should we consider playing the depth of the head? First, we are able to expand the tonal capabilities of our mallets without losing resonance and pitch definition. As discussed above, moving toward the center of the timpano darkens the sound but sacrifices pitch definition and resonance. Playing the depth of the head allows us to produce a dark sound with full resonance and pitch clarity. Second, playing the depth of the head permits us to progressively darken or lighten the sound. There are many times in which we would like to play a roll that becomes progressively darker. The opening section of Mendelssohn's *Fingal's Cave* has a hairpin roll over two bars. The timpanist is asked to mimic the effect of a wave moving toward the shore, falling on the rocks, and flowing out to sea. One way of musically depicting this natural sequence is to begin the roll on the top of the head, progressively play to the bottom of the head, and then progressively retreat to the top of the head. Combined with a crescendo and diminuendo, this technique effectively depicts the movement and power of the sea. Third, playing the depth of the head gives timpanists the tools to more effectively interpret our parts. In Romantic music, the timpanist must go beyond the light, flowing, articulate sound found in the Classical music of Mozart. It becomes important to change the color of the sound to match the changing emotion of the music. For example, there is a long roll sixteen measures before rehearsal 6 in the last movement of Dvořák's *Symphony No. 9* (the "New World"). In measures 4 through 6 of that roll, the music becomes darker and then lighter again. To support this, the timpanist can play on the top of the head at the beginning of the roll, play progressively deeper into the head throughout measure 4, and retreat to the top of the head by measure 7 (see example 1.1).

1.1. Shading tone

The tonal effect of becoming darker and lighter can be used effectively in the fourth movement of Brahms's Symphony No. 1. At measure 375, the timpanist begins a roll on the top of the head, allows the mallet to progressively penetrate the head until the *forzando* at the beginning of measure 376, and then retreats toward the top of the head. In the last two measures of the roll, the timpanist can again play deeper into the head, supporting the progressive darkening sound of the orchestra. In this passage, the effect of darkening and lightening the color of the roll by playing the head is reinforced by the crescendo and decrescendo in this passage. In sum, playing the head permits timpanists to interpret and play the part more expressively.

Playing the Head: Techniques

Playing the head requires the timpanist to master the art of stick control. By controlling the penetration of the stick into the head, the timpanist can change tone. In what follows, it must be emphasized that individual or alternating strokes always "pull the sound" out of the drum. That is to say, the timpanist does not play *into* the head, but *off* the head with a lifting motion. Playing the head requires the timpanist to change the character of the lifting motion so that the stick slowly falls into or rises out of the head. This is accomplished by beginning the roll in a way that Fred Hinger suggests in his book, *Technique for the Virtuoso Tympanist*. In placing the stroke, Hinger refers to an upward resistance that is felt. A timpanist can get a feel for this resistance if he or she grips the stick very loosely, plays a *forte* roll, and barely touches the head (Hinger 1981, 2). The timpanist will notice that while playing *forte*, very little sound is produced as the sticks make minimal contact with the drum. In order to play in this manner, resistance has to be created to pull the sticks away from the head before they penetrate the head too far. How is one able to play progressively deeper into the head? Simply, begin to relax. As the timpanist relaxes, the sticks naturally fall deeper into the head. The challenge for the timpanist is to learn to control the degree of relaxation—and hence the penetration—that is necessary to achieve the desired tone quality.

It is necessary to point out that even when playing a roll in a relaxed fashion, the timpanist is still lifting the stick off the head. The difference between playing in a relaxed mode or one with resistance has to do with using the natural rebound of the head. In playing with resistance, the timpanist is actively (one might say almost consciously) lifting the stick off the head. However, when playing relaxed, the timpanist begins to use the natural rebound of the head to help get the stick off the head, and to assist this rebound, the timpanist provides a certain amount of lift. Thus, relaxing is synonymous with the timpanist putting less lift into the stroke. It is not hard to imagine the effect of relaxing when playing a roll: the process of relaxing allows the sticks to fall deeper into the head, producing a much richer tone.

What is described above refers to the roll; the same principle applies to a legato, marcato, or staccato stroke. It is possible to darken any of these strokes by playing on the top of the head and progressively playing deeper into it. The color will be fuller for the legato stroke because of the darker qualities of the stick. A staccato stick will become darker, but because its nature is to produce a lighter sound with more upper partials, it will not sound as dark as a legato stick. Nevertheless, there are times when the timpanist wants a staccato and a progressively darker sound. For example, consider the first entrance of the timpani in the first movement of Dvořák's "New World" Symphony. While this is a dark, threatening passage that requires the maximum of articulation, getting progressively darker on each of the three notes in measures 10 and 11 produces a profound, disturbing effect on the listener—just what is needed! Allowing the stick to progressively penetrate the head will give an increasingly darker sound. By contrast, the opening four measures of the third movement would not, in my estimation, need to be darkened. Here it is important that this passage be played cleanly with no tonal shading. See the companion Web site for a marked timpani part.

Changing Tone by Changing the Grip

As described above, the timpanist's style has an impact on the sound that is produced. Parts of that style include standing or sitting, the amount of motion the arm and upper body put into a stroke, the construction of the sticks, the choice of timpani, and the kind of grip. Without doubt, the grip is one of the most important factors in tone production. Where the stick is held, the extent to which the hand is turned over, the amount of contact the stick has with the hand, and the balance point of the stick are important factors shaping the tonal characteristics of a stroke. First, how the stick is held is important. The French grip permits timpanists to play more easily near the top of the head, and this produces a clearer, more transparent tone without an overabundance of lower partials. The German grip produces a much darker sound, in part because the stick penetrates the drumhead to a greater extent. A remarkable range of tone can be made by starting a roll with a French grip and slowly rotating the thumbs inward (continuing to grip the stick with the thumb and forefinger). Turning inward even one-eighth of a turn produces a noticeable darkening of the sound. Thus, simply rotating the position of the hands can be effectively used to darken the sound that is produced.

There are two other factors that influence tone production. The first is the degree of finger contact with the stick. Among those who use the French grip, some use very little third, fourth, and fifth finger contact with the stick. This produces a lighter sound—one that emphasizes the upper partials. Cloyd Duff and his students believe that allowing the fingers to "ride the stick" improves the quality of sound. It effectively adds body or color to an already lighter sound without losing its clarity or transparency. Second, where one holds the mallet impacts tone production. Holding the stick with the butt flush with the end of the hand produces a darker sound than holding the stick where the end of the stick protrudes—perhaps three inches from the back of the hand. In the latter case, the sound is very thin and devoid of character. This bodiless sound results from the mallet head playing very much off the top of the drumhead. In the former case, holding the stick at the butt permits the stick to ruthlessly penetrate the head, producing a more articulate, stifled, and darker sound. Somewhere in between these extremes is the place where the best sound is produced for normal playing. Knowing where to hold the stick is important in getting the proper sound for the proper passage. For example, beginning at rehearsal 12 of Maurice Ravel's *Bolero*, the timpanist can progressively bring out more timpani tambre by turning over the hand, wrapping the fingers around the stick, and holding the stick more toward the butt end. By using more arm as the dynamic increases, the timpanist can progressively make each note darker and heavier.

Tightening or loosening the grip on the mallet can shape tone. Slightly tightening the grip between the thumb and first two fingers (or between the thumb and all the fingers) produces a more articulate, brighter, and intense sound.[3] To produce a roll with a lot of tension, the timpanist can tighten up the grip (pinch the stick) and play the roll slightly faster than normal. This can be used successfully in the first long roll in Tchaikovsky's *Overture to Romeo and Juliet*. Begin the roll in a normal way, but as the tension and dynamic in the orchestra builds, begin to progressively pinch the stick and play slightly faster. This produces a sound that is full of tension—just what is needed in this passage. Often it is important to build tension toward the end of a piece so that the music can be harmonically resolved. Composers will write a series of quarter or half notes—each of which can be played with greater and greater intensity until the final note is reached and the music is resolved. To increase the tension in each successive note, the timpanist can progressively pinch the stick and play a little more into the head with each note as the music drives toward the end. For example, in the last movement of Brahms's Symphony No. 1, Brahms builds tension so that the symphony can be resolved in the last measure (see example 1.2). He does this by writing four staccato quarter notes in the four measures (measures 453–456) preceding the final rolled measure. Each of these quarter notes can be played with greater intensity and the final roll can be played with a stinger that announces the final resolution of the symphony. Thus, the timpanist can help create the musical tension that is necessary for the effective resolution of the piece.

1.2. Intensifying individual notes

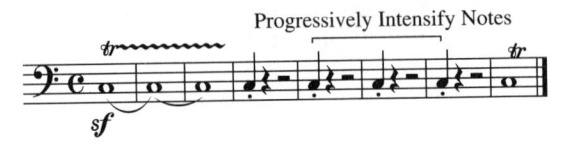

Stick Selection and Tone Production

Timpani mallets are constructed to provide different degrees of articulation and to produce different shades of tone color. Regarding the latter, larger, softer, and heavier sticks produce a darker tone than do smaller, harder, and lighter sticks. However, because smaller, lighter sticks tend to be more articulate, while larger, heavier sticks tend to produce a legato sound, timpanists often find themselves in the position of playing with an articulate stick when the part calls for a legato sound. The primary way of handling this problem is to play the passage with the articulate stick but playing it in a legato fashion. As with any stick, there are limits to which an articulate stick can effectively produce a more legato sound or a legato stick produce a more articulate sound. Nevertheless, the tonal characteristics of any stick can be modified by the timpanist's playing style, grip, and playing the head. Special mallets can be constructed to produce a specific tone. For example, to achieve a very bright, legato sound, a timpanist can fashion a stick that is light, made with a larger head, and covered with softer felt. The stick could be made of bamboo, the mallet core made of cork, and the outside covered with soft, German felt.

The history of stick making is marked by attempts to find materials that will produce the proper tone for the musical context.[4] In the seventeenth century, when the timpani were finding a place in the orchestral repertoire, wooden or ivory sticks were common. However, timpanists soon covered their mallets with other materials to produce better tone. The evolution of tone started when timpanists cloaked their wood or ivory sticks with chamois, cloth, wool, or leather. The second revolution came when Hector Berlioz—a timpanist, composer, and conductor—developed the sponge stick. This was the first real advance in stick construction, permitting a significant improvement in tone quality. Sponge sticks gave way to felt-covered sticks in the late nineteenth and twentieth centuries, and felt sticks remain the most popular stick covering today. They are popular because they can be crafted and picked to produce a wide variety of tones.

Some composers require a lighter or darker stick. On the one hand, Brahms's symphonies consistently call for specific sticks: those that produce a dark and often articulate sound. The first symphony begins with a relentless series of timpani strokes that must be dark and fully resonant, and the first measure of the fourth movement includes a roll that must be so dark and sound so heavy that only a larger, heavier, softer stick will suffice. On the other hand, Wolfgang Amadeus Mozart, writing in a Classical (often happy and playful) style, requires a brighter stick.

Using Physical Gestures to Color Tone

Tone can be shaped by the use of wrist, arm, and body. Most timpanists concerned with tone production emphasize the contribution that the wrist plays in producing a good tone and they teach that good tone production results when the wrist—not the arm—is used to place the stroke. Because the wrist is more flexible and responds quicker to the rebound of the timpani head than the arm, timpanists believe that the primary motion in placing the mallet on the timpano head must flow from a limber wrist. After striking the head, the wrist is used to quickly bring the mallet off the head, allowing the head to "sing" resonantly. Timpanists who use the arm to place the stroke inevitably drive the mallet into the timpano head. Not only does this arm-driven motion create a heavier, articulate sound, but it also dampens the head and it prevents the head from ringing fully and resonantly. Thus, for those timpanists who want their heads to sing, the primary stick action flows from the wrist. However, there are occasions when the use of the arm is important in obtaining the requisite sound.

The arms can be used to enhance tone production in two ways: first, to bring out more color, and second, to articulate a passage more effectively. Bringing the forearm into play is one way of darkening the sound of a stroke. As described above, the heavier the stick, the darker the sound. When the forearm is brought into play, the timpanist is simply adding more weight (the weight of the forearm) to the stroke. When the stick makes contact with the timpano head, it penetrates deeper into the head and brings out the color of the drum, so that the audible fundamental with all its partials is heard in its glory. In the fourth movement of his Symphony No. 1, Brahms begins with a roll that ends on the first beat of the second measure (see example 1.3).

1.3. Full-bodied note in Brahms's Symphony No. 1

The first beat must be darker and heavier than the roll that precedes it. This dark ending is achieved by adding the weight of the arm in the placement of the stroke, and just after the stick reaches its deepest penetration, the wrist is used to bring the mallet smartly off the timpano head—taking advantage of the natural rebound of the head. During this stroke, the timpanist should hold the stick very loosely, and during the rebound, the timpanist should *feel* the mallet recoiling from the head. The result is a fully resonant, heavy, full-bodied legato sound that shakes the soul. This stroke can be used in any place where it is necessary to create a very heavy and resonant sound. Second, the arms can also be used to achieve the maximum articulation of a passage. Holding the stick in the normal staccato manner, the arm moves up and down, one to three inches, with each stroke placed on the head. At the same time, the mallet head is sharply placed and brought off the timpano head. The effect of the arm movement is to allow the mallet head to penetrate the drumhead more than normal and this effectively muffles the overtones, producing a more articulate sound. This technique is very difficult to master since it requires synchronized arm and wrist movement. When performed well, this technique produces the greatest degree of articulation with good tone quality.

Finally, the position of the human body relative to the timpano can shape timpani tone. To permit the sound to leave the drum and stage in an unrestricted manner, the timpanist should get out of the way of the sound. After playing the final note in a passage, timpanists can let the mallet rebound from the drumhead and simultaneously bring the stick up and toward them. This allows the timpanist to (1) let the stick rebound and follow the sound upward, and (2) get the stick away from the drum. In this way the timpanist avoids influencing the flow of the sound. There may be times when it is advisable to keep the sticks near the head, impeding or distorting the sound as it leaves the head. Keeping the mallets and wrists over the drum after playing a part tends to articulate the passage. The body can be used in other ways to shape timpani tone. In *forte* or *fortissimo* passages where a roll ends with a distinct "stinger," or where an articulated note follows a roll, it is sometimes helpful for the entire body to rise and fall *slightly* and *gracefully* so the stick is able to create a distinct, articulate note. In this stroke, the body never leaves the stool; it is simply used to give the stroke more articulation and color. Stopping the roll a little early helps the timpanist prepare to articulate the successive note. Brahms's Symphony No. 1 provides a good example (see example 1.4). At M in the fourth movement (measures 268–273), a half note roll is followed by an eighth note. These eighth notes need to be articulated—especially the last two eighth notes on the low G drum—and the above technique is particularly useful in articulating a low G note. See the companion Web site for a marked timpani part.

1.4. Articulating notes on low drums

Choice of Drums

Timpanists know that the size of drums affects the tone.[5] Compared to smaller drums, larger drums provide more tone color and a fuller, more voluminous sound. A B played on a 29-inch drum will sound much fuller, more colorful, and more resonant than a B played on a 26-inch timpano. Also, the pitch will be focused better on the larger drum because the note is played on a tighter head. As a general rule, if a note can be played on two drums (as the B above), play the note on the larger drum. The note will have a stable pitch and much more tone color. Of course, there are always exceptions. On the one hand, tight heads produce a more articulate sound; if a timpanist needs a legato sound, it might be best to use the smaller rather than the larger drum. Rolls are more difficult to play on a tight head than on a looser head. When rolling on a low A, it makes more sense to execute the roll on a 29-inch timpano than on a 32-inch drum—the roll will sound more seamless and less articulate than one played on the larger drum. On the other hand, if an articulate sound is needed, one may choose to play on a larger drum with a tighter head. A low A is much more articulate on a 32-inch drum than on a 29-inch drum. Finally, there are times in which a timpanist may want to play articulate notes on the larger drum and rolls on a smaller drum with a looser head. Pitching a 29- and a 26-

inch timpani to d would allow the timpanist to play articulate notes on the 29-inch drum and rolls on the 26-inch timpano.

Tone quality is also affected by the synergistic relationship between the size of the drum, mallet weight, and stick composition. To bring out the resonance and tone color of a drum requires the proper stick. A large and heavy-headed stick striking a small (23-inch) drum produces a sound that lacks life, and a very small and light mallet striking a large (32-inch) drum produces a thin sound with less body. A smaller drum usually requires a lighter stick with a smaller mallet head, and conversely, a larger drum responds better to a heavier stick with a larger head. Therefore, if the tone quality, not articulation, is the primary concern in executing a passage, it is necessary to select the right stick to elicit the proper color. However, to get the proper tone, one may need to use a stick that is lighter or heavier than one would use ordinarily for any particular drum. Stick selection for tone production is more critical on the outside drums (32-inch and 23-inch in a four-drum set) than on the inside drums (29-inch and 26-inch). The inside drums respond fairly well to a variety of sticks. It is the outside drums that do not respond well to sticks that are either too large (in the case of a small drum) or too small (in the case of a large drum) for them.

Acoustically, different sizes of timpani have different tonal characteristics. A note played on a larger drum sounds softer than a note played on a smaller drum. Compare a 32-inch drum with a 23-inch drum struck in the upper compass of the range. The larger drum has a more voluminous sound—it has a big, broad, and transparent sound. It has volume and it fills up the musical space well. The smaller drum is much different. Strike it one time and the sound will be more compact, smaller, more focused, and less transparent. When alternatively playing smaller and larger drums, the smaller drum sounds louder than the larger drum (Lundin 1953, 53–58). On the one hand, if the goal is a balanced dynamic between two or more drums, the timpanist must put more energy into the larger drum than into the smaller drum. As a result, the larger timpano will speak at the same dynamic level as the smaller drum. On the other hand, if the goal is to execute a decrescendo descending from a smaller to a larger drum, the timpanist should place a similar amount of energy into each drum, realizing that the audience will hear a natural decrescendo that is a function of bowl size. That said, adjacent timpani, for example 26-inch and 29-inch drums, demonstrate less aural dynamic difference than timpani that are not adjacent (31-inch and 26-inch timpani). In the case of adjacent drums, it is easier for the timpanist to balance the sound between the drums but more challenging to create dynamic differences. For an explanation of choosing the right drum, visit the companion Web site.

Playing In and Around the Playing Spot

There is an optimum playing spot on each timpano that is a function of the diameter of the drum. On smaller drums, the playing spot is relatively closer to the counterhoop than on larger drums. The playing spot, like a sweet spot on a tennis racket, is the point at which the head produces the most resonance, has good pitch definition, produces a long ring, and has the best balance of partials. To find the playing spot on any drum, start to play successive, single strokes beginning at the center of a timpano and moving to the counterhoop. As you do so, you will notice that the tone at the center of the timpano is very percussive, filled with lower partials, and without a defined pitch, resonance, and ring. As you move toward the counterhoop, you will notice that the head begins to sing more, the pitch becomes more discernable, and the head resonates and rings more. When you reach the playing spot, you will notice that the stroke produces a note with good pitch definition, much resonance, a nice ring, and a good balance of partials. As you move closer to the counterhoop, the lower partials are lost—as is the resonance and ring. The sound becomes very thin. By experimenting with each drum, the timpanist will locate the optimal playing spot on each drum. This spot will give the timpanist the best tone production, and this is the area in which over 90 percent of the strokes will be made.

Rolls are most always executed in the playing spot; but there are exceptions. The playing spot provides a continuity of sound that is not found toward the center or edge of the drum. At either extreme, the sound becomes more percussive and defeats the purpose of a roll: to produce sustained sound with a definite pitch. The playing spot also produces a nice balance of partials that gives color to the roll. It also provides full-bodied resonance and pitch definition that is essential in a good roll. However, there are times in which a timpanist may want to roll outside the playing spot. Measured rolls are typically a series of semiquavers played at a quick tempo. To sound more articulate, they may be played between the playing spot and the center; however, so doing reduces the resonant quality of the drum. Where a roll must come from nowhere, some timpanists will begin to play very near the counterhoop and move slowly toward the playing spot as they crescendo. Like a measured roll played toward the center of the drum, rolling between the counterhoop and playing spot sacrifices tone quality. This author has found that timpanists can come from nowhere at the playing spot if adequate attention is given to beginning "inaudibly." Of course, there may be times when playing near the counterhoop is either called for by the composer or for some special, tonal effect.

Some timpanists recommend playing outside the playing spot as a matter of practice or to achieve a particular effect. Erwin C. Mueller has written about the performance practices of Edward Metzenger, one-time timpanist with the Chicago Symphony Orchestra. Mueller reports that Metzenger divides the timpano head into four concentric circles. The innermost circle is around the center of the drum. Moving from the center of the drum, there are three successive playing rings: the staccato, the semistaccato, and the legato rings. The staccato ring is the playing spot closest to the center ring and it provides the timpanist with the greatest amount of articulation, but with less resonance. The semistaccato ring produces less articulation but more resonance. The legato ring, perhaps three to five inches wide, creates the greatest amount of resonance and the least amount of articulation—except for the part of the head closest to the counterhoop. Most of the playing is done in the legato ring; however, the timpanist moves into the semistaccato and staccato rings whenever greater articulation is needed. Where successive notes are played with articulation (a staccato followed by a legato, for example), the timpanist can play the short note in the staccato ring and the longer note in the legato ring (Mueller 1976, 25–29, 277). While Metzenger builds a whole system of playing around the head's differing degrees of articulation and resonance, timpanists can take advantage of the differing tonal characteristics of a drumhead without adopting Metzenger's entire system. For those who want to play in the playing spot most of the time and take advantage of the resonance and pitch definition that come with it, one can move occasionally toward the center to take advantage of the head's greater articulation. This is particularly true when playing articulate phrases at the *piano* or *pianissimo* levels. Playing with articulate sticks in the playing spot often does not produce the articulation that is needed. To achieve a more staccato sound, moving slightly toward the center will produce a shorter note and still provide the timpanist with some resonance.

Finally, the timpano head can be mounted to produce a more articulate or a more sonorous sound. As discussed above, calfskin, Remo plastic, and composite heads appear to have a backbone that runs through them. Playing at 90 degrees from the backbone produces a darker, less resonant, more percussive sound. The most resonant sound is found on either side of the backbone and one of those four playing spots is usually better than the others. For the timpanist who wants the greatest amount of resonance, the head should be mounted in a way that puts the most resonant part of the head near the timpanist. For those timpanists who want to play on a darker and more articulate part of the head, the head should be mounted so that the darkest part of the head is located near the player. Evans Strata heads give a more consistent sound around the head than the Remo Renaissance head. With either head, the timpanist can find the section of the head that produces the most desirable tone (the sweet spot) and mount it near the player.

Tone Producing Strokes

All strokes—staccato, legato, marcato, and bounce—produce a tone and their own degree of articulation. There are a number of strokes that can be used to create the proper kind of tone color and articulation. Staccato strokes are typically made with staccato sticks. The sticks are lightly pinched between the thumb and first two fingers. These strokes are made by smartly snapping the mallet off the head. The effect of the small mallet head and the quick penetration is a short sound: more punctuated, less colorful, and with fewer lower partials. The staccato sound, in addition to sounding short, is also bright. The legato stroke is played with a mallet with a larger head and a much looser grip. Compared with a staccato stroke, the head of the mallet remains on the timpano head slightly longer, and this produces a much broader, colorful sound. Between the staccato and the legato is the marcato stroke. A marcato stroke seeks to produce a marked, sonorous sound. Using a general purpose mallet that is firmly held, the timpanist individually places each stroke into the head as one would drive a nail with a hammer, then rebounds quickly to avoid a lifeless thud. Finally, a full-bounce stroke produces a very heavy, dark sound. Using a large, soft stick, gripping the stick very loosely, and placing the stroke deep into the head, the timpanist catches the bounce of the head—bringing the stick up high. This produces perhaps the largest, broadest, darkest, most soul-shaking sound produced by few instruments. In the opening bars of Brahms's Symphony No. 1, the timpanist can use a bounce stroke to good effect. A variation of the bounce stroke can be used to effectively punctuate notes. This stroke, using any stick, is executed as described above, but the timpanist abruptly stops the stroke when it strikes the drumhead, catches the bounce, and immediately lifts the stick about six inches from the drumhead. The effect is to punctuate the note (make it more staccato) by dampening the resonance of the head but still allowing it to ring.

The Grip

The tightness or looseness of the grip radically affects the sound that is produced by the timpanist. For legato playing, mallets should be held "looser than you can possibly imagine," as Paul Yancich of the Cleveland Orchestra recommends—an approach echoed by timpanist Didier Benetti (Kruse 2003, 30). Gripping the stick loosely and getting off the head produces a broad, singing note that brings out the color of the timpani. By loosely holding the mallet, the mallet head is allowed to sufficiently penetrate the timpano head, resulting in a round, full legato sound. For French-style staccato playing, the mallet is pinched between the thumb and first two fingers, producing a shorter, less colorful sound. By so pinching the stick and snapping the wrist to get the mallet head off the timpano, the stick does not penetrate the head as much as a legato stroke does. This produces a thinner sound, and the listener hears a more articulate, less colorful note. Between holding the stick loosely and tightly, there are varying degrees of looseness or tightness. The timpanist can use the relative looseness or tightness of the grip to shape the articulation and sound to fit the music.

In gripping the stick, another issue centers on what to do with the third, fourth, and fifth fingers. Some timpanists prefer to have these fingers "ride the stick." The fingers are wrapped lightly around the mallet handle and they literally follow the motion of the stick as it moves up and down in the timpanist's hands. The tonal effect of riding the stick is to produce a dark, broad colorful tone. This method captures much of the color of the drumhead and bowl. Other timpanists, such as Saul Goodman, Ernst Pfundt, Heinrich Knauer, and Otto Seele, recommend holding the stick with the thumb and first two fingers—the last two fingers free of the stick except in loud rolls (Goodman 1948, 21, 33; Pfundt 1849, 9; Knauer n.d., 9; Seele 1895, 7). This permits the timpanist to play lighter and, some would say, more sensitively. The effect of playing in this manner is to produce a sound that emphasizes more of the upper partials—the sound is thinner and less colorful.

The German style of playing palms down produces a darker sound than the French style.[6] By varying the tightness of the forefinger-thumb grip and by changing the tightness with which the remaining fingers grip the stick, the sound can be made lighter or darker, more legato or staccato. As described above, there are times in which a timpanist may want to produce an extremely dark, heavy, legato sound. In those cases, timpanists may want to use a German grip, holding the stick very loosely, and executing a bounce stroke. A good example is in Georges Enesco's Rumanian Rhapsody No. 1 (see example 1.5).

1.5. Tonal shading in Enesco's Rumanian Rhapsody No. 1

At rehearsal 19 the composer writes a rather perplexing part. Enesco places tenuto marks over eighth notes—seemingly contradictory. How does a timpanist play an articulated, long note? Part of the answer to this question can be found at rehearsal 12; he puts tenuto marks over dotted quarter notes and asks the timpanist to play heavily. The tenuto marks indicate that he wants a darker, heavier sound. The other part of the answer to this question takes into consideration the musical context at rehearsal 19: Enesco calls for a very heavy, dark, somewhat articulate orchestral sound. Given these two clues, it is clear that Enesco wants the timpanist to produce a very dark, articulate sound. To execute this part, the timpanist can use a larger, heavier, more articulate stick, play palms down, hold the stick very loosely, and use a bounce stroke. This produces a very heavy, dark, somewhat articulate sound that is perfectly shaped to the musical context. Finally, beginning at rehearsal 19, the articulated eighth notes beginning each phrase can be played in staccato fashion. This produces a very sharp, dark, big sound that supports the darker orchestral sound. The tenuto-marked notes are played very broadly. See the companion Web site for a marked timpani part.

Psychological Openness to the Music

Serious music, and especially orchestral music, has a unique ability to convey deeper and more varied emotions than other musical forms (Bloom 1988, 68–81). The canon of serious music reaching back to ancient Greece is filled with emotion. To most composers, the musical pallet gives them the means to express various emotions. Anger is ferociously released in the opening lines of Beethoven's Symphony No. 9 and pathos in the second movement of his Symphony No. 7. Utter hopelessness fills the beginning measures of the fourth movement of Tchaikovsky's Symphony No. 6. Joy animates the strains of the chorale in Sibelius's *Finlandia*. While timpanists might disagree with the specific emotion that the composer is trying to convey, there is little doubt that much serious music attempts to convey the feelings, often nuanced, that are part of the human spirit.

The timpanist's challenge is to open his or her soul to the music, to be moved by it, and to use timpani technique to shape the part to convey the emotional meaning of the piece. The timpanist must first be open fully to the music and then the timpanist must fully submit to it. Opening oneself to the music involves (1) clearing one's emotional state of all contending emotions or feelings, and (2) allowing the music to excite the timpanist's emotions. Clearing the emotional pallet involves purging the musician's soul of all emotions that may prevent him or her from feeling the music. For example, all of us have at one time or another felt feelings of anxiety or nervousness. The presence of anxiety is a major impediment to emotionally capturing the spirit of the music. Sublimating anxiety, that is, pushing it into the unconscious, can be useful if emotions are not entirely purged. However, sublimated emotions often creep into the timpanist's sound: for example, the timpanist may unconsciously grasp the mallet too tight. Percussionist John Beck takes these ideas a step further. If the timpanist is angry, fearful, or passive, the timpanist is likely to play barbarously, timidly, and insensitively. Playing well requires the timpanist to be confident, alert, and sympathetic to the music (Papastefan 1978, 87). Thus, clearing one's emotional pallet allows the music to penetrate the musician's soul. The soul is opened, and the timpanist is relaxed and observant. Once the emotional pallet has been cleared. then the music can seep into the soul and stir the soul in ways that help the musician understand the music and effectively play the part.

Once the timpanist has opened his or her soul to the music, the timpanist must submit to the music. In submitting to the music, I simply mean that the timpanist should develop an understanding of the meaning of the music the composer wishes to convey and then find the techniques that will permit the musician to express the composer's intentions. Studying the score, listening as the conductor crafts the sound of the orchestra, listening to recordings, appreciating the performance practices of the period in which the music was written, and understanding the composer's style can help the timpanist develop a meaningful vision of the music. This is not to say that the musician slavishly replicates some abstract notion of the part played. Rather, the timpanist marries the music (the object) and the timpanist's understanding of the music (the subject) and this marriage constitutes one's subjection to the music. In this subjection, the performer uses all facets of his or her art to achieve a personal, idiomatic, dynamic interpretation of the music. Finally, the timpanist must use the tone production techniques to produce the sound required by the music and interpreted by the conductor. Learning to play gaily, tragically, angrily, happily, or joyfully requires the timpanist to develop the techniques and approaches to playing the drums that will permit the musician to support the meaning of the music. It is at this point that playing the head, exploring various forms of articulation and musical punctuation, and choosing the appropriate sticks and drums become important.

The Theory of Contrast

The theory of contrast is an approach to playing the timpani that addresses a significant challenge every timpanist faces: the timpani are not instruments that lend themselves to evoking a wide range of emotions and articulations. A violin can play very sadly or joyously. A great violinist can make a violin "weep." The trumpet is capable of producing shorter notes than a timpano. A series of sixteenth notes—played with good tone quality—can be executed much more effectively by a trumpeter than by a timpanist. This is not to say that timpanists cannot play short notes: they can, but they cannot achieve the degree of articulation a trumpeter can. Thus, the timpanist has greater challenges in playing a series of short notes than the trumpeter. The theory of contrast is an approach helping timpanists find ways to coax the appropriate sound from the drum. The theory is based on the principle that any one technique to elicit a specific sound may be, in itself, insufficient in producing that sound. Therefore, it will be necessary to combine various techniques, the physical properties of mallets, and the tonal capabilities of the timpani head to the end of producing a particular sound. As timpanist Mark Yancich of the Atlanta Symphony Orchestra says, timpanists must "pile nuance on nuance" to get the proper sound.

The theory of contrast has several applications. The first two concern articulation and tone. Timpanists can achieve different degrees of articulation by "piling on the nuances." In themselves, smaller, lighter, harder sticks are often not enough to get the articulation the timpanist needs. Instead, timpanists must add other techniques to achieve the degree of articulation they desire. They can slightly pinch the sticks, play in an individuated manner, snap the sticks off the head, and play slightly more toward the center of the drum. In short, the sound created by employing one articulation technique differs from the sound produced by massing several techniques. Second, the tonal range of the timpani is relatively limited. Staccato and legato sticks do not sound very different to many people. For example, if a heavy dark roll is needed, the timpanist would select a heavier stick with a soft, large head, allow the mallet head to penetrate the timpano, employ a German grip (or a modified French grip), and let the stick naturally rebound with the head (keeping the stick slightly longer on the head). This same principle applies to single strokes. To produce a very dark sound, one could use a German grip; employ a bounce stroke that thoroughly penetrates the timpano head; choose a heavy, soft, large-headed mallet; use some arm; and be very relaxed when playing. Thus, augmenting any one technique with other techniques produces a sound that markedly contrasts with that of a single technique.

Third, it may be important to support tonal contrasts in the orchestra. Often the timpanist wants to produce a sound that becomes darker or becomes more intense, and to do so requires the musician to contrast the strokes so the sound can become darker or more intense. If the music becomes progressively darker and if it appears that the timpani part should become darker, it is possible to move from a brighter to a darker sound. If there are a series of notes that become progressively darker, the timpanist can play the earlier notes off the top of the head and progressively penetrate the head more and more to pick up the darker colors. As the mallet head penetrates the drumhead with each successive stroke, timpanists can (1) slowly move from a French to a German grip, (2) bounce the stroke more and more, and (3) raise the butt of the stick with each successive stroke. All these have the effect of producing darker sound. The same technique can be applied to a roll. Sometimes it is necessary to tonally taper a roll from dark to light. In so doing, the timpanist begins the roll by playing at the bottom of the head and allowing the sticks to follow the natural rebound of the head. To make the roll brighter, the timpanist can progressively roll toward the top of the head: lifting the roll from the bottom to the head, as it were.

Fourth, timpanists can produce sounds that are more relaxed or more intense. It is not uncommon to find the final notes in Romantic symphonies becoming more and more intense until the harmonic tension is resolved. Greater intensity can be produced by progressively tightening up on the grip of the stick. The effect is to produce a sound that progressively sounds harsher to the timpanist, but to the audience is filled with greater intensity. A relaxed sound can be produced by holding the mallet very loosely and by playing very fluidly.

Finally, dynamic contrasts are important in the timpanist's art. If a wide contrast is needed, such as the last crescendo roll in Tchaikovsky's *Overture to Romeo and Juliet*, the timpanist can exaggerate the dynamic difference to achieve the desired effect. A roll or series of notes can be exaggerated by beginning softer than required or becoming louder than is specified in the part. This is particularly true for rolls that begin at *mezzo forte* and crescendo to *forte*. The dynamic difference is often not enough to produce the effect desired by the composer.

The theory of contrast is one way of providing a more dynamic performance by augmenting a particular technique with other techniques to achieve the proper tonal effect. It is helpful in giving timpanists a broader pallet of colors from which they can paint the part.

Conclusion

In this chapter, the author has examined the factors that influence timpani tone. The brand of timpani, mallets, playing style, the grip, composition of the drumhead, method of striking the timpani, and playing spot are important in shaping tone and articulation of a particular stroke. Timpanists are called to develop a sound that allows them to effectively execute their parts in an orchestral context. Beyond the purely rhythmical nature of the timpani, timpanists have the opportunity to tonally shape their parts in ways that support the spiritual nature of the music. Being aware of the tonal capabilities and limitations of the timpanist's art is a prerequisite for playing well. The next three chapters will examine the interpretation of timpani parts in the Baroque and Classical eras.

2

Musical Interpretation and the Timpanist

> A musician cannot move others without moving himself being moved. He will have to feel all the emotions he hopes to call up in his audience ... when the passage is languishing and sad, the performer must languish and grow sad.
> —C. P. E. Bach 1773, III: 13

As Aaron Copland reminds us in his book, *What to Listen for in Music*, the performer is the principal interpreter of the music—the middleman (Copland 1957, 267–268). The performers' tasks are to render—in light of their education, training, and experience—what they consider to be the musical meaning of their parts. As middlemen, they serve the composer by giving a conscientious, faithful interpretation of the piece, and they serve the audience with an aural, mental, spiritual experience. The timpanist's interpretation of the part is framed by many factors. Among them are the period in which the composer was writing, the composer's intentions in writing the music, the overall structure of the music and the specific lines of the piece, and the conductor's interpretation of it. These factors limit and empower the artist to shape the part in ways that elicit the musical meaning of the piece. Classicism often limits the performer's use of dynamic contrasts and tonal coloring. Large crescendos and decrescendos are not only less common in Classical music, but are also less pleasing. The timpanist is restricted in the dramatic use of crescendos to highlight the musical line. Then, the thinner orchestration of Mozart's symphonies requires mallets that produce a more transparent, articulate, fluid sound. Thus, the Classical compositional style places limitations on the tools timpanists have to convey the meaning of his music. But musical styles are equally liberating for the timpanist. Each style authorizes the timpanist to explore ways in which the meaning of the music can be conveyed. The giddiness of Mozart's symphonic finales empowers the timpanist to develop the technique, select the mallets, and shade the tone that is appropriate to the light-hearted nature of the music. In the same way, the anger that Beethoven elicits from the orchestra in the opening measures of Symphony No. 9 requires timpanists to select a stick and put themselves in the right psychological frame of mind to play the first entrance powerfully and angrily.

The Romantic style, on the other hand, offers timpanists greater opportunities to exercise their art. Romantic music is more emotional, lyri-

2.1. Darkening rolls in Sibelius's *Finlandia*

cal, free, and dramatic. Therefore, timpanists exercise more technical and interpretative skills, shaping their part in a way that supports the music. For example, a crescendo may be used to build tension or excitement; but timpanists may want to add color to the crescendo to make it sound progressively darker and heavier. The second and third timpani entrances in Sibelius's *Finlandia* serve to make the point (see example 2.1). The opening section of this music musically depicts the oppressed spirit of the Finnish people. Timpanists can play bars 10 and 12 as *fortepiano* crescendo rolls. So doing helps create the tension that is essential to transmitting the sense of oppression that Sibelius wishes to portray. However, in executing the crescendo, timpanists can darken the roll as it builds; thus, the tense, dark roll reinforces the oppressive tone that reflects the musical intentions of the composer.[1] Timpanists can also draw upon their skills and techniques to create a heavy sound. The first two measures of Brahms's *Tragic Overture* are a case in point. It is clear from the title of the piece that the composer wishes to convey his thoughts on human tragedy. The timpanist's entrance must be authoritative and very heavy—with the heart of a person who has lost a loved one. Timpanists must use the appropriate technique and the proper mallets to create a very heavy, dark, inescapable sound. In this case, timpanists would use a darker stick, accent the first note of the roll to strengthen the tragic effect of the roll, and play in a heavier manner so as to bring out the darkness and color of the drum. Thus, the Romantic style offers many opportunities for the timpanist to dynamically and tonally shape timpani parts to fit the requirements of the music. See the companion Web site for a marked timpani part of Sibelius's *Finlandia*.

The Composer's Style, Psychology, and Intentions

Knowing the composer's general style, psychological states, orientation toward life, and intention in composing the music can help a timpanist interpret their parts. Typically composers develop a compositional style that differentiates them from their fellow composers: Beethoven sounds different from Mozart, who in turn sounds different from Wagner. The particular composer's style helps timpanists determine (1) the attitude they will bring to the part, (2) what sticks to use, and (3) how much liberty they can use in tonally and dynamically shaping their parts, for example. Brahms's symphonic works are often thick, dark scores that require heavy, dark sticks—the so-called Brahms's sticks. Brahms's writing is often darkly passionate, which suggests timpanists should shape the dynamics, articulation, and color of their parts often. The ebbing and flowing of passion in his symphonies offer opportunities for the timpanist to shape the intensity and dynamics of each phrase. Sibelius's compositions often express deep, titanic, natural forces from the natural world and the human psyche. His timpani parts are typically very nuanced: he expects timpanists to effectively and tonally shade their parts and to successfully employ crescendos and decrescendos to highlight the subterranean forces at work in his compositions.

The psychological backdrop of a composer may be helpful in interpreting a piece. One of the most profound, and well-written, psychological profiles of a composer is J. W. N. Sullivan's *Beethoven: His Spiritual Development*. Sullivan chronicles the impact of Beethoven's early life experiences and his growing deafness on Beethoven's Weltanschauung. Sullivan demonstrates how the themes of fate, suffering, and heroism culminate a long process in which Beethoven fatefully accepted his suffering and heroically transcended his fate (Sullivan 1960, chaps. 2, 3, and 4). Knowing about Beethoven's struggle with deafness helps the timpanist interpret many of Beethoven's works. Beethoven's *Egmont Overture* opens with a foreboding theme: one that foreshadows the fateful turn of events that, in Wolfgang Goethe's *Egmont*, will lead the heroic Count Egmont to his death. Yet the final strains of Beethoven's overture are filled with the nobility of the hero who, despite his earthly fate, has secured an eternal place in the hearts of all liberty-loving people. Knowing this, the timpanist can interpret each discrete part of the overture. In sum, the psychological background may be helpful in interpreting a piece of music

Most music is composed with a purpose. Having an understanding of the composer's compositional purpose is helpful in interpreting the piece, and subsequently, the timpani part. The intention may be programmatic as in Bedrich Smetana's *The Moldau*, it may explore a dimension of the human experience as in Brahms's *Tragic Overture*, or it may musically state and develop a theme as in Brahms's *Variations on a Theme of Haydn*. Let's return to Beethoven again to illustrate how the composer's purpose can help the performer understand the music and authoritatively play the part. In the *Coriolanus Overture*, Beethoven reflects on the life of the Roman general, Coriolanus, and on the twin themes of tragedy and heroism. William Shakespeare's *Coriolanus* put in bold relief Coriolanus's tragic, yet heroic life. From his rise to power as a great and admired general, through examples of the hubris that doomed his political career, and to his fateful death, Shakespeare chronicles the life of Coriolanus. Beethoven develops a musical picture of the universal properties of human tragedy and heroism woven into Coriolanus's life. The overture's two principal themes—

representing the tragedy and heroism of Coriolanus's life—are placed in stark relief over and over again in the overture. Only in the final measures—in death—is the struggle between the tragic and heroic figure resolved. Thus, knowing something about the universal themes that pushed Beethoven's pen helps the musician develop a deeper appreciation of the meaning of his music.

Ultimately, the composer's intentions are revealed in the musical score. The score can help timpanists determine how their part is integrated into the harmonic, melodic, tonal, dynamic, and rhythmic fabric of the piece. The score is particularly helpful in defining the amount and kind of articulation, melodic or harmonic support, and dynamic contrast demanded by the music. Comparing the timpani part to the score can reveal when to muffle a note or when to let it ring through. If all instruments end a phrase on an eighth note, the score might suggest that the timpanist should immediately muffle the drum rather than carrying the tone over into the beginning of the next phrase. The score can also help the timpanist determine when to muffle the drum for harmonic reasons. Since the timpani is a legato instrument, a note must be allowed to sound and ring to achieve the full effect of the drum. Letting the drum ring full and resonant often supports the harmonic structure of the music. If, however, there was a key change immediately following a timpani passage, the timpanist would likely muffle the drum to avoid any unwanted dissonance. Finally, and as discussed fully below, the score can aid the timpanist in determining the kind and character of accents and the dynamic shaping of phrases. For example, timpanists can crescendo an ascending line and decrescendo a falling line. Perusing the score is critical in interpreting Francis Poulenc's Concerto for Orchestra, Strings, and Timpani. Poulenc scores each instrumental section at a particular dynamic level. While the organ is playing *forte* and timpani may be written at *mezzo forte*. In these cases, the score is helpful in identifying those parts in the score where timpanists should adjust their dynamics to contour their part to other instruments in the orchestra.

Phrasing and Articulation

In interpreting music, the musical phrase is important. A phrase is a musical idea: the phrase may be one or more measures long. Hermann Keller reminds the musician that a musical phrase is much like a verse in poetry or an unbroken sentence: it may pause, slow down or speed up, grow louder or softer, and grow more intense or more relaxed (Keller 1965, 13). Above all, a phrase has a spiritual meaning that is shaped by its rhythm, melody, harmony, tone color, articulations, and dynamics. For Keller, the greatest masters of music give performers the latitude to phrase passages according to the demands of the piece (Keller 1965, 16–17). Let us examine some of the ways timpanists can breathe meaning into a musical phrase. First, the phrase may be shaped dynamically. Often it makes good musical sense to increase the music's dynamics as the melody ascends and decrease the dynamics when the melody descends. At the end of the third movement of Max Bruch's Violin Concerto No. 1, the violin line ascends and descends. Timpanists may shape this part by growing louder as the violin line ascends and becoming softer as the line descends. This has the effect of not only reinforcing the violin line, but it also gives the music a sense of "surge and decline." Phrases or motives may be played progressively louder until the final downbeat is reached. This has the effect of pushing the music forward rhythmically, gradually intensifying the feeling of the music, and giving the downbeat or tonic note the strongest accent. There are times in which a phrase is written at one dynamic level but the orchestration suggests a crescendo. In that case, the phrase can be played at the marked dynamic level for several counts or measures, then decrescendo every so slightly (almost inaudibly), and in the final measures crescendo to the end. This method establishes the dynamic level at the beginning of the phrase and then permits a crescendo into the final measure to bring out the meaning of the music. A good example can be found at the end of the first movement of Dvořák's Symphony No. 9 (see example 2.2). The timpanist plays the first measure at *fortissimo*, "inaudibly" decrescendos to *forte* in the next bar, and then crescendos to *fortissimo* in the last four measures of the roll. See the companion Web site for a marked timpani part.

2.2. "Inaudible" decrescendos

A succession of legato notes may need to be phrased, too. A legato note is a broad, connecting note that allows other notes of a phrase to flow easily one into another. Phrased legato notes are notated in one of two ways. First, a series of notes may be slurred. Second, a composer may write a tenuto mark above (or below) the note—signifying that the note should be played its written value. However, the musical context often determines whether or not notes should be played in a legato fashion. Where it is clear that the composer meant notes to be tied more closely together, the notes may be treated as legato notes.

Legato notes present particular problems to the timpanist. On the timpani, the sound of a single legato note decays fairly rapidly. At slow tempos, a legato note becomes something less than a legato note: the relatively rapid decay of the note prevents a real legato note from sustaining its tone. Perhaps this is why George Frideric Handel wrote rolled notes in the first movement of the *Royal Fireworks*. At this very slow and deliberate tempo, single legato notes may not sustain the sound in the way a roll would. The decay of the note is particularly problematic if the timpanist is playing in the upper register of the drums or on smaller drums. In the drum's upper register, the tightness of timpano head prevents the note from resonantly ringing for a longer period of time. This is less true with notes played in the drum's middle and lower register. The dynamic level of legato notes played on smaller drums decays quicker than those played on larger drums. Once again, this limits the ability to produce a legato sound on these drums. For these reasons, some timpanists argue that the only truly legato note is the trilled or rolled note: a note that sustains both the tonal character and dynamics of that note. The theory of contrast helps the timpanist bring out a legato note. A legato note will sound more legato if it is preceded and/or succeeded by staccato notes. For example, in the second movement of Beethoven's Symphony No. 7, the principal phrase can be articulated in this manner (see example 2.3). This allows the timpanist to make subtle distinctions between the preceding staccato notes and the legato note.

2.3. Varying articulation

Playing in a staccato fashion punctuates specific notes in a phrase. Technically, the performer attempts to clearly articulate one note from the next. The duration of any note is less than half that of the written note. Since the seventeenth century, a staccato note has been notated by a dot or wedge above or below the note (Turk 1982, 342). But, there is considerable controversy over the meaning of the wedge and dot. Hermann Keller surmises that after 1600 dots were employed to simply shorten the note, while wedges were used to shorten and add weight to the note. However, publishers were notorious for using whatever symbol they desired—a problem for musicians playing the music today. In the eighteenth century, both the wedge and dot shortened the value of the note by one-half in duple and one-third in triple meter. During the nineteenth century, the wedge was often used to indicate a sharp, short staccato note, but its use died out by the end of the 1800s (Keller 1965, 48–51). In addition to using these two markings, a staccato note can be notated by placing a rest after or before that note, thus shortening the value of that note. In the Classical and Romantic periods, composers often chose to write shortened notes by using the rest (Keller 1965, 48).

As described above, timpanists have gone to great lengths to play staccato notes. As Cloyd Duff reminds us, a timpano is a legato instrument: its nature is to ring full and resonant. Thus, the timpanist takes special pains to shorten the note—many times with less than complete success. For example, timpanists have played with one mallet, placing the other mallet somewhere on the timpano head to shorten the note. Timpanists have resorted to any number and variety of sticks to give different note values, they have placed mutes made from leather or felt on the heads to shorten the note, they have draped cloth over the heads, they have played on a tighter head, and they have adopted a number of different grips and playing styles to shorten the notes. (See figure 12 for an example of a

Figure 12.   Leather Timpani Mute: 2¼" × 3¾"
and 1.5 oz.

leather mute.) It is also possible to give the *impression* that notes are shorter by placing them in the context of long notes. See, for instance, the example above. In Symphony No. 7 Beethoven composed a figure where two eighth notes are placed between quarter notes. If the quarter notes are played more legato and the eighth notes more staccato, then the eighth notes sound more staccato than if all the notes are played staccato.

Staccato and legato strokes are at the opposite ends of the spectrum. In the middle are such strokes as nonlegato and portato—as well as many other terms denoting degrees of shortness and weight: marcato, martellato, staccatissimo, leggiero, and leggierissimo. For the timpanist, nonlegato, portato, and marcato are more common denotations found in the orchestral repertoire. Nonlegato signifies a note that is neither legato nor staccato. Timpanists typically play this as a marked or pointed note, letting the timpani ring the full duration of the note. This author considers legato as the norm with nonlegato, staccato, marcato, and portato strokes being variations of it. Keller describes portato as a holding together of what is separated. Portato markings are much less common. This timpanist doubts they can be effectively played. In Mendelssohn's Symphony No. 5 *(Reformation)*, he uses a portato figure in the last movement (see example 2.4). One can play this with very articulate sticks in a legato fashion or with general sticks in a staccato fashion. The former suits the author because it preserves the continuity of the musical line that Mendelssohn wished to convey. Finally, marcato is often found in the repertoire. Marcato, signifying a "marking," can be effectively used where there is a pointed, heavier,

2.4.   Mendelssohn's portato figure in Symphony
No. 5

Musical Interpretation and the Timpanist   41

marchlike rhythm. In Sergei Rachmaninov's Piano Concerto No. 2, the musical line, nine measures after rehearsal 10, calls for sixteen measures of marcato strokes. Marked "Maestoso. (Alla marcia.)," this part requires the timpanist to push the music forward in a marchlike manner that must be articulate and heavy. In conclusion, whether defined as nonlegato, portato, or marcato, these terms intellectually signify the sound and articulation of a particular note. Ultimately, timpanists are called to use the technical resources at their disposal and their personal skill to create the articulation that is needed for the passage being played. It is at this point that these terms become intellectual abstractions signifying little more than a kind of sound. See the companion Web site for a marked timpani part.

The emotional effect of legato, staccato, and marcato has not lost itself on composers or performers (Keller 1965, 98–99). Some of the most touching and tender music has been written in legato fashion. For the timpanist, much of the third movement of Beethoven's Symphony No. 9 should be played very softly (at *piano*) and tenderly with long legato strokes—strokes that allow the timpani to ring full and resonant. An examination of the score will reveal that many phrases in the strings, woodwinds, and brass are slurred—played in a connected, legato fashion. The timpani, to match the legato playing of the other instruments, must play in a similar manner. Anything more articulate would ruin the feeling that Beethoven wished to convey. On the other hand, Brahms was a master at using the staccato note to add energy and strength to his music. In the last four measures of the *Tragic Overture*, Brahms writes four and one-half measures of articulated, staccato notes, giving the music incredible strength. These notes are followed by three quarter notes articulated with wedges, and Brahms wants these notes to be played not only short, but also increasingly heavier. The effect is to further intensify and strengthen the phrase as the music moves inexorably toward harmonic resolution. Finally, using a marcato stroke can effectively convey the martial feeling that accompanies some music. See the companion Web site for a marked timpani part for Brahms's *Tragic Overture*.

Another dimension of phrasing concerns accents. Accents may be dynamic, melodic, agogic, tonal, or metric. Dynamic accents are stressed notes. The most common accented note is indicated by a carrot or, in the nineteenth century, a tenuto mark over the note. Melodic accents are notes that are stressed due to their position at the peak of an ascending line. No extra energy is needed to stress these notes; the phrase naturally stresses them. Melodic accents are relatively rare in the orchestral timpani repertoire; however, the opening line in Richard Strauss's *Burlesque* provides a suitable example (see example 2.5). The f in the third and fourth measures represents the top of the phrase and these notes appear to be naturally accented. The notes leading up to and away from it do not have the stress of the f. Agogic accents are notes whose greater length of tone calls the listener's attention to them. In the *Burlesque*, for example, the length of the f in measure 2 appears accented for another reason. Where there is a single short note or a series of short notes followed by a longer one, the longer

2.5. Natural accents in Strauss's *Burlesque*

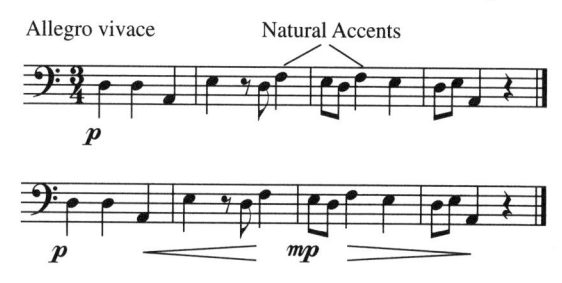

note appears to be accented. The f of the second and third measures is accented due to the position of the quarter notes immediately following the eighth note(s). To understand this effect, play this phrase on one timpano. Timpanists need to be particularly aware of agogic accents because they often swallow up the smaller notes that precede them. For example, in the fourth movement of Beethoven's Symphony No. 7 (see example 2.6), the rhythmic figure of two sixteenth notes followed by the eighth note is rendered less forceful because the two sixteenth notes are swallowed up by the agogic accent. If the goal is a musical gesture consisting of notes played at the same dynamic level, it is necessary to compensate for the agogic accent by stressing or bringing out the smaller notes. This is accomplished by putting a bit more energy into them. This figure would be played with two accents over the sixteenth notes, making sure that the four notes are of equivalent volume. See the companion Web site for a marked timpani part.

2.6. Accenting "short notes" to bring them out

The choice of and use of sticks can be used to affect an agogic accent. First, it is sometimes useful to think in terms of playing with a small-headed, light, hard mallet in one hand and a larger-headed, heavier, soft mallet in the other. While this method would not be appropriate to Wagner's *Funeral Music*, this passage makes the point. Playing the first sixteenth note with the more staccato stick and the second sixteenth with a legato stick effectively produces the aural impression of a shorter and a longer note. Of course, the primary disadvantage is that there will be some difference in the tone color produced by each stick. An alternative to using two different sticks is to play the small note staccato (just out of the playing spot toward the center of the drum) and the larger note legato (in the playing spot). Phrasing in this manner effectively accents the legato note.

Embellishment accents are simply ornaments that add stress to a note or phrase. Ornaments underwent a significant development in the Baroque period; however, only later did they have an impact on the timpani.

The grace note, tremolo, dot, wedge, stroke, slur, accent, fermata, and caesura made their way into the timpani parts. Regarding grace notes, rarely more than four grace notes precede the principle note; one to three grace notes are the most common. The grace notes are played slightly before the beat; although, there are times when playing them on the beat is more effective. The grace notes are usually played slightly softer than the principal note or at the same dynamic level. If the grace notes were played at a stronger dynamic level, the principal note would be swallowed up. There is certain eloquence in playing the grace notes one or two dynamic levels below the principal note, and it gives the aural impression that stress is placed on the principal note. Richard Wagner uses grace note ornaments to accent the downbeat in measures 11–13 of his introduction to *Die Meistersinger zur Nürenberg*. Playing the grace notes at the same dynamic level seems an appropriate way to accentuate the downbeat. As an alternative, increasing the dynamics of each grace note and accenting the principal note effectively moves forward the motion of the music. Where the music is rushing toward the downbeat of the next measure, playing a series of grace notes with increasing volume effectively draws attention to the downbeat and emphasizes its importance. See the companion Web site for a marked timpani part. Finally, sticking grace notes may depend on the tempo of the piece or the effect the timpanist wishes to project. As the nineteenth century German timpanist, Ernst Pfundt notes (1849, 20–21), the grace notes can be played hand to hand (at more slow tempos) or they can be played with one hand (at slower tempos or where each note should sound the same).

Timpanists encounter two final accents: tonal and metric. The tone color of a note can also give the impression of accent. A brighter note sounds accented when compared to one that is darker. Return to the *Burlesque*. The f is much brighter than the other notes. This brightness gives the f an accent that the other notes do not have. In this case, the brightness of the f is due (in part) to the drum on which it is played. If this solo is played on 31-inch, 26-inch (or 29-inch), 26-inch, and 23-inch timpani, the f will be played on the 23-inch drum—the drum that has the least resonance and transparency; the drum with the brightest and most focused sound. As a result, the f will be tonally accented compared to the notes of the other drums. If the unaccented notes are balanced dynamically with the brighter note, attention needs to be paid to either putting more energy into the lower notes or placing less energy in the higher notes. Finally, metric accents occur once an order of notes has been firmly established in a common rhythmic pattern. In John Phillip Sousa's "Stars and Stripes Forever," the listener imagines an accent on the first beat of each measure once the rhythmic pattern of the piece is established. The timpanist can create tension in a rhythmically ordered part by displacing the accent from the first beat, in this case, to another beat of the measure (Boatwright, 1956, 52–55). For example, in the third movement of Eduard Lalo's *Symphonie Espagnole*, timpanists can accent the third and fifth notes in the second and subsequent measures after rehearsal 2 (see example 2.7). By

2.7. Displacing accents in Lalo's *Symphonie Espagnole*

slightly accenting these notes, the musical line is made more sensuous and compelling—just as the author believes Lalo intended. See the companion Web site for a marked timpani part.

In discussing dynamic, melodic, agogic, tonal, or metric accents, it is important to remember that they can often supplement one another. In the *Burlesque* example cited below, the f was accented melodically, agogically, and metrically. A melodically accented note can be given even greater weight if timpanists add a dynamic accent. Indeed, by using crescendos and decrescendos, timpanists can give greater weight to some notes than to others. In the *Burlesque* (see example 2.8), crescendo from the first through the second beat of the third measure and decrescendo through the rest of the phrase.

2.8. Dynamic shading to strengthen accents

This highlights even more the f in the third measure—shaping the phrase in a pleasing manner. Timpanists can also use staccato and legato strokes to effectively accent one note over the other. In Richard Wagner's "Funeral Music" from *Die Götterdämmerung* (see example 2.9), play the first note staccato (and slightly into the head) and the second note legato. The second note is given an agogic accent and this kind of accent fits the phrase better than a dynamic accent. A dynamic accent would simply stress this note. In this musical context, stress is not the issue; rather, we want to play the first and second figures in a similar manner. Playing both figures as short-long provides a sense of aesthetic beauty that is pleasing to the ear.

2.9. Effectively articulating Wagner's "Funeral Music"

Using dynamic contrast is an integral part of phrasing. In part, dynamic phrasing is a function of musical style. During the Classical period, most composers (such as Haydn and Mozart) avoided using crescendos and decrescendos. This was in part a function of the nature of the Classical style and the evolution of musical notation. By the latter part of the Classical period, composers—perhaps led by the Mannheim school—found it more acceptable to incorporate crescendos and decrescendos in their compositions. This practice became common in the Romantic period. With a greater stress on the emotions, composers found that the use of dynamic contrasts conveyed the emotional meaning of the music to a greater extent. The use of dynamic contrast was an important part of conveying musical meaning.

The use of crescendos and decrescendos (written or unwritten) is an important part of shaping a phrase. A crescendo has the effect of increasing the emotional response of the listener—especially when it accompanies a transition to the tonic. Tchaikovsky's *Romeo and Juliet Overture* is a case in point. The crescendo roll from *piano* to *fortissimo* five measures from the end of the overture raises the emotional response of the listener. Crescendo rolls are often effective at the end of pieces, even though they are not notated as crescendos. They have the effect of increasing or deepening the emotional response of the listener. Crescendos are also effective in the final notes leading up to the resolution of the piece to the tonic. In the last movement of Brahms's Symphony No. 1, the four notes beginning five measures from the end of the piece can be played by giving each note a slightly greater dynamic (see example 2.10). So doing helps build musical tension as the music rushes toward the final resolution in the last bar. As described below, progressively increasing the amount of tension in each note further creates greater musical tension that is gloriously resolved in the final measure. It is not uncommon to use a crescendo in a previous measure to move the music forward into the next measure. See the companion Web site for a marked timpani part.

2.10. Intensifying notes to effectuate a final resolution

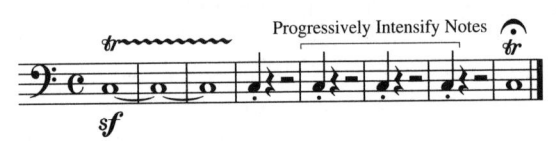

Decrescendos provide the timpanist with the opportunity to ease musical tension, and in conjunction with crescendos, they can be used to shape the musical line more effectively. If employing a crescendo can increase musical tension, using a diminuendo can dissipate it. Brahms disperses musical tension one measure before letter B in the fourth movement of Symphony No. 1 (see example 2.11). After an accented entrance filled with tension, Brahms helps release that tension by writing a diminuendo. However, shaping a phrase can be effectively accomplished by using a crescendo and diminuendo—following the ascending and descending line in the melody or harmony. The undulating melody of the violins at letter E of the first movement of the Bruch Violin Concerto makes

2.11. Descrescendo: dispersing
musical tension

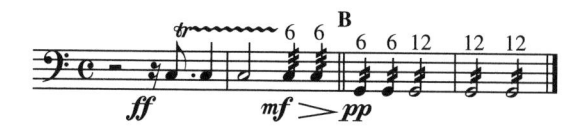

this point. The ascending and descending string line provides the timpanist with the opportunity to crescendo and diminuendo with them, creating an emotional surge and decline over three measures. Sometimes the timpanist must diminuendo in order to execute an effective crescendo. In the opening measure of Brahms's Symphony No. 1, the thundering timpani strokes are written at *forte*, but the timpanist is expected to crescendo to a *forte* by measure 9. The timpanist cannot begin the part *mezzo forte* and crescendo to *forte*, and to crescendo from *forte* to *fortissimo* would destroy the musical line. So the only other alternative is to begin to diminuendo "inaudibly" from measures 5–7 and then crescendo in bar 8. (An inaudible diminuendo is one in which successive notes are played at successive lower dynamic levels—so gradual that individual notes do not appear to have different dynamic markings, but collectively there is an dynamic diminuendo.) To make a crescendo more effective, the same principle can be applied to passages that are not so marked: gradually diminuendo so that the crescendo can be made more effective. Finally, a hairpin roll or *messa di voce* (a roll that crescendos and then diminuendos quickly and usually within one measure) can be effectively used to add character to a rolled note. Brahms uses this roll effectively in many of his orchestral works. In the Symphony No. 2 he uses it in the first movement. Eight and six measures before K, the timpani are given two half note tremolos that are played soloistically. In the fourth measure before K, the timpanist is asked to play a hairpin roll—once again, soloistically. The key to executing this roll is to start the roll at a normal speed, open up the roll (play it gradually slower) during the crescendo and gradually increase the speed of the roll during the decrescendo until the normal speed is reached. Cloyd Duff and his successor, Paul Yancich, in their tenure at the Cleveland Orchestra, used this roll effectively and this technique allows the sound to fully blossom. See the companion Web site for a marked timpani part for Brahms's Symphony No. 1 and an effective way to execute rolls.

Timpanists often overlook phrasing grace notes. Alfred Friese and Alexander Lepak note that grace notes may be played open and not crushed (Friese-Lepak 1954, 34). It is a matter of interpretation on how open the grace notes should be played. Clearly, a grace note played too close to the principal note destroys the effect of the grace note figure; therefore, there must be some separation between the grace notes and the principal note. In most cases, the grace notes should be tightly grouped, placed slightly before the principal note, and played in a way that the grace notes are clearly heard. However, there are times when the most effective grace

2.12. Opening grace notes

notes are opened very widely.[2] The second movement of Bruch's Violin Concerto No. 1 serves as an illustration (see example 2.12). At letter H and two measures before letter L, Bruch writes two grace notes preceding the principal eighth note. The emotional context at H is passionately noble, while two measures before L the music is exceedingly tender. The timpanist can play the grace notes very close together, which gives additional weight to the principal note. However, weight is not needed at these points. A heavy downbeat two measures before L conflicts with the very tender moment that Bruch so effectively scores. Playing the two grace notes very open—*almost* to the point of playing them as rhythmically defined sixteenth notes—effectively portrays the sentiment Bruch wishes to convey. Playing the two grace notes with the stronger hand and the principal note with the weaker hand conveys this feeling. Executing the grace notes with one—and the stronger—hand articulates them effectively, and the effect of the principal note as an accented downbeat is diminished by playing that note with the weaker hand. The grace notes at H are written at *fortissimo* and one might expect that Bruch wished to use the grace notes to accent the downbeat. In fact, this music is very noble and to play the grace note figures very tightly brings down this noble music by their sheer weight. Opening these notes up has the effect of supporting the nobility of this music. See the companion Web site for a marked timpani part.

Often, phrasing requires the timpanist to consciously use either one or two hands. For example, in the first movement of Beethoven's Symphony No. 7, Beethoven writes this figure at measure 89 (see example 2.13). This is often sticked LLR, RRL, LRL, or RLR. On the one hand, this part can be played hand-to-hand. Since this galloping music must move forward fluidly, playing it in this manner is preferable since there is no hesitation in the movement of the line. Accenting the sixteenth note prevents it from being swallowed up by the following eighth note. See the compan-

2.13. Alternating strokes to clarify rhythmic lines

ion Web site for a marked timpani part. Music that gives the sense of walking can be played with two hands. Just as alternating left and right steps are weighted differently, playing with two mallets, each penetrating the drumhead in different degrees, can give the sense of walking. On the other hand, there are times in which double sticking is clearly preferable to playing hand-to-hand. First, double sticking faster parts tends to articulate the parts better than playing hand-to-hand. So parts that need to be cleanly articulated might benefit from double sticking. For example, Dvořák writes nice solo figures at the beginning of the third movement of the "New World" Symphony (see example 2.14).

2.14. Double sticking to improve rhythmic lines

This can be effectively sticked **LRLL** for left-handed or **RLRR** for right-handed timpanists. This sticking articulates the eighth notes and improves the flow of the musical line. Second, the musical line might sound better where some phrases are double sticked. Third, if the timpanist desires evenness of sound, playing a passage with one hand may be preferable to playing a passage hand-to-hand. At the very beginning of Beethoven's Violin Concerto, the timpani play five solo notes. These notes are so exposed that timpanists often play them with one hand to minimize the differences that can arise in playing a part hand-to-hand. See the companion Web site for a marked timpani part for Beethoven's Violin Concerto.

Tonal phrasing involves shaping the tone of a phrase to support the musical intentions of the composer. Because the timpani are capable of producing a variety of tones, it is possible to use that capability to paint a musical phrase in a way that is pleasing to the ear and supports the color of the orchestra. The author has described some methods of shaping timpani tone. First, the tone can move from brighter to darker. In the opening bar of the fourth movement of Brahms's Symphony No. 1, the timpanist executes a roll on the c drum and ends with a single stroke on the G drum. Because this roll crescendos from *piano* to *forte*, the roll conveys a dark, powerful meaning. By beginning the roll more brightly and progressively getting darker, the roll adds a darker, more sinister meaning to the music. When reaching the G—the first beat of the second measure—the timpanist produces a very heavy stroke that brings out the entire lower partials of the drum. Tonal phrasing permits darker passages to become lighter. Occasionally, a roll at the end of a phrase ends one musical thought and establishes the conditions for the beginning of the next musical idea. Rather than playing the entire roll in a dark manner, the timpanist can make the roll progressively brighter. By starting the roll at the bottom of the head and progressively ascending to the top, the timpanist can brighten the sound, make it more transparent, and phrase the musical line more effectively. This technique is particularly effective if the roll is written as a diminuendo. In the fourth movement of the "New World" Symphony (seven measures after 12), Dvořák writes a *fortissimo* roll that diminuendos to nothing eight measures later. Beginning at the fifth measure of that roll—after two measures of diminuendo—the timpanist can begin to brighten the color of sound until the end of the phrase is reached. This feathering out of the tone is particularly effective in this passage because Dvořák is making a diminuendo and is lightening the forces of the orchestra. Dvořák progressively eliminates the brass and then thins out the woodwinds: the result is a brightening of the sound. Thus, timpanists can support the rest of the orchestra by brightening their sound, too.

Dampening or muffling notes are an important part of phrasing. There are three fundamental reasons to dampen a note for the purpose of phrasing. First, the nature of the timpani is to ring full and resonant. However, there are times when the ring must be stopped. Timpani are dampened at the end of a phrase where it is clear a ring would interfere with the subsequent musical line. Second, timpanists muffle timpani for harmonic reasons. It is not uncommon in Romantic music for the keys to change abruptly. To let a note well written for one key to bleed over into the new key often creates a dissonance that is so objectionable that the note must be muffled. Finally, there are times when in playing two consecutive notes, the first note should be muffled so the second can be heard. This muffling might be for dynamic or aesthetic reasons. Often composers in the Classical and Romantic periods wrote a subito dynamic marking: an immediate change in dynamics—from *forte* to *piano*, for example. Without muffling the *forte* note, the *piano* note is rarely heard. In these cases, timpanists must develop the dexterity to quickly muffle the louder note so that the softer note can be heard. Beethoven uses *subito* dynamic changes often. In the third movement of Symphony No. 7, he writes a difficult phrase that requires the timpanist to muffle very quickly and effectively (see example 2.15). In this and other examples, the luftpause is my notation for muffling. Muffling is done immediately after the note on the downbeat. This sticking gives the timpanist enough time to get into position to muffle the penultimate note. Finally, there may be aesthetic reasons to muffle a note prior to playing the final note in a figure; for example, the timpanist may want the final note to ring without any interference from the previous note. Often one note—the dominant or subdominant beneath the tonic—is written prior to the tonic. Acoustically, the lower notes have a tendency to detract from the power of the tonic. Where the presence of the tonic is very critical to the musical line, it may be important to muffle the lower note so the tonic is allowed to establish its place in the music.

2.15. Muffling to execute soft passages

Whether a timpanist is left- or right-handed can affect phrasing of timpani parts. Timpanists are trained to play evenly with both hands; that is, strokes made by either hand should sound similar—in tone, articulation, and dynamics. However, most timpanists are either left- or right-handed. As such, they will naturally begin or end a note or passage with their favored hand. As Fred Hinger notes, the strong hand tends to play more affirmatively than the weak hand; thus, the stronger hand should play the pulse of the rhythm. This leads to a more effective rhythmic phrasing of timpani passages. However, there are times in which the leading note (the note leading up to the primary beat) should be emphasized. In these cases, timpanists can play the leading note with the strong hand leaving the weaker hand to play the subsequent note. As Hinger notes in the fourth movement of Tchaikovsky's Symphony No. 5 (measures 523–526), the quarter note preceding the downbeat of each measure can be played with the stronger hand and the downbeat with the weaker hand. This phrases the passage most effectively (Hinger 1983a, 17). See the companion Web site for a marked timpani part.

Learning how and when to articulate passages is a fundamental skill timpanists master. The timpani are in many ways sustaining instruments, and as such, it is more difficult to get an articulate sound out of a sustaining instrument than it is to coax a legato sound out of it. Therefore, timpanists struggle to find ways to articulate passages effectively. This includes using mutes, harder sticks, free fingers, mechanical mutes, articulate parts of the timpano head, the grip, and arms to achieve the proper articulation. Absent directions by the composer and conductor, the timpanist must recognize when a passage must be articulated or punctuated. As described earlier, articulation marks developed predominately in the Classical period. Common articulation marks are the dot above the note, indicating that it should be played *secco* or short; the wedge, which articulates and adds weight to the note; the caesura, which indicates an immediate end to the musical line; the luftpause, which terminates a note; the tenuto and slur, which broaden the note; and the fermata, which sustains a note for an indeterminate amount of time. The composer will often describe the articulation by writing *secco* (short), *con sordini* (with mutes), *marcato* (marked), and *marcia* (in marching style) into the part. Each of these articulation markings and terms suggest how the composer wants to articulate or stress a note or phrase; how this was accomplished is left up to the timpanist (Cook 1988, 17; Lampl 1996, 61–74; Van Ess 1970, 4–5). Let's briefly examine methods of articulating passages and leave an extended discussion of articulation to the chapters on Baroque and Classical music.

Dampening is a technique that produces varying degrees of articulation. As discussed above, drums may be dampened with the timpanist's fingers, with timpani sticks, or with muffles made from felt, leather, linen, or some other suitable material. By putting one or more fingers on various parts of the timpano head, timpanists can articulate a note and give it the appropriate tone color. In many cases, the fingers are the least effective way of developing a staccato sound. The timpanist can place a timpani mallet on the appropriate part of the drumhead to achieve even greater articulation. The size of the mallet head and the amount of pressure the timpanist exerts on the timpani head help determine the tone and level of articulation that is accomplished. This technique can be used successfully in the "heartbeat" section (the measures after letter U) of Tchaikovsky's *Romeo and Juliet Overture* (see example 2.16).

2.16. Muffling with a timpani mallet

After coming off the huge, dark F roll played with soft, large-headed timpani mallets, the timpanist must quickly exchange them for a staccato mallet. The staccato mallet is necessary to cleanly articulate the triplet figures at letter U. With the larger stick placed at or near the center of the timpano head, the timpanist can play the passage with the more articulate stick. By slightly accenting the first note of each triplet, each figure is given a "heartbeat" and this effectively pushes an otherwise languishing part forward. Finally, the most effective way of articulating a note is to use a muffle or mute. Muffles may be placed anywhere on the timpano head; however, the most common place is in a radius of a foot from the middle of the head. Given the physics of timpano head movement, the timpano head is most dramatically dampened at a point opposite the playing spot about three or four inches from the counterhoop (at the twelve o'clock position). This spot is used rarely (except for special effects) because it effectively destroys the tonal characteristics of the timpano head. However, there are two other spots that effectively articulate a note: at the three and nine o'clock positions. These spots add articulation without sacrificing too much tone. By experimenting with the placement of the muffle and the location of the stroke (in or outside of the playing spot), timpanists can achieve the right amount of articulation with the proper tone. The position of the mute will vary with the needs of the musical gesture.

The tonal music of the Baroque, Classical, and Romantic periods was divided into musical ideas that were stated, developed, or reworked in some fashion. Especially during the Classical period, these musical ideas were divided into phrases, phrases were compounded into periods (larger musical thoughts), and periods into larger musical ideas: themes. Since phrases and periods had a beginning and an ending point that were melodically, harmonically, rhythmically, or stylistically determined, they could be punctuated—just as we end a sentence with a period, explanation point, or question mark. The cadence—the point of repose that marks an end of a phrase, period, or theme—is a point at which the timpanist may be asked to punctuate the musical idea. Often, this punctuation is a matter of playing a bounce stroke into the drum: a staccato note played "into the head" of the drum, finishing with a bit of stick lift. So doing makes a shorter, darker, pointed sound; but, the lift prevents the timpanist from driving the sound into the head, and produces an appropriate tone. This sound tells the listener that the phrase has ended and another musical idea is about to begin. At the twenty-first measure of the Allegro con brio of Beethoven's *Egmont Overture*, Beethoven ends one musical idea and begins the next. It is at this point that the timpanist could punctuate this phrase because Beethoven clearly wanted to end the phrase here. The corresponding notes in the brass, viola, and bass parts are marked *forzando*—further suggesting that Beethoven wanted to end the phrase. However, cadence points are not always so punctuated. The composer may desire a degree of continuity between the first and second phrases. In this case, the end of the phrase should be played as written without any attempt to punctuate it. See the companion Web site for a marked timpani part.

Carrying forward our literary metaphor, a passage can end with an explanation point or question mark. The timpanist may do this by accenting the note. Placing a stinger on the end of the roll can effectively conclude the piece. This adds not only excitement, but also a sense of finality to the music. Some composers clearly indicate that the timpanist should end the piece with an accented note. Sibelius did this in *Finlandia*. However, timpanists can use a stinger when it is not so marked. Stingers can be used at the end of Brahms's or Tchaikovsky's Symphony No. 4, for example. A stinger can be used elsewhere. Former Cleveland Orchestra timpanist, Cloyd Duff, uses a stinger to terminate the roll at the end of the first movement of Brahms's Symphony No. 4. Brahms builds so much excitement into the music that a stinger seems appropriate. However, using a stinger within a symphony or movement may give a false sense that the piece has ended, and waiting to the end of the piece to place a stinger gives the stinger its greatest effect. Thus, careful consideration should be given to the use of a stinger within a symphonic work. Finally, not all pieces of music ending with a roll should be played with a stinger. Music that ends in an uplifting and ethereal manner, rather than music that ends dramatically, should be allowed to soar. A stinger would prevent the music from continuing upward; therefore, a timpanist would want to avoid using a stinger in those situations. Requiem masses often end on an uplifting note, intending to transport the listener to a higher plane. In cases like this, the timpanist would want to end the piece without any punctuation. Finally, a rising phrase may imply a question mark. In that case, the timpanist could play a sustained, legato stroke with lots of lift to mimic the rising inflection of a vocal question.

For those pieces that do not end with a roll but a single note, it is possible to use a stinger—an accented note—to give the piece a greater sense of finality. However, for this to be successful, notes leading up to the final note must be distinguished from the final note. Increasing the amount of tension in each note preceding the final accented note, increasing the dynamic level of each note, and accenting the final note can accomplish this. For example, the final three timpani strokes in Beethoven's *Egmont Overture* can be played with increasing intensity and volume. This heightens the excitement created by the flute's triplet figure in the penultimate bar, and brings a glorious overture to an appropriate end.

There are times when the timpanist gives a send-off to another instrumental section. The send-off is usually one note that connects the end of one phrase harmonically, rhythmically, or melodically with the beginning of the next. Often these notes can be played in legato fashion with plenty of lift. The legato stroke provides a broad, full sound that connects the end of one phrase with the beginning of the next. Lifting the stick—drawing the sound out of the drum—lifts the musical line into the next phrase.

Creating Emotion

If the primary function of music is to convey emotional meaning, then the primary role of the timpanist is to help convey that meaning. Yet many would question whether this is possible. In fact, the timpanist has a supportive role in creating emotion. While the timpani lack the expressive quality of the lyrical violin, the nobleness of the French horn, and the plaintive voice of the English horn, the timpani support the orchestra in creating a certain mood. Can the timpanist convey the feelings of anxiety, love, sudden anger, gaiety (and happiness), pathos (and sadness), or nobility? Yes, and in interpreting their parts, timpanists must understand the emotional effect the composer wishes to convey and use their technique, sticks, timpani, and timpani heads to create the desired effect. Anxiety is one emotion that composers use frequently, and the timpanist must be able to create an anxious mood. Intensifying one note, a series of notes, or a roll can do this. Anxiety increases emotional tension in a person and puts the listener on edge. In playing a single note "anxiously," the timpanist can play staccato, harsher sounding notes. Oftentimes this is needed at the end of a movement that builds up and suddenly releases musical tension in its final bars. It is not uncommon for composers to write a series of four or six staccato notes that support the growth of harmonic tension at the end of a piece. Timpanists may intensify a series of notes by playing each successive note shorter and harsher. Using the theory of contrast, this means that the first note should be played more legato. Each successive note should be played more staccato and with increasing tension in the arms and upper body. Each note should sound somewhat more tense and pointed. The final notes should have a very little "crack" to them. A little crack may sound objectionable to the timpanist, but because of the acoustics of the timpani and concert hall, the audience will not hear an objectionable crack—just a sound that is filled with tension.

Finally, rolls can be shaped to increase anxiety. Relying on the theory of contrast, timpanists can begin a roll very relaxed and as the tension builds, they can increase the speed of the roll to the point that they overplay the head; in other words, they play the roll faster than they should to intensify the sound. To this the timpanist can add additional nuances: gradually pinch the stick, use more staccato (harder) sticks, gradually play into a more staccato part of the head, and play on a tight head. By aggregating these techniques, the timpanist can heighten the tension of the roll that nicely complements the increasing tension in the orchestra. Tchaikovsky's *Romeo and Juliet Overture* provides a good example of how a timpanist can intensify a roll to reflect the growing tension in the music (see example 2.17).

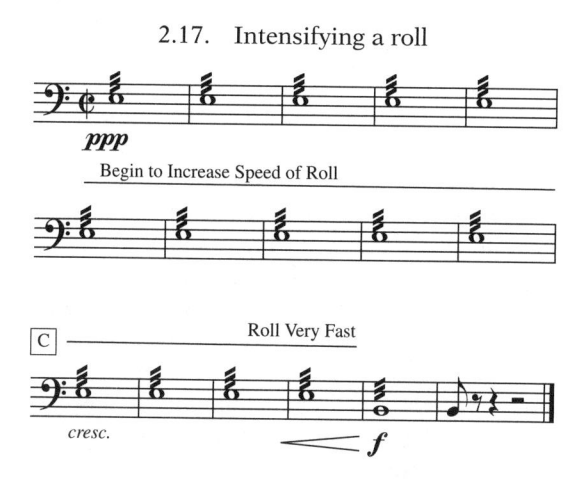

2.17. Intensifying a roll

This exposed roll begins at measure 76. By playing the roll as a normal legato roll, the timpanist is able to establish a nice roll in a very exposed section. By letter C, the timpanist should begin to speed up the roll, and four measures after C, the roll should be as intense as the timpanist can make it. The B should be played at the normal speed. The timpanist can use a medium-hard stick and play on a 26-inch drum. The stick will aid in developing a tense sound as the tension increases in the music. The e played on the 26-inch drum is preferable to the e played on the 23-inch timpano. First, the head is tighter on a 26-inch drum and is more likely to produce the tense effect that is desired. Second, the volume of sound and tone that is produced by the 26-inch drum is much better than that of the smaller drum. See the companion Web site for a marked timpani part.

As there are times when music must become more intense, there are also times when very tense music is relaxed. In these cases, timpanists may employ the above procedures in reverse order: begin by overplaying the head with a medium-hard stick and a staccato grip and then gradually slow the roll down and loosen the grip. The semistaccato stick may not be the best rolling stick, but where the effect is to release tension, this mallet can be employed to that end. If the timpanist has the choice of drums, he or she might want to play the roll on a larger drum. For example, a tense A roll that becomes more relaxed might be more effectively played on a 29-inch timpano rather than on a 31- or 32-inch drum. By the same token, an A roll that becomes more intense might be better played on a 31-inch timpano. In the former case, the head will be looser and will sound more relaxed; while in the latter case, the head will be tighter and it can be overplayed to create a tense sound.

Timpanists can use techniques to create the impression of sudden anger, love, and gaiety. Sudden anger is another emotion that is frequently found in serious music. In many cases, the composer will write a *forzando* over an individual note to indicate that the note should be stressed. To produce the effect of sudden anger, the note can be played in a staccato manner with a sharp attack and lightening recoil. Played in this way, the sound should slightly "crack." There are times when the music should sound loving, and often this music is quite slow. In these cases, the timpanist should play very tenderly with a legato stick. By holding the stick "looser than you can possibly imagine," using a long legato stroke, and playing on the top of the head, the timpanist can produce a very tender sound with no sense of attack. Music that sounds very cheerful and gay is often written uptempo. To lightly and cleanly play these parts, the timpanist must use a lighter, more staccato stick, play on the top of the head, and play hand-to-hand. The ensuing strokes will sound light and flowing—exactly what is needed in cheerful music. Cheerful music is less convincingly conveyed using a heavier, darker, legato stick. Those sticks can be used to create a sense of pathos or tragic loss.

Some music depicts the pathos of human life, and pathos weighs heavy on the human spirit. It grounds human emotion in the dark realities of human life. Death, tragedy, loss, and depression are but a few of these earthly realities. In conveying pathos, composers typically write slow, dark, dirgelike, and often weeping music. The final movement of Tchaikovsky's Symphony No.6, the "Pathétique," and the second movement of Beethoven's Symphony No. 7 provide vignettes of human loss and spiritual exhaustion. It has been said that Tchaikovsky's final movement expresses the darkness that lies behind those who find life hopeless. The heaviness of this music requires a dark sound, and using heavy, soft sticks that bring out the fundamental and lower partials of the timpani can produce that best. In many ways, Beethoven's second movement of Symphony No. 7 is a funeral dirge—slow, dark, and filled with pathos. As in Tchaikovsky's Sixth Symphony, the timpanist must elicit a broad, heavy, dark sound that is commensurate with the dirgelike character of the music. For example, the figure at letter G should be played with a soft pair of mallets capable of bringing out the lower partials of the timpani (see example 2.18). Because the music is so heavy, the timpanist can also use a bounce stroke (described above) on the quarter notes to bring out as much of the timpani's color as is possible. The eighth notes should be heavily articulated, using lots of arm and wrist recoil. The pathos of this passage is strengthened by the heavy, dark strokes of the timpani. See the companion Web site for a marked timpani part.

2.18. Using a bounce stroke to elicit color

The timpani can reinforce the noble or heroic nature of melodic and harmonic lines. Heroic or noble music must transcend ordinary life and lift one to the level of the sublime. To express the noble and heroic qualities of music, the timpanist must create a sound that is filled with color and that projects well. A sound that is too dark, too bright, or too articulate will not convey heroic feelings. A general purpose or medium stick, lifting the sound out of the head, will achieve a heroic or noble sound. Beethoven was a master of writing heroic music—in part because his life was heroic. The first two measures of Symphony No. 3 set the tone for the heroic music that follows. In each of these measures, Beethoven asks each instrument to play a single, short, full-bodied, transcendental note. The first two timpani notes need to reflect this sound and can be played with a medium mallet, held in a staccato manner, and executed with a bounce stroke that lifts the sound out of the drum. The timpani part at the beginning of the final movement of Beethoven's Symphony No. 5 can be played in a similar manner (see example 2.19). After fifty measures of growing tension, Beethoven writes three melodic and ascending quarter notes (a third apart) that lift the listener upward. The first three timpani notes can be played with a medium stick using a very loose grip and a bounce stroke with lots of lift. This will give the requisite color and transcendental quality to the music. The next five eighth notes are intended to punch out the melody in an authoritative manner. This effect can be achieved by playing each note in marcato fashion. Marcato strokes give point and color to the sound and adequately convey the noble character of this music. See the companion Web site for a marked timpani part.

2.19. Bounce stroke to improve phrasing

Aids in Interpreting Music

What resources do timpanists have at their disposal to aid them in interpreting their part? Examining the score, listening to and watching the conductor, and listening to the way the orchestra plays a particular passage can help the timpanist determine how to punctuate a musical line. The score is perhaps the most useful aid. The score provides ready reference to the overall architecture of the music, the musical phrases, dynamic markings, rests suggesting where to muffle, and articulation markings. These components of the score help timpanists rhythmically and tonally shape their parts and determine the appropriate articulation. The score is particularly useful in interpreting Romantic music because composers in this era expected so much more out of an orchestra: tonally, dynamically, rhythmically, harmonically, and melodically. The timpanist must refer to Francis Poulenc's score to the Concerto for Organ, Strings, and Timpani to properly interpret the timpani part. Because Poulenc scores each instrument at a particular dynamic level, timpanists must write into their parts the strongest or weakest dynamic played by an instrument at each of their entrances. Then the timpanist can play at the proper dynamic level relative to the strongest or weakest instrument. Since Poulenc often reserved the highest dynamic level for his melodies, timpanists should play their melodic parts at that dynamic. Poulenc scores long chords whose purpose is to connect notes in rising or falling arpeggios. Against this harmonic backdrop, he will occasionally score a short note for the timpani. But he does not expect it to be played as a short note! The notes, often in the root of the chord, are intended be played staccato but sustained the duration of the chord. Finally, Poulenc uses meter changes to begin or terminate a musical phrase. Knowing this helps the timpanist convincingly begin and end those phrases.

The conductor often gestures or uses facial expressions to express the type of sound and phrasing he or she expects of the orchestra, and the alert timpanist will pick up on the meaning of these expressions. Common gestures include large, sweeping, side-wise movements connoting legato phrasing. Upward gestures can mean a strengthening the dynamic line and downward gestures, a weakening of that line. Small, quick, hand motions often denote short, staccato playing. The shaking of a hand or fist can indicate greater intensity. The conductor will often discuss phrasing with a particular section or instrument, and the conductor's interpretations of a particular passage or phrase, although for one instrument, may have implications for the way the timpanists interpret a part. If the conductor asks for a diminuendo in a descending melodic line in the violins, timpanists may want to add a diminuendo their parts. Finally, musicians, by their musical training, are expected to phrase their parts. Listening to one instrument or one instrumental section phrase a passage provides an insight into phrasing. Because the timpani and trumpet often double each other in Baroque and Classical music, it is essential for both to have a common approach to interpreting the passage. Conferences often focus on how long to hold notes and whether to dynamically shade a phrase. A conference between the timpanist and members of the trumpet section may or may not be necessary. On the one hand, it is not necessary in cases where the members have played together for some time and have a common understanding of how each person interprets a part. Conductors develop an interpretation of a particular style or composer. Where the orchestra shares this interpretation, it limits the number of interpretation issues. On the other hand, where there is a difference of opinion in how to interpret a passage, a conference may be required to resolve multiple interpretations. Ultimately, the conductor is the arbiter of thorny issues.

In conclusion, this chapter has described the interpretation of timpani parts. An understanding of the style, psychology, and intentions of the composer is very helpful in determining how to play a particular part. These factors shape the overall character of the music that the composer writes. Tone, phrasing, dynamic contrast, accents, and articulation are important in shaping the musical line to effectively convey musical meaning. Tonal phrasing is often overlooked by timpanists and can contribute significantly to the emotional quality of the timpani part. Understanding the emotions the composer wishes to convey is the first step in interpreting a timpani part. Subsequently, timpanists draw on their own artistic resources to support the kind of emotional ambiance that the composer wishes to create. Finally, studying scores, paying close attention to the conductor's exhortation to other instruments, and listening to the orchestra can help timpanists more effectively interpret and play their parts.

3

Interpretation of Baroque Music

The interpretation of timpani parts in the Baroque and Classical periods is, at times, shrouded in mystery. Our knowledge of the timpani, timpani mallets, bowl shape, timpani heads, the composer's understanding of the use of the timpani in the orchestra, and scoring for the timpani is limited. In a two-hundred-year period, the timpani underwent a transformation. The size of the drums and the tonal quality of the instruments increased. In some cases, we know the drums composers had available to them, but in other cases we can only speculate about the kind of drums that composers had in mind when they wrote for the timpani. We have few documents describing the timpani sticks used in the seventeenth and eighteenth centuries. Therefore, we are left to speculate about the quality of sound production that a timpanist could produce. During the Baroque and the early to middle Classical period, timpanists were quite secretive about their art, and, with few exceptions, they did not leave a written record of the drums, performance practices, techniques, and playing styles (Virdung 1993; Arbeau 1972; Speer 1697; Eisel 1738; Mersenne 1957; Altenburg 1974, 30–35; Titcomb, 1956, 56–66). The seventeenth and eighteenth centuries witnessed the gradual introduction of the timpani into the orchestra. Undoubtedly, composers puzzled over how the timpani could be used effectively in communicating musical ideas. In some cases, timpani notation was not standardized: composers did not agree on how to notate a roll. Consequently, the interpretation of timpani parts must be a very personal one—one informed by our limited understanding of the timpani and its use in the Baroque and Classical eras. In this chapter, the author will examine stylistic concerns, musical notation, and phrasing issues that bear on the interpretation of music in the Baroque. The author will leave it to others to discuss whether or not this music is best played on original instruments.

    The Baroque era begins around 1600 and ends in the mid-1700s. Historically and intellectually, this was a period of great change on the Continent and abroad. Economically, trade during the preceding three hundred years led to the rise of a prosperous middle class, and the English philosopher, John Locke, was among the first to lay the intellectual foundation for the rise of capitalism and modern democracy (Locke 1980). Politically, monarchies dominated the Continent, but after the Glorious Revolution in Britain, the Parliament gained a greater share of political power than it had before the revolution. Despite the rise of the middle class, the landed aristocracy remained the most efficacious force in politics and music. The Age of Discovery enriched many nations and produced a self-confidence and grandeur of spirit. The Reformation led to the Counter-Reformation. Across Europe, religious differences were in part responsible for continuous political conflict. For many Catholics, religious art and music was expected to inspire and instruct. Music, rooted in human sense, opened the soul to the Holy Spirit. Rather than corrupting the soul, music could ennoble it (Artz 1962, 158–161).

Music reflected the wealth, power, majesty, and grandeur of this era: the Baroque. Often divided into the early (1600–1685) and late (1685–1750) Baroque periods, music was sensuous, grandiose, glorious, ornate, mammoth, heavy, complex, and sumptuous. Composers used massive sonority, ornament, movement, tone color, and dynamic contrasts to express their musical ideas. It was not uncommon in the late Baroque for composers to combine a number of smaller pieces into a sonata da camera, suite, partita, or overture—allowing each section to speak a different mood. Bach used particular musical gestures to represent certain moods. Drawing on the doctrine of affections, sorrow and sadness were associated with descending musical phrases, and this was effectively used in the B-Minor Mass (Schweitzer 1966, II: 64–65). In choral music of other composers, the choice of musical instruments and voices often reflected the libretto. Heaven was represented by voices in the angelic boy's choir and hell by the growling bass voice, for example. Effort and hardship were represented by slower rhythms, while hurry and rapture were written to quicker tempos. The evolution of instruments, especially the violin, provided composers with more sonorous and flexible instruments. The modern violin produced greater tone color and dynamic contrasts, and it was more effective in expressing deeper emotional themes. Movement, tension, swelling, and the contrast between light and dark passages were possible with improved instruments and larger ensembles. Baroque music became very emotional or dramatic—and very personal as well. Thus, Baroque music became much more sumptuous, ornate, powerful, and emotionally colored than earlier music (Artz 1962, 204–218; Blume 1967, 111–117; Van Ess 1970, 150–154).

Timpani, Mallets, and Tone in the Baroque and Classical Eras

Contrary to conventional wisdom, the evolution of the larger drums, evolving bowl shapes, better drumheads, new mallets, and new playing style suggests that the timpani could be treated as a tonal (as well as a rhythmic) instrument. Throughout the Baroque and into the Classical period, the diameter of timpani increased. This means that the tone quality of the instruments improved. Jeremy Montagu, James Blades and Edmund Bowles report that timpani in the seventeenth century ranged in size from 17 to 34 inches. There is some dispute about whether or not the drums were, on the whole, smaller than what we use today. While 17-inch drums (smaller drums) were common in many orchestras, James Blades suggests that other drums measured between 24 and 30 inches. Bowles and Montague place the diameters of seventeenth-century drums between 18 and 24½ inches, and John Papastefan agrees with H. C. R. Landon that smaller drums were preferred because larger timpani reverberated more than smaller drums. To complicate this picture, instrument historian, Nicholas Bassaraboff, argues that larger drums were present in Eastern Europe and Russia, but not in Western Europe during the Baroque. In the fifteenth and sixteenth centuries, very large drums were reported in Hungary and Russia (Bassaraboff 1941, 33–35). At the end of the sixteenth century, Thoinot Arbeau describes a Turkish drum measuring about 30 inches in diameter, and Sebastian Virdung, at the beginning of the sixteenth century, describes the very large military drums (*die grossen Heerpauken*) used to summon men to the battlefield. In Virdung's words, "die grossen Heerpauken" were "enormous tubs of great noise" and they were capable of "a smothering and drowning of all sweet melodies and of the whole of Music" (Arbeau 1972, 18; Virdung 1993, 114–115). Not to be outdone, Henry G. Farmer discoved a 40- and 38-inch pair of late eighteenth century timpani (Farmer 1962, 129). In conclusion, it appears that timpani were usually smaller than those used today; however, larger drums were circulating and one must conclude that some court orchestras owned larger drums. These would have produced a better tone than smaller drums (Montagu 2003, 78–87).

While smaller-sized drums were common in the early Baroque, musical scores of this period attest to the use of larger drums in Western Europe. Nicholas Hasse's *Auffzug 2. Clarinde [und] Heerpauken* (1656), Heinrich Biber or Andreas Hofer's *Salzburger Festmesse* (1682), and Jean-Baptiste Lully, *Thesée* (1673) are scored for timpani in G and c (Bowles 2002, 18–19). Andre and Jacques Philidor, court musicians to King Loius XIV, wrote a march scored for two timpani in G and c and e and g (Blades 1970, 237-240). In the eighteenth century, many of Bach's sacred cantatas are written in for G and c timpani (Nos. 31, 41, 43, 59, 63, 71, 74, 130, 137, and 172) or for A and d timpani (Nos. 11, 34, 80, 110, 149, 191, 195, 201, 205, and 206 for example). In No. 143 the lower drum reached down to an F—presumably the lowest, recognizable note on larger timpani of his time (Blades 1970, 245). Bach could have scored the timpani an octave higher and that would have been appropriate for the use of small drums; however, he did not. This attests to his preference for using larger, more sonorous drums. It also suggests that he had access to these drums. Since he wrote for larger drums when he lived in Köthen, Weimar, and Leipzig, larger drums must have been available in other parts of Germany. Other composers could have written parts to fit smaller drums if they desired; however, they chose not to do so. Rather, they wrote parts that could be played on modern 26- to 29-inch timpani. Second, if smaller drums were used, the tone would not have been very good. Bowles rightly concludes that tuning small drums down to A and d would have produced a "belting" tone. Additionally, articulation would have been very difficult to achieve on drums with very loose heads. Where the timpani were employed rhythmically, composers would have preferred drums capable of better articulation. This would mean that when timpani were written in G and c, larger drums with tighter heads would have been preferable to smaller drums with slack heads. Composers would not have scored for instruments unable to articulate a part or play it tonally. Finally, the existence of larger drums suggests that they were available to European composers, and for this reason, composers would have scored for them. It is unimaginable that Bach, a sensitive and demanding composer, would want timpanists to play on very slack heads. He would have asked for the larger drums (Altenburg 1974, 121–122; Terry 1932, 50–61; Bowles 1976, 58–59; Papastefan, 1978, 61; Blades 1970, 230–231).

There is one further piece of evidence suggesting that timpani increased in size in the eighteenth century. By examining Bowles images of historical timpani of the time, the number of tension rods increases. In the seventeenth century, there were approximately six to seven tension rods on the larger of two drums; however, in the eighteenth century, seven to eight tenion rods are common. Assuming that the tension rods were not added to improve the sound quality of the drum, it is reasonable to conclude that the increased number of tenion rods reflected a modest increase in the size of the drums.

Well into the classical period, timpani larger than the traditional 19- to 24-inch drum were available to some composers (Montagu 2002, 80). When Handel came to London in 1784, Charles Burney notes that Ashbridge of Drury-Lane made two larger drums (Bowles 2002, 457). These drums were larger than the orchestra's drums and they provided superior tone (Burney 1979, 7–8). We do not know the size of the Ashbridge timpani; however, Jeremy Montagu, noted instrument historian, says that two surviving timpani of the eighteenth century were 27½ and 33 inches (Montagu 2002, 85). These middle-sized drums suggest that Ashbridge could have produced drums of like or similar size, and they would have produced a much better tone than 19- to 21-inch or alleged 36- and 39-inch double-bass timpani (Farmer 1960, 95; Blades 1970, 254–255). Finally, anecdotal evidence suggests that drums in the 25- to 29-inch range were used at this time. O. Vandenbrock, in his *Traite general de tous les instruments a vent a l'usage des compositeurs* (1794, 56–57), tell us that the preferred notes on the larger and smaller drums were B and c, and d and e-flat respectively. These are suspiciously close to the range of a contemporary 29- and 26-inch Dresden drums. Choice notes on these timpani range from A to c on the large drum and from d to f on the small drum.

The size of the Ashbridge timpani helped produce a better sound, but Burney suggests something more tantalizing: he writes that Ashbridge built timpani that were more cylindrical than hemispherical. Hemispherical drums tend to produce a more focused sound with a strong fundamental. Cylindrical timpani tend to be slightly more transparent, the fundamental note is strong but not overpowering, and they would emphasize the upper partials to a greater extent. This accounts for their greater transparency. At a time in which timpani heads were thicker than they are today, hemispherical drums would produce a very strong and focused tone. However, the cylindrical drums would have modified the acoustical spectrum of the drums and would have produced a more tonal, transparent sound. Thus, the changing size and shape of the timpani suggest that attempts were being made to achieve better timpani tone—appropriate to the concert hall.

The drums available to Handel were two tenor (19- and 21-inch), two bass (the Ashbridge "Tower" drums of around 27½- and 33-inch), and two double-bass (possibly 38- and 39-inch) artillery drums. Blades documents Handel's frequent use of the larger Tower drums. Of course, these six drums would provide a broader pallet of tone color from which a composer could choose. Thus, Handel was not restricted by the tight, focused sound produced by smaller drums or the belting tone that resulted from playing on slack timpani heads.

As the diameters of the timpani changed through the Baroque and Classical periods, so did the shape of the timpani bowl. Donald Bowles, in *The Timpani*, provides a photographic history of the timpani (Bowles 2002, 88–348). For the Baroque and Classical periods, his images of timpani include period prints, woodcuts, paintings, statues, and contemporary photographs of historical timpani. In combing through these pictures, it appears that the timpani bowls were constructed in three basic shapes: hemispheric, parabolic and semiflat-bottomed. In the following analysis, the author selected images of timpani using two criteria. First, timpani had to be placed in a non-military setting. These timpani would have been used in a concert venue. Second, the author culled photographs of historical timpani and prints, paintings, drawings, and woodcuts of timpani. These images would most accurately describe or represent timpani bowl shape. Figurines of angels playing timpani mounted on eighteenth century organ cases were omitted. The author was concerned that these would be less historically reliable, since the goal of the craftsman was to ornament the organ, not accurately depict the drums in a social or historical context. After classifying their shape as hemispheric, parabolic, or semiflat-bottomed, the timpani were grouped into roughly 25-year periods: 1600–1650, 1651–1700, 1701–1725, 1726–1750, and 1751–1775. Bowles does not produce images of timpani from 1776-1800, the final years of the Classical period, so this period is necessarily omitted.

The findings are interesting. In the two periods from 1600-1700, the dominant bowl shape was hemispherical. Eighty percent were hemispheric, ten percent parabolic, and 10 percent semiflat-bottomed. Although it is important to note that Michael Praetorius sketched two drums that were round in shape. 1701–1725 was a transitional period. There was expansion of the non-hemispheric bowl (fifty percent hemispherical, twenty-five percent parabolic, and 25 percent semiflat-bottomed). In final two periods, 1726–1750 and 1751–1775, the semiflat-bottomed bowl dominated other bowl shapes. From 1726–1750 and 1751–1775, seventy-seven and eighty-three percent respectively were semiflat-bottomed bowls. Clearly, the changing shape of the timpani bowl suggests that timpanists were searching for timpani that would produce the best tone and pitch. They found this in the semiflat-bottomed and parabolic bowls. The greatest evolution of the timpani came in the Baroque. Timpani tone and intonation would have been better after 1725 than before it, and composers of the Classical period would be writing for timpani whose bowl produced the best intonation and tone possible for that time.

Changing methods of tanning the timpani head and the artistry of the tanner provides more evidence that composers and timpanists were concerned with timpani tone. In 1732, Joseph F. C. Maier's *Museum Musicum* (1954) tells us that timpani heads were half-tanned so they sounded brighter. The tanning process concluded with brushing the head with brandy and garlic, and placing it in the sun or by a gentle, small fire to dry. It is clear by Maier's account that orchestral timpanists were seeking an alternative to the dark, percussive sound produced by cavalry timpanists. Instead, the need for better sounding orchestral timpani heads led to experimentation in hide tanning that produced a brighter sound. Johann P. Eisel's 1738 *Musicus autodidaktos*, describes the same tanning process; however, he adds that heads should be made by a parchment or harness maker (Eisel 1738, 66–67). A parchment maker would have been able to produce a thinner skin, and this thin skin would have produced superior tone quality for the orchestral timpanist than was possible with thicker heads. Maier and Eisel's comments on making timpani heads clearly convey one conclusion: timpanists and composers were searching for a different tone than what was common for the period. Undoubtedly, the quality of timpani tone was improving in this period and this advance would have led composers to score for timpani more often.

Timpani mallets, I suggest, were capable of greater tone color than is normally inferred from eighteenth-century sources. Prior to the time the timpani found their way into a refined musical setting, timpani mallets were made of a hard material, such as wood or ivory. These were particularly useful on the battlefield: the timpanist could clearly articulate a marching cadence and produce a great noise to create terror in the opposing troops. Virdung and Praetorius provide a drawing of a timpani mallet that looked like a short sword with a tapered shaft that ends with a knob or ball (Bowles 2002, 93; Praetorius 1619). This mallet appears to have been made only for producing great noise. As the timpani were integrated into the orchestra, the sticks undoubtedly changed. This may have been one reason for the development of the cartwheel stick. They were made from lighter beech wood or boxwood, they were eight to nine inches in length, and a rosette the size of a silver crown was attached to the end. "It is the edge of these small rosettes that strikes the skin of the kettledrum, and makes it give out a sound much more pleasant than if it were struck with a side-drum stick" (as cited in Titcomb 1956, 60; Eisel, 1738, 66–67; Bowles 2002, 404–405). Shortening the sticks would have made them lighter, and lighter sticks would have produced a more sonorous and less percussive tone quality—all other things being equal—than heavier sticks. Lighter sticks would have facilitated playing in a more delicate and musical manner that brought out timpani tone.

Bowles provides images of timpani sticks from 1237 to the late 1980s. While is it is not possible to describe material from which the mallet is made, nor it exact length, it is possible to identify if mallet had a ball- or cartwheel type head. Prior to the Baroque, all timpani sticks recorded by Bowles were ball-type mallets or side drum sticks. Beginning in the early Baroque, the cartwheel stick, which ended with the small rosette, made it first appearance. In all drawings, prints, paintings, and woodcuts of the Baroque and Classical period, all timpani sticks are cartwheel sticks. The only time ball sticks make their appearance is in the hands of organ case angels playing timpani (Bowles 183, 231, 235). One can only suspect that cartwheel sticks produced a better sound than the ball stick; however, timpanists probably kept a ball stick in their stick bag and used them on the proper occasion.

Improved mallet construction provided timpanists and composers an opportunity to explore a wider variety of tonal shading. By 1738, Eisler makes it clear that timpanists were using various materials to shape the tone of their instruments. To deaden the ring of the drum, the timpanist could drape the drums with cloth (Eisel 1738, 68–69). When the knobby, wood-headed stick gave way to the wood *covered* stick, timpanists were able to explore the nuances of timpani tone. Certainly by 1750, covered sticks were more broadly used in orchestral settings. In 1738, Eisler notes that timpanists were covering their sticks with leather, gauze, or wool. These advances were made for one reason: to improve timpani tone and to give timpanists the resources to rhythmically and tonally play their parts. By 1802, Koch reports that chamois or wool mallets were a requirement for timpanists (Bowles 2002, 69). However, Blades reports seeing a set of Austrian mallets where "traces of softer covering (now almost gone) could clearly be seen on several ends" (Blades 1970, 250).

At some time in the eighteenth or early nineteenth century, the covered cartwheel stick was created. A doughnut disk of differing diameters, thickness, and materials was sandwiched between two disks of wood. Made of different materials, such as wool, linen, or chamois, these sticks provided greater tonal and rhythmic articulation (Bowles 2002, 69). As the Baroque passed, timpanists employed a growing number of sticks capable of producing a broader spectrum of timpani tone and articulation. It is only reasonable to conclude that composers, like Bach and Handel, understood the kind of tone color the timpani produced (Blades 1970, 249).

There is evidence that timpanists were familiar with the tonal characteristics of the timpani head. Daniel Speer and Eisel describe the unusual echo of striking the drumhead near the counterhoop and then in the center of the drum. In the process of discovering this echo, they would have noticed the differing tonal characteristics of drumhead (Eisel 1738, 68; Speer 1974, 220). Since timpanists played on different parts of the head, they would have understood that different playing spots produced different tones. While the playing spot was important, so was the kind of stroke that vibrated the head.

Bowles's book demonstrates that the timpanist's grip and style of playing changed by the high Baroque. First, the only grip used throughout the Baroque and Classical periods was the German or palms down grip. Unending images detail timpanists holding the sticks in what appears to be a near death-grip on the sticks. However, there is evidence that the grip changed in high Baroque or early classical period. A1770 drawing shows a German timpanist holding his left stick with this thumb and forefinger, the remaining fingers having no contact with the stick at all. This appears to be the case with the right hand too (Bowles 2002, 252). In three years (1730, 1757, and 1773), angel sculptures positioned on organ cases are holding their sticks in a similar manner. Therefore, by the Classical period, timpanists were exploring different ways of holding the stick to play more tonally, more softly or loudly, or more or less articulately. Second, the playing style of timpanist evolves in the Baroque. In the Baroque and Classical periods, there are six images of timpanists playing in orchestral settings. Prior to 1740, four drawings picture timpanists flinging their sticks high above their head and landing, however delicately or indelicately, on the timpani head (Bowles 2002, 121, 152, 171, 177). In two orchestral drawings after 1740, the timpanists are depicted playing in a more reserved fashion and closer to the drum. This development suggests that timpanists became increasingly concerned with stick control, the reserved execution of their parts, and timpani tone.

By the Classical period, continental timpanists were experimenting with different tone producing playing styles. Evidence of this can be found in Sir George Smart's writings. In 1794, the Haydn-Salomon orchestra was rehearsing for a concert. Smart, not a timpanist by training, played the drums that day. Smart reports that Haydn, a one-time timpanist, approached him about his playing style. Haydn pointed out that Smart was bringing the drumstick straight down. Instead, Haydn recommended a glancing stroke because German timpanists discovered that a vertical stroke stopped the vibration of the head. The oblique stroke allowed the head to vibrate, giving a superior tone (Smart 1907, 3).

In sum, there is little question that timpani tone production became important to musicians during the High Baroque and Classical periods. Larger drums, more tonal bowls, better heads, cartwheel mallets, covered mallet heads, alternative grips, reserved playing styles, new strokes, and expanding knowledge of how to produce different tones gave timpanists a larger color pallet from which they could draw in painting their parts. Seventeenth- and eighteenth-century writers discussed above provide evidence that timpanists were aware of timpani tone and knew how to shape the tone to achieve certain effects and execute specific passages. Because of the technical advances in stick production, head and bowl construction, playing style, and the availability of appropriate sized drums, composers in the eighteenth century could effectively use the timpani in their compositions. The development of the timpani in these periods suggests that timpanists should treat their instruments as tonal as well as rhythmical instruments. Using covered mallets is certainly permissible in the proper orchestral context.

Technical Considerations in Interpreting Baroque Music

The author does not purpose to engage in a discussion of the relative benefits of performing with period instruments or modern-day timpani. Conductors bring with them predilections about how Baroque music should be played. Their understanding of the Baroque style and performance practices of the day shape their conception of the music to be performed. For that reason, it is helpful for timpanists to be conversant with advances in Baroque musical notation and performance practices.

Timpanists are aware that there are a number of musical issues in Baroque music deserving careful thought: double-dotting, articulation, phrasing, dynamics, accents, and the treatment of mood or emotion. More narrowly, timpanists are concerned with the notation of rolls, writing parts, and improvisation. Double-dotting notes was not uncommon in the Baroque. Double-dotting simply extended the length of the note by one-half. The purpose of the double-dotting was to provide a degree of exhilaration that could not be obtained by playing the part as written. Where composers did not double-dot their parts, it was left to the musicians to double-dot in the appropriate circumstance (Quantz 1966, 67; L. Mozart 1951, 157–158). Most dotted notes were not lengthened by "adding another dot," according to musical scholar, Robert Donington. Notes could be double-dotted if there were enough dotted notes in a consistent rhythmic pattern, and if the double-dotting would not make the music sluggish. For the timpanist, the opening movement of Handel's *Royal Fireworks* provides a good example of the appropriate use of double-dotting. In the first forty-three measures of this movement, double-dotting the quarter note can lengthen it. This example meets Donington's three double-dotting criteria. First, there are enough dotted quarter notes to establish a consistent rhythmic pattern. Second, the notes are part of a distinctive rhythmic pattern. In fact, this pattern dominates the first forty-three measures of this movement. Finally, while it might be argued that double-dotting these notes might slow the piece down, double-dotting them definitely gives the part the nobility that Handel desires. But a double-dot would not be added to measures 9 and 10 of the La Rejouissance. Donington's second condition is not satisfied: these two measures are not part of a distinctive rhythmic pattern characterizing the music (Donington 1974, 380–381, 386).

Related to double-dotting is the issue of two against three rhythms. During the Baroque it is not unusual to find two against three rhythms.

See, for example, the Sanctus of Bach's B-Minor Mass (see example 3.1). At first blush, the timpani and violins appear to play a similar rhythmic figure. The eighth note followed by the four thirty-second notes in the timpani seem to square rhythmically with the dotted eighth followed by the

3.1. Interpreting rhythms in Bach's Mass in B Minor

sixteenth figure in the strings. The trumpets and choir are playing or singing triplets. Did Bach intend to write a very awkward duple and against triple figure? This has been a subject of debate. On the one hand, Gallant style performance practice of the day suggests that these timpani and string parts should be played as triplet figures. It was common for composers to expect parts in duple meter to be played in triple meter when the two occurred against each other (Donington 1974, 464, 467; Spitta 1951, I: 563; Schweitzer 1966, I: 350). Therefore, timpanist Nicholas Ormrod believes the best way to execute this passage is to play the figure as part of a triplet: a quaver and four semiquavers (Option 2). This approach would be stylistically correct and rhythmically elegant—avoiding the disjointed feeling that comes with a three against two rhythm.[1] On the other hand, conductor Helmuth Rilling believes that Bach intended to write a two against three rhythm and concludes that it is best to play four semiquavers on the last note of the trumpet's triplet (see Option 3).[2] As there is no consensus among timpanists on how to interpret this passage, perhaps the best advice is to use your best judgment and the conductor's interpretation of how to execute this rhythmic gesture.

Timpanists need to be aware of the manner in which "inequality" can be used to push a phrase forward. Inequality (*notes inegales*) refers to the practice of lengthening the first of two notes, effectively shortening the second or vice versa. The purpose of this practice was to make the rhythm and melody more graceful. The lourer and couler are two common kinds of inequality found in Baroque music. The lourer represents a practice of lengthening the first of two slurred notes and shortening the second. In a couler there are two slurred notes, the second of which is dotted. In this figure, the first note is shortened and the second is lengthened. How much the long note is lengthened is a matter of musical taste. Finally, there is the issue of when to use inequality. Both Robert Donington and Mary Halford in her introduction to Couperin's *L'Art de Toucher le Chavecin* nicely summarize rules guiding the use of inequality. Halford argues that inequality is permitted in the following circumstances: stepwise notes with time values shorter than the lower figure of the time signature, notes falling in pairs, melodies which would be made more elegant, groups of notes uninterrupted by a rest or other notes with greater time values, notes that are slurred, and pickup notes to inequality-eligible notes. Inequality is forbidden where the musical phrase consists of broken, leaping, repeated notes (Quantz 1966, 123); with triplets and syncopated notes; in very slow or fast tempi, making the phrase too sluggish or the rhythm indistinct (Quantz 1966, 123); in mixed grouping of notes; in slurs over three or more notes; where dots or strokes are added above or below the notes (Quantz 1966, 123; Couperin 1974, 49); and in allemandes or marches (Couperin 1974, 11).[3]

What implication does inequality have for the tied notes in measure 145 of Bach's B-Minor Mass (the Gloria)? Spitta believes that Bach was thoroughly familiar with the French style and Francois Couperin, and Bach copied the French style pieces of N. Grigny and Charles Dieupart (Spitta 1951, I: 202). In so copying, Bach would have been familiar with the French ornamentation and compositional practices—to include the use of slurs to indicate inequality. Should these two sets of slurred notes be played unequally? The timpanist should be prepared to play this figure in one of three ways. First, play it as written because to play it with inequality would make the final two beats of the measure less eloquent. One could play the first note as usual. The second note is an A and will naturally project less. The next three notes could be executed as a diminuendo: effectively emphasizing the A, giving less weight to the d, and finishing with a phrase-ending quieter note. This would achieve what Bach intended: a stressed first note and an unstressed second note. Second, play this part as a lourer because it meets the Halford's test for playing an unequal pair of notes. While this might fit the rhythm of the music, it certainly makes the line more impetuous and less pleasing. Third, play this as a couler. This is recommended by Ormrod; however, this author does not believe that the tied eighth notes were written as a couler; played as a couler, the figure would not fit well with the rhythm in the voices and strings (Ormrod 1997, 56–57). See the companion Web site for a marked timpani part.

Early Baroque music is typically underphrased. Articulation as a form of phrasing is not *compositionally* important to seventeenth-century music, but musicians used performance practices of the day in playing a part. It becomes more critical in the High Baroque and a growing number of composers ornament their scores with articulation markings. Leopold Mozart notes that dashes and dots are used to clearly articulate notes in a score.

Daniel Turk, writing about fifty years later, adds that staccato notes are played half the length of a legato note (L. Mozart 1951, 45–47; Turk 1982, 345–346). Bach, in Cantata No. 130, takes special pain to articulate eighth notes in the wind and timpani parts in measure 55 and after. Bach places a dot above each note. Obviously, he is sensitive to the problem timpanists have in playing articulate notes. Between measures 55 and 72, all eighth notes in the timpani, brass, and winds are written staccato; this is not true for instruments that can play shorter and longer notes. For example, in measure 63, the trumpets and timpani both have dots above their eighth notes (see example 3.2).

3.2. Articulating underphrased parts

However, in the next measure, Bach has the trumpets play undotted eighth notes, while the timpani is marked with the dotted eighths. In the following examples from the Mass, the timpani part is written in c and G but should be played d and A. Possibly, Bach was aware that timpanists have difficulty articulating notes on low drums and consequently used articulation marks to more effectively write the timpani parts. Perhaps more suggestive, Bach's scoring reveals that timpanists were able to produce staccato and legato notes: if it is possible to write staccato notes, then it infers that notes could be played in a more legato fashion. Because Bach is clearly differentiating legato and staccato strokes, it is important for timpanists to use a technique capable of producing the appropriate articulation and tone. Using a stick other than wood or ivory at the appropriate time would seem to be suggested by this analysis.[4] See the companion Web site for a marked timpani part.

In conclusion, timpanists were capable of playing a broader range of tones and articulations than is ordinarily supposed and Bach's scoring for timpani suggest that he understood this. In addition to larger drums and better heads, timpanists used a variety of sticks and understood how different parts of the timpano head would produce different tones. While the tone was not comparable to the tone we achieve today, it was much better than what is commonly supposed (Mersenne 1957, 555–556; Altenburg 1974, 122).

In a chamber orchestra, timpanists exercised some influence over the phrasing of Baroque music. The fermata gave musicians the freedom to determine the length of the note, and when placed over a rest or bar line, the musician controlled the amount of silence that fit the musical line. The luftpause, which separated musical phrases, gave the musician the opportunity to determine the amount of tone taken out of the earlier note. Also, musicians were able to determine how much silence to place between unmarked phrases. Composers occasionally used ligatures over groups of notes to slur them. Finally, Donington noted that musicians exercised some discretion in prolonging or shortening notes for expression (Donington 1974, 407–409). Thus, musicians had some latitude in phrasing a musical line. For timpanists, phrasing included muffling a note and playing a roll or possibly schlagmanieren (ornamental cadences) under a fermata.

Ligatures, ties, or slurs occur with increasing frequency in the Baroque. Used in 1597, slurs defined which note falling within the slur was given a longer or shorter value (Donington 1974, 595–597). The slur was used to tie notes, show extreme legato, to place notes in a phrase, and, in conjunction with dots and dashes, to show how notes should be bowed. Slurs could be used to indicate tonguing on wind instruments and note groupings on keyboard instruments. Thus, slurs were used to shape note values, to indicate legato, and to phrase (Donington 1974, 407–408; Butt, 1990, 186–206). For the timpani, slurring was used most often to phrase notes (as in the B-Minor Mass described above) or to connect notes.

Baroque composers are unlikely to employ crescendos and diminuendos; although, as the period progressed, the use of dynamic terracing increased. In the early and middle Baroque, composers did not use crescendos and decrescendos. Instead, they used them to alternate between loud (*forte*) and soft (*piano*) passages (Quantz 1966, 133). Composers gave musicians the latitude of playing either loud or soft, and C. P. E. Bach notes that musical context determines what dynamic to play (C. P. E. Bach 1949, 162–164). The choice was structured by the passage, other markings, and the presence or absence of a choir. In measure 25 of the Gloria of the B-Minor Mass, Bach scores the orchestra and chorus very lightly and it is apparent that he intended a quieter section. In measure 29, the full choir and orchestra enter and Bach most likely intended the music to be played at a louder dynamic level, for example, *forte*. This movement alternates between louder and softer dynamic moments based on the entrance of the choir. Schweitzer believes that Bach should be played with alternating dynamics, and musicians should avoid the terracing that occurs ever more frequently after the beginning of the eighteenth century. That said, Schweitzer argues that a rising line might justify a slight crescendo; however, a descending line would never justify a decrescendo (Schweitzer 1966, II: 376, 380). Writing in 1762, C. P. E. Bach says that discordant notes should be played more loudly than concordant notes because discordant notes arouse human feeling while concordant notes quiet it. He adds that concluding cadences should be played loud (C. P. E. Bach 1949, 163). For example, in the Gloria from the B-Minor Mass, the last two measures may be played significantly louder than the preceding measures.

It is clear that composers began to use dynamic markings in the early eighteenth century. Given the emotional nature of Baroque music, it is reasonable to consider the conditions under which crescendos and decrescendos could be employed. Karl Hochreither in his *Performance Practice of the Instrumental-Vocal Works of Johann Sebastian Bach* argues that it was not unusual for musicians to swell and ebb to effectively play a part (Hochreither, 2002, 136), and Donington suggests that terracing dynamics should follow the rise and fall of musical tension. Since pitch and emotion often rise and fall together, it makes sense to terrace dynamics based upon the rise and descent of the musical line (Donington 1974, 416, 420, 422). This is particularly important in the later Baroque when dynamic shading became more common. While crescendo ($\diagup$) and decrescendo ($\diagdown$) markings were used in the early eighteenth century, *fp* and *pf* also made their appearance. Donington believes that composers gave musicians the latitude in determining how to play these markings. The marking *fp* might suggest either a decrescendo from *forte* to *piano* or a *forte subito piano*. The *pf* might suggest a crescendo from *piano* to *forte* or a sudden *forte* (Donington 1974, 418). Frederick Neumann advises Bach instrumentalists to be aware of markings such as *piu p* (a decrescendo). Dynamic markings made over several measures (for example, *piano* in one measure and *forte* in the next) might suggest a crescendo, and *piano*, *piano*, and *pianissimo* over three measures could indicate a decrescendo (Neumann 1993, 169–170). According to Winton Dean, in his classic study of *Handel's Dramatic Oratorios and Masques*, dynamic shading was accomplished by using *f-p-pp* to indicate a decrescendo and *p-mf-f* to indicate a crescendo (Dean 1959, 118). In sum, the latter Baroque was a period of remarkable creativity—composers exploring new ways to effectively communicate the passion and drama of their music to the musician and, ultimately, to the listener. Regarding dynamic markings, timpanists should be attentive to changing scoring and performance practices.

Articulation markings became increasingly important in the Baroque. As far back as the ancient Greeks, composers distinguished longer from shorter notes (West 1992, chap. 5). And this was certainly the case in the Baroque. As described above, the ligature or slur was used to group notes, indicate legato, phrase musical lines, and determine the value of notes. Regarding staccato markings, the Baroque composers used a vertical dash or a wedge (pointing up or down) to indicate staccato notes. By the end of the Baroque period, the dot indicated a lighter or less abrupt staccato. While musicians were expected to know how and when to articulate in the absence of staccato or legato markings, the evolution of musical markings gave composers greater control over the score and the performance. The dot provided composers a new means of expression. The wedge or vertical line denoted a note that was not only shorter, but also more heavily stressed. In sum, the dot gave the composer a shorter note, but one that was not stressed as heavily (C. P. E. Bach 1949, 154; L. Mozart 1951, 78–79; Turk 1982, 342).

Accents were used also in Baroque compositions. In cheerful music, Leopold Mozart believed that violinists should accent the highest note in a musical phrase. A vertical line above the highest note marked these notes. Baroque musicians became familiar with what we now call the agogic accent. Notes were stressed by prolonging them slightly. Violinists were expected to give (1) a weight accent by pressing down on the bow; (2) a slight accent to the note; and (3) various weights to the accented note. The *forzando* was considered by Baroque musicians and composers to be less weighty than the weighted accent and was given to finer gradations. The *forzando* gave composers and musicians the ability to shape a phrase more effectively, to strengthen agogic accents, and to emphasize the longer notes in a phrase of shorter ones (L. Mozart 1951, 219). Finally, the attack accent allowed string players to begin a phrase with a strong, decisive, crisp attack. Or it could be used within a phrase to emphasize a note without making it overly heavy. For wind instruments, the attack accent could be done through tonguing (Quantz 1966, 132; Donington 1974, 429–431). Timpanists should consider stressing, accenting, or prolonging notes in the proper orchestral context.

The emotional character of Baroque music—much more emotional than Classical music and more elegantly refined than Romantic music—would allow the timpanist to explore the nuances of color. As described above, the timpani of the Baroque would support the prevailing orchestral color. On the one hand, in Handel's *Messiah*, the timpanist could play "For Unto Us a Child is Born" in a light, bright manner. On the other hand, "Worthy is the Lamb" could be played in a darker, nobler manner. With the proper size drums, a growing variety of timpani mallets capable of producing different tone and articulation, and a deeper understanding of timpani tone, timpanists could explore the kind of tone production most appropriate to a musical phrase.

The timpani roll or tremolo has a long, confusing history. The primary issue concerns how the roll was executed. How is a roll played when it is marked with a tremolo sign versus a roll notated as sixteenth or thirty-second notes?[5] Should sixteenth note rolls be played as measured (metered) or as open rolls? In the B-Minor Mass, Bach writes a tremolo over the half note in measure 157 and over the whole note in measure 165 of the Gloria. At measure 157, Bach clearly desires a sustained sound (see example 3.3). The timpani support the sustained d in the flutes, oboes, and first violins, and they provide a foundation for the first and second trumpets that are playing legato. At measure 165, the timpani is rolling on an A that provides support for the bass line in the continuo (playing alternating a and A) and in the vocal bass parts. How is Bach expecting this to be played? The consensus among musicologists and timpanists is that it was played as a bouncing, double stroke or "mammy-daddy" roll (LLRRLLRR). This would have provided a continuous sound; however, this roll would not have sounded very resonant (Benvenga 1979, 38). The rapid mammy-

3.3. Importance of sustained timpani rolls

daddy stroke would dampen the head to some degree. To produce a sustained sound on less than ideal heads, the timpanist would use gauze or wool-covered sticks. Would a double stroke roll produce enough sound for a mid-eighteenth-century orchestra? Yes, these orchestras were small by today's standards. Indeed, it was not unusual for Bach to be playing with eighteen or twenty musicians (Terry 1932, 9). With an orchestra this size or even somewhat larger, a double stroke roll would most likely produce the sound that Bach needed.

In the latter part of the eighteenth century and in the nineteenth century, timpanists became adept at playing single stroke as well as double stroke rolls. This raises the question, "how would composers notate the score to specify whether the roll was a single or double stroke?" We don't know the answer to this question, but let me suggest a probable story.

A long time ago timpanists belonged to a secret society. They learned how to beat the drums, how to put skins on them, and how to put the drums in tune. They developed the most intricate practice of playing these drums: flinging their arms into the air and crossing their hands over one another in ways that were truly miraculous. They learned to make one note last a measure or two by rapidly striking the drum twice with one hand, twice with the other, and so on and so forth. This they

Timpani Tone and the Interpretation of Baroque and Classical Music

called a double stroke roll. This secret knowledge was kept among them, and they pledged never to divulge this knowledge to anyone else.

There came a time when a composer asked the timpanists how they played the drum and how they made that sustained sound. But true to their trade, the timpanist refused to tell the writer their secrets. So, the composer did the best he could as he wrote music for these noble drums. One day, the composer thought to himself, "I have written single notes for these beautiful drums and I have combined them into wonderful rhythms. But I need a note that will sustain over two or three measures. I have heard the timpanists play these notes, I guess I will notate them with a tremolo sign—a sign which other instrumentalists knew how to play." Some time later, the composer brought the music to the rehearsal for the first time. The timpanist looked at his part and noticed the wonderful part the composer had written: it was filled with notes where he could throw his arms in the air and cross his hands over one another. But then he noticed a new sign: the tremolo! The timpanist thought to himself, "This note is like the one my friends play in the violins. It is a sustained note. I will play this with double strokes on the drum." Over the years, he passed this idea on to other timpanists and whenever they saw a tremolo sign, they played a double stroke roll. One day this timpanist's student was practicing, throwing his arms up in the air, and crossing over his hands as he struck the drums. He was playing a series of very fast notes, alternating sticks, on one drum. He said to himself, "This sounds very much like the double stroke roll my teacher taught me. It makes the same sustained sound that the double stroke roll does, but it has more volume and better tone quality. I will call this sound a single stroke roll." Like other timpanists, he passed this new roll on to his pupils, but they kept the method of playing this new roll a secret.

Many years later, a new composer heard a timpanist practicing his rhythms and the two different kinds of rolls. The composer thought, "That timpanist is making two kinds of sustained sounds, and one is much more beautiful than the other." He noticed that there was a difference in how the rolls were played. One was played using double strokes and the other using single strokes. But the composer thought, "How do I tell these timpanists how to play a single stroke roll and how to play a double stroke roll? My composition professor taught me to use a tremolo to notate the double stroke roll. What should I use for a single stroke roll?" He thought and thought and thought. Then it occurred to him, "I can write the single stroke roll as a single note with hash marks through it. This will tell the timpanist I want a single stroke roll and not the double stroke roll."

Well this solved his problem—for a while. One day he was talking with another composer who was faced with the same notation problem. The first composer said, "My friend, we know that there are two kinds of rolls and that the best roll is the single stroke roll. More and more timpanists recognize this and are using the single stroke roll. So

Interpretation of Baroque Music

I have been using the tremolo sign to indicate a single stroke roll. The timpanists are familiar with what this sign means—they will play a single stroke roll. Don't bother making a new sign. It will complicate your work." Well, the two parted company, each notating single stroke rolls in different ways.

One day, many, many, many years later, a timpanist was going to play works by these two composers. When looking at the parts, he became confused. One was filled with tremolos. "This is certainly a roll," the timpanist, "but is it a single or double stroke roll?" Then, he looked at part by the other composer. Here he saw very many measures with semiquaver and demisemiquaver notes. He thought, "How should I play these notes? Does he want me to play individual notes or a single stroke roll? I am truly confused."

Historically, a tremolo indicates a double stroke roll in the Baroque, but in the late Classical period the notation of rolls begins to change. Perhaps the development of the single stroke roll, on larger drums, with marginally better calfskins, and in larger orchestras led composers to write semiquavered (sixteenth) notes to indicate a roll. Haydn appears to appropriate this method. Other composers, such as Mozart, continue to use the tremolo. But what if the tremolo and demisemiquavered notes appear in the same measure? What do they mean? This occurs in the last measure of Beethoven's Symphony No. 5 (see example 3.4).

3.4. Beethoven's final rolls: an enigma?

Was he attempting to distinguish the two rolls? Probably not. Haydn, who usually writes semiquavered notes to indicate a roll, uses a tremolo sign to notate a single stroke roll in a bar with a fermata. Beethoven, a close student of Haydn, appears to have appropriated this notational practice, and the final roll should be a single stroke, open roll, not a double stroke roll.[6]

However, notating a single stroke roll with sixteenth notes leads to another problem. If a composer notates rolls as semiquavered notes, when do timpanists play semiquavered notes individually as a measured roll (played in time as individual strokes) and when do they play them freely (as an open roll)? The problem is most acute in Beethoven. At times, Beethoven uses sixteenth notes to indicate a measured roll, and at other times he uses them to indicate a single stroke, open roll. Studying the score and listening to the context in which the timpani part is played are the best ways to discern Beethoven's intent. Beethoven writes very well for the timpani and clearly indicates when he wants the timpanist to play measured notes. For example, in the last movement of Symphony No. 7 (see example 3.5),

3.5. Measured rolls in Beethoven's Symphony No. 7

Beethoven indicates measured sixteenth notes at measure 94 (nineteen measures after B) and again at measure 318 (twelve measures before H). Beginning at measure 94, the sixteenth note figure adds a degree of tension to the music that Beethoven desired. In measure 106 (letter C) the measured notes support the rhythmic character of the music—especially the strings, which are playing sixteenth notes, too. This same pattern holds true for the figure beginning at measure 318. This passage should not be played as an open roll. See the companion Web site for a marked timpani part.

How have other composers handled the notation and meaning of a roll? In the first movement of Franz Schubert's *Unfinished Symphony*, Schubert uses thirty-second-note hash marks to indicate rolls. Often, these rolls are associated with sustained notes in the orchestra. However, the semiquaver figures should be played as measured notes. For example, eight measures before H, the semiquavered half notes rhythmically support the same figure in the strings. Peter Ilyich Tchaikovsky is inconsistent in his use of hash marks to indicate a roll. In his symphonies, *Swan Lake*, *Nutcracker*, and popular overtures, he uses semiquaver, demisemiquaver, and hemidemisemiquaver notes to indicate an open roll. This inconsistency is not as serious as it appears! In slower pieces or movements, he notates the roll with sixty-fourth or thirty-second notes. In quicker movements he uses sixteenth or thirty-second notes to indicate a roll. The tempo of the music obviously dictates how he notates a roll, and the timpanist must interpret the part accordingly. This is evident in Symphony No. 6; rolls in the last, slow and tragic movement are marked with hemidemisemiquaver notes. Rolls are marked in the other sprightlier movements with demisemiquaver notes. Interestingly, in the third measure of T of the first movement, the demisemiquavered figure should probably be played as a measured figure rather than as an open roll (see example 3.6).[7]

In sum, the modern timpani roll evolved from the double stroke roll to the single stroke roll. In the seventeenth and early eighteenth centuries, the roll was a double stroke roll and notated as a tremolo. Toward the end of the eighteenth century, thinner skins, larger orchestras, and better sound-

3.6. The problem of the demisemiquavered roll

ing timpani encouraged timpanists to experiment with rolls. The single stroke roll and double stroke roll were used side by side in the early part of nineteenth century; although, it was left up to the timpanist to decide when to use the appropriate roll. Composers notated the single stroke roll with either a tremolo sign or demisemiquaver or semiquaver hash marks: the choice was the composer's to make. Timpanists are left to their own devices in determining if a demisemiquaver or semiquaver figure is a roll or should be played as individual notes—a rhythmic figure different from a roll. By the nineteenth century, it became clear that the single stroke roll was preferable to the double stroke roll (Pfundt 1849, 7–8).

Henry Purcell and Johann Sebastian Bach

The above interpretative principles can be applied to the timpani parts of Henry Purcell, Johann Sebastian Bach, and George Frideric Handel. The author will discuss Purcell's *The Fairy Queen*, Bach's B-Minor Mass, Handel's *Messiah*, and his *Music to the Royal Fireworks*. Henry Purcell is often credited for being one of the first composers to integrate the timpani into the orchestra. In Act IV of *The Fairy Queen*, Purcell writes a rhythmic part that doubles the organ line. The opening measure is soli with the organ: the timpani playing the tonic and subdominant. The timpani part also strengthens the base line. The part is straightforward and should be played with articulate sticks with no tonal or rhythmic phrasing.

Bach used timpani in forty-nine of his orchestral works and cantatas. He often employed them in music that was joyous or dramatic (Pollart 1976, 76–77). For example, Bach's first use of the timpani in the B-Minor Mass, hereafter called the Mass, is in the inspiring Gloria—neglecting it in the preceding movement, the more somber Kyrie. He uses the timpani in parts of the Sanctus that are bright and cheerful. He concludes the Mass with a very nobly written timpani part that adds depth and drama to the movement. In Bach's works, the timpani play a largely rhythmic role, and the timpani are freed often from their dependence on the third or fourth trumpet. Liberating the timpani from the trumpet occurred in other Bach pieces, for example, Cantata No. 31; however, by Cantata No. 91 Bach feels particularly free to give the timpani its own voice—linking it less and less to the trumpets and rhythmic figures of other instruments.[8]

The Gloria of the Mass opens with the timpani playing single tonic and dominant notes. These should be played very legato and this gesture is repeated beginning in measure 77 and should be executed in the same manner. In the sixth bar, the sixteenth notes can be played as written or

3.7. Dynamic terracing in Bach's Mass in B Minor

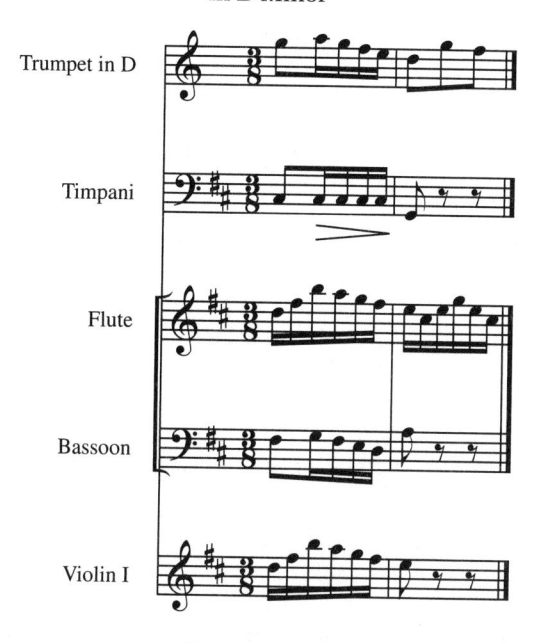

they can be phrased with a very slight diminuendo (see example 3.7). This could be done because there is a descending line in the trumpets, winds, first violins, and continuo. Ultimately, the conductor will provide guidance on dynamic phrasing. At measure 24, the musical line moves from the dominant to the tonic. A slight crescendo on the sixteenth notes pushes the music forward nicely. Throughout the Mass, there are other opportunities for the timpanist to phrase a series of sixteenth notes by playing a slight crescendo or decrescendo, and the timpanist might be aware of those points by looking carefully at the score. For example, in number 21, the Osanna, an ascending figure occurs at measure 27. If a slight crescendo is given to the sixteenth notes, the figure is nicely phrased. The music naturally ascends from the dominant to the tonic. This nicely reinforces the voice and instrumental line. However, this convention should be used sparingly and used only in ascending musical lines. Schweitzer believes that the dynamic terracing is compatible with Bach's writing. Ascending lines could be played *forte* and descending lines *piano*. However, musicians should avoid a diminuendo at the end of a cadence (Schweitzer 1966, I: 359, 361). There may be times when the music, often played *forte*, permits no dynamic phrasing. Baroque music often requires alternating dynamic contrasts. At measure 25 of the Gloria, the altos sing their part with a thinly scored orchestra of flute, oboe, and continuo. Two measures later (measure 27), the tenors enter, instrumentally augmented by the timpani, trumpets, and the second flute and oboe. The timpani part should be played quite softly in measure 27 to establish a quieter musical ambiance. However, in measure 29 the entire orchestra and choir burst forth and the timpani should do likewise—thus providing the dynamic contrast that Bach requires. Timpanists can play these five measures at *forte* with no need for any unusual phrasing. However, they should be aware that the A can be swallowed up quite easily by the rest of the orchestra, and therefore, they should take care that the A is brought out. See the companion Web site for a marked timpani part.

There are four additional issues in the Mass. The first, interpreting the lourer in measure 145 of the Gloria, is treated above (see example 3.8).

3.8. Phrasing in the Gloria

Second, should the timpanist use a double stroke or a single stroke roll? In measure 157, Bach uses a tremolo to indicate that the timpanist should play a double stroke roll—a roll that is usually played as a single stroke roll by timpanists who are not concerned with authentic reproduction of timpani performance practices. Because modern drums, especially Dresden drums, are so resonant and mallet quality so improved over eighteenth-century sticks, and because Bach has produced such a beautiful work, one is inclined to take advantage of modern drums, sticks, and techniques to play these rolls as single stroke rolls. Third, should the timpanist roll at the end of movements where a note is held by a fermata? In the final two measures of the Gloria, Bach has the timpani rhythmically doubling the trumpets. On the one hand, if Bach wanted to treat it as a roll, he would have written a tremolo sign. In Cantata No. 19, he composed a roll in the penultimate measure, followed by a single note in the final measure. Given his compositional style, one must conclude that the half note should be played as a single stroke. Additionally, a double stroke roll would not be very resonant and might sound less glorious than Bach would have wished. If the fermata is not held very long or if the orchestra is small, a roll would not be needed. A single well-placed note might sound long enough to have the effect Bach wished. On the other hand, if the note were held very long, it would make sense to roll—especially because the single stroke roll produces a very nice sustained note. The most convincing evidence is that Bach could have written a tremolo in the final measure, but he didn't. Additionally, Bach often composes the timpani part in detail. In so doing, he takes away the timpanist's liberty to ornament their parts with schlagmanieren.[9] For a similar opinion on whether or not to roll long notes, see James Blades's *Percussion Instruments and Their History* (1970, 248). My guess is that Bach wants the timpanist to play a single note, and this practice can be applied at the end of other movements of the Mass (and in other pieces) where the timpanist is asked to play a whole or half note. A final issue concerns the treatment of the introductory figure in the Sanctus (see example 3.9).

3.9. Rhythmic interpretation of the Sanctus

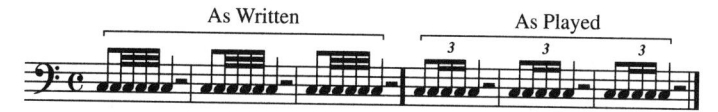

This figure should be played as a triplet figure and not as it is written. There are two reasons for this. As explained earlier, Baroque composers often expected timpanists and violinists to play this rhythmic gesture as a triplet figure. Second, the rhythm of this part of the Sanctus is based on a triple meter figure. The triplet is initially introduced in the voices and trumpets and later given to other instruments. To provide rhythmic integrity to the piece, the timpanist should play these notes as triplets.

What mallets should be used in playing Bach? Short of playing on original drums with eighteenth-century mallets, the music in Bach's Mass often calls for covered medium-to-hard sticks. Small, harder sticks can be used to articulate the rhythmic passages. Throughout the Gloria and Sanctus, the timpanist should use an articulate stick. The first four notes should be played more legato. However, in measure 5, the three eighth notes can be played marcato and the sixth measure should be played very staccato. In the Sanctus, the opening and repeated rhythmic gesture should be played with very articulate sticks. After measure 49, a less articulate stick could be used. In more articulate passages, timpanists should play in a *very* staccato manner to bring out these notes. Finally, a soft legato stick can be used in the final twelve measures of the Mass. This is necessary for two reasons. This music is slower and more somber, and a softer stick will convey this feeling. Because the half notes must sustain for some time, the timpanist has two options. Roll the half notes or use a single stroke that will ring as long as possible. Since Bach did not write a tremolo over the half and whole notes when he could have done so, timpanists should not roll these notes. In fact, rolling these notes interferes with the melodic and harmonic lines: it obscures the ascending and descending voices. The timpanist could use a softer, legato stick and employ a bounce stroke to bring out as much of the color of the timpani as is possible. This will produce a sustained sound carrying though the end of the phrase.

Articulation is very important in the Mass. First, many of the timpani entrances are played staccato. Bach, like many other Baroque composers, writes timpani parts in the more glorious, up-tempo choruses. At quicker tempos, the timpanist should play more articulately to effectively separate the notes. Second, there are times when the last note of a phrase should be well punctuated. In the Number 4 of the Gloria at measure 41 (see example 3.10), the phrase ends on the first beat of the measure for the brass and timpani. At this point, the timpanist could articulate this part by using a staccato stroke, playing into the drum, and finishing with a lifting motion. This stroke will articulate the phrase effectively and it will give a send-off to

3.10. Punctuating a phrase in the Gloria

the strings, continuo, and choir. See the companion Web site for a marked timpani part.

George Frideric Handel

George Frideric Handel wrote very well for the timpani in *Music for the Royal Fireworks* and the *Messiah*. Handel primarily used the timpani in a rhythmic manner, and he made use of the larger Tower drums on special occasions. James Blades, in his history of percussion instruments, suggests that Handel used these drums because they produced a superior sound. This was undoubtedly the case. Blades reports that these drums were probably 36 and 38 inches in diameter. Other drums at Handel's disposal were cavalry drums measuring 19 and 21 inches, and double-bass kettledrums measuring 39 and 35 inches (Blades 1970, 254–255). Since drums between 26 and 30 inches were not uncommon in Europe, one suspects that Handel had access to these drums, too. Perhaps the Ashbridge timpani were of similar size. Thus, he possessed a wide variety of drums capable of producing acceptable tone. This meant that Handel, like Bach, could be very demanding about the kind of tone the timpanist produced.

Handel scored excellent timpani parts in *Music to the Royal Fireworks* (1749), and the interpretation of those parts requires an understanding of performance practices of the day. What size drums should one use? Timpanists can use three drums in this piece: a 31- or 32-inch tuned to A, and 29- and 26-inch timpani tuned to d. In the first movement, the timpanist can play A and d on the larger drums. This is particularly important because the timpani part reinforces the rhythmic line, and by playing the notes on these drums, the timpanist places the notes in the uppermost register of the timpani. The sound will be more articulate—just what is needed for this part. In the Minuet II, the timpanist can use the 26-inch drum for the d and either the 29- or 31-inch drum for the A. Since this music is less articulate, playing on slightly looser heads provides more resonance and a broader tone—just what is called for by this music.

The music opens with a slow, deliberate Overture. Since the music is written in the French style, the dotted quarter notes should be double-dotted, and today it is common for conductors to ask for double-dotted notes. Thus, the first (and subsequent) measures of the piece should be played in this manner (see example 3.11).

3.11. Double-dotting Handel's *Fireworks*

To play this successfully, the timpanist must also take care that the sixteenth note is brought out. This is particularly true of all the A notes because putting more energy and articulation into this note prevents it from being lost—especially when the A is followed by a d. The d, because of its tight sound, tends to drown out the A. A second issue concerns whether or not to roll the dotted quarter and the half notes in this introductory section. Handel gives us some help. Two measures before the Adagio, he writes a tremolo above a quarter note (which is notated on the following dotted quarter in some editions). This roll is probably misplaced; therefore, this author is not inclined to play it.[10] If this roll is intended, rolling the notes in small orchestras might obscure the delicate brass and string lines—another argument for not rolling these notes. Even at this slow tempo, the timpani would sustain these notes. Therefore, one could argue that the roll is unnecessary—and maybe even detrimental to the sound of the overture.[11] This said, when the *Fireworks* is played by a very large, contemporary orchestra in resonant concert halls, the timpanist might wish to roll this note. How Handel's timpanist treated this part in the original performance is unknown: Handel employed an orchestra consisting of one hundred musicians—forty-three string and fifty-seven wind players—at the premier in Vauxhall on Friday, April 21, 1749 (Cudsworth n.d., iii–v).

The three-measure Adagio can include two measures of schlagmanieren. Daniel Speer notes that a good timpanist will use a roll followed by an appropriate schlagmanier, and ending with a single stroke (Speer 1974, 219–220).[12] The Adagio is really structured for schlagmanieren. The first measure could be a roll on d. In the next measure, the timpanist could employ a series of individual strokes, and this measure would be followed by a single, well-placed stroke on the A drum.

Mallet selection is relatively simple in the *Royal Fireworks*. The beginning of the Overture should be played very broadly with less articulate sticks or even general purpose sticks. The Allegro of the Overture should be played with very articulate sticks. Here the tempo is quicker and the timpani doubles the trumpet parts; thus, very articulate sticks should be used. The Overture can be played with medium-hard sticks, but not the most articulate. There is a trade-off in using medium-hard mallets: it may not be possible to change the sticks to a more articulate stick required in the Adagio. If the conductor asks for no rolls or schlagmanieren in the measure preceding the Allegro, then it is possible to change sticks in that measure: from less articulate to the most articulate stick. However, if the conductor moves quickly into the Allegro, the timpanist does not have the time to change sticks (unless the conductor is willing to wait for the timpanist to do so). Unable to change mallets, the timpanist's is forced to use medium-hard sticks throughout the Overture. The La Rejouissance may be played with articulate or very articulate sticks depending on the speed at which the movement is taken. If taken at a very quick tempo, it should be played with very articulate sticks. The Minuet II is typically played more deliberately, with a great amount of dignity, and Handel does not write a strongly rhythmic part. Therefore, it is best to play this section with medium mallets—sticks that bring out the depth and color of the drums.

Attention must be paid to articulation in the *Royal Fireworks*. In the Overture at the Allegro, care must be taken to bring out the sixteenth notes—especially if the two sixteenth notes are tied to a rest or eighth note. By giving each of the sixteenth notes more energy, the notes are brought out clearly compared to the following eighth notes. Using a staccato grip and stroke also helps articulate each of these notes. In Le Rejouissance, the timpanist can use a staccato stroke to bring out some unique characteristics of this part. In the second and third full measures, the eighth note can be played slightly into the drum and the quarter note played more legato. This rhythmic pattern is played by the instruments supporting the melody and should be brought out distinctly. Playing short-long in this manner clearly contrasts the eighth and quarter note. The quarter note should be played legato because the legato note will ring through the measure more effectively than a staccato note, and this note must ring throughout the measure. This sticking should be used in measures 9 through 12, where similar demands are placed on the timpanist and orchestra. In the seventh measure of Menuett II b and c, these three quarter notes need to be played staccato—matching the other instruments of the orchestra that are also playing this figure. Finally, the three quarter notes in measures 9, 11, 13, and 14 of the Menuett II c should be played in a marcato manner, and the quarter note downbeat played legato. This is noble, yet martial music, and a marcato stroke provides a marchlike flavor to the music. As discussed below, Menuett II c must sound qualitatively darker than Menuett II b—to provide some contrast between the two sections. The marcato stroke also produces a darker sound than a legato stroke, thus achieving this effect.

There is some dynamic shaping that the timpanist can use to effectively play the *Royal Fireworks*. In the Overture, attention must be paid to muffling. Baroque composers often dynamically shape a piece by playing alternatively loud and soft passages. This is the case here. Measure 14 and the first two counts of measure 15 are played *forte*—supporting the entire orchestra (see example 3.12). However, only the strings play in the second half of measure 14 and the first two beats of measure 15, and they normally play *piano*. To prevent the timpani from bleeding over into the quieter string line, the timpanist should muffle the drums after the last *forte* note in measure 14. There are other places too numerous to mention where this occurs, so the timpanist must be prepared to muffle the timpani in the proper places (for example, measures 16, 19, 48, 52, 56, 60, 64, and 67). It is not uncommon to play this music with added crescendos and

3.12. Muffling in the Overture to *Fireworks*

Interpretation of Baroque Music

diminuendos. The three quarter notes in measures 75 through 77 can be made progressively softer (see example 3.13). In so doing, the timpani and brass can get out of the way of the melody in the violins. From measures 86–118, much of the timpani part can be dynamically crafted. In the following extract, the author indicates one way this passage can be shaped. In measure 86 the rising line in the strings and brass can be supported by

3.13. Dynamic shading in the Overture

a small crescendo in the timpani. At measure 90, the timpani part must come down to *mezzo forte* or *piano* so that a crescendo can be made in measure 94—once again supporting a rising line. After rising to a *forte* in the first half of measure 95, the timpanist can drop back to a *mezzo piano* and begin a crescendo that grows quickly in measure 98 and culminates in the first beat of measure 99. This crescendo effectively supports the rising lines in the brass and strings. In measure 95, the line begins to ascend in the strings and trumpets. In measures 96 and 97, the horn line ascends. The timpanist can crescendo throughout these three measures to support the ascending lines in the brass and strings. However, the timpani part can be played even more effectively if measure 98 is played with an even greater crescendo. This crescendo in the timpani dynamically doubles the rising trumpet, first violin, and viola parts and it creates an even more noble quality to the music. Finally, play a long crescendo (from *mezzo piano* to *fortissimo*) between measures 108 and 115. This crescendo adds some drama to the music since there is no rising line in this section (with the exception of measures 111 and 112 in the trumpets and the horns). The remainder of the Overture is written very similar to the section just described and can be played in a similar fashion.

In La Rejouissance, the timpani part may be played without dynamic shaping. This happy music should be well articulated and flowing. The Kalmus timpani part indicates a series of crescendos and decrescendos throughout this movement; however, as the dynamic markings rarely follow the line of the music or add any important drama to it, it would seem reasonable to disregard them.

The same cannot be said of the Minuet II b. More dynamic shading gives this music nobility and beauty. Timpanists need not play the crescendos indicated in the Kalmus score—playing Minuet II b at a *piano* dynamic throughout gives the timpanist an opportunity to contrast Minuet II b with Minuet II c—which one will play with greater nobility and dynamic terracing. Measures 9, 11, and 13 are an exception. Play each quarter note with increasing loudness until the downbeat of the following measure. This dynamic shading follows the line of the trumpets and prevents this quieter music from becoming too "boring." Playing these quarter notes slightly more staccato and then playing the downbeat more legato allows the timpanist to shape these notes in two ways. First, a legato stroke at the beginning of measures 9, 11, and 13 provides a tonal foundation to each of these three measures. Second, a legato note naturally decrescendos over the duration of the measure, and this reinforces the downward line in the violins and the brass.

In Minuet II c, the timpanist can take greater liberties with dynamic shading. Played at *forte*, the timpanist can crescendo slightly on the three quarter notes in measures 9 and 11—playing the quarter note in the succeeding measures very legato (for reasons explained above). But, timpanists can crescendo in bars 13 and 14 up to *fortissimo*. This effectively augments the nobility of the music so that the *Music for the Royal Fireworks* can be brought to an effective end—especially if a stinger is added.

Since the original version of *Fireworks* did not include rolls (with one exception two measures before the Adagio in the Overture), most timpanists are inclined to play this music without them. First, Handel could have included rolls in the slow, majestic Overture. However, knowing he could have written these half notes as rolls and did not is the strongest argument for not using a roll on these notes. However, taking some license in the Adagio could be in order. The trumpets, timpani, and conductor should agree on how to handle these three measures. The timpanist could roll on the first measure of the Adagio, use schlagmanieren in the penultimate measure, and follow it with a roll on the last measure. This would give the trumpets the opportunity to play a solo lick in the first one and a half measures of the Adagio and let timpanists play their part in the second half of the Adagio. Rounding out the Adagio with timpani and trumpets would be consistent with performance practices of the period. Second, a roll on the last note of the Overture would effectively ennoble this movement. Third, a roll (followed by a stinger) in the final measure of the Menuett would conclude the piece triumphantly.

There is some tonal shading that the timpanist can employ in the *Royal Fireworks*. The nature of the Overture is slow and noble. The slow tempo requires the timpani to sound colorful, broad, and long, and placing each stroke well into the head and using some arm can achieve this. This stroke produces a sound that is more full-bodied than can be otherwise attained with a more articulate stick. Furthermore, since the half notes are not rolled, the darker sound will carry through the measure more effectively. The rest of the piece needs no special tone coloring. Play the Overture's Allegro very lightly with articulate sticks. This moves the piece forward and the timpani's rhythmic pattern nicely supports the trumpet's rhythm. See the companion Web site for a marked timpani part.

Handel's *Messiah*, written in 1741, revised in 1788 by Wolfgang Amadeus Mozart, and edited by Prout, has straightforward timpani parts. This analysis is based upon the Prout edition that includes Wolfgang A. Mozart's augmented timpani part. This edition is often heard in concert halls and churches today. There are no surprises in the chorus "For Unto Us a Child Is Born." This part can be played on two drums: a 31- or 32-inch and a 29-inch drum that reaches a d. Playing a 29-inch c and d gives a lot of articulation to these notes, and this is needed at this point. To emphasize the articulation, a medium-hard stick should be used: especially because it is more difficult to articulate the G on this larger drum. As the G is likely to be swallowed up, the timpanist can put a little more energy into these notes. In so doing, the G will sound as loud as the c and d. This part can be played with no embellishments or double-dotted eighth notes. Since the sixteenth notes are apt to be lost, accenting them will bring them out. "Glory to God" can be played on 29- and 31-inch drums for the same reasons cited above. Six measures before rehearsal letter D, one can diminuendo throughout that bar. "Why Do the Nations" is played in a straightforward manner, with an articulate stick, bringing out the sixteenth note, and playing on 31- and 29-inch drums. The entrance of the piece can be tricky. Some conductors conduct it in two and others in four, so it is important to know how it will be conducted. The tempo can be tricky, too. The previous chorus, "The Sound is Gone Out," is taken at a more relaxed tempo than "The Nations"—which is quicker and more nervous. Therefore, there is a psychological tendency for the timpanist to start "The Nations" at a slower tempo than is actually taken. Placing a metronome marking at the beginning of the movement reminds the timpanist of the tempo.

The "Hallelujah" chorus, one of the most beautiful timpani parts written, is without serious problems. The timpanist could use a 31-inch and either a 29- or 26-inch timpano to play this part. Playing a d on the 29-inch timpano takes advantage of a very articulate head—one that matches an A played on a tight 31-inch head. The principle disadvantage of using the 29-inch timpano comes in the last two measures where a roll is marked. A roll on a 29-inch timpano tends to sound a little choked and the timpanist must play a little more rapidly to get a nice roll. This is not a huge problem: the music builds in intensity throughout this chorus and an intense roll fits the nature of the music. Putting a stinger at the end of the final roll is better executed on the 29-inch timpano, too. Playing a d on a 26-inch timpano avoids the problem of rolling on a tight head, but one sacrifices a degree of articulation and focused sound that is achieved on the 29-inch timpano. Using 29- and 31-inch timpani best serves the purpose of this music; although, the timpanist can bring in a 26-inch timpano for the d roll.

The "Hallelujah" chorus provides some opportunity for dynamic shaping and muting. For example, slightly crescendo one bar before rehearsal letter B (see example 3.14). This transfers musical tension to the rising soprano line beginning at B. A decrescendo can be placed one and one half measures before rehearsal letter C. This follows the descending line in the brass. Muting is very important in this movement. After each "hallelujah" phrase, both drums should be muffled. This holds true for other places where the timpani should not intrude into the silence of the

3.14.   Dynamic contrasts in the Hallelujah

piece (three measures from the end) or where the timpani would bleed into solo voices (three measures after rehearsal letter F).

Finally, timpanists should bring out the sixteenth notes and make a decision whether or not to use schlagmanieren in the penultimate measure. To bring out the rhythm and to move the piece forward, the timpanist must ensure that all notes are played evenly. This means slightly accenting the sixteenth notes and using more articulate sticks. By so doing and by playing on the 29- and 31-inch, or on the 32-inch timpani, the timpanist can give this music drive and destination. Finally, conductors call for different beatings in the penultimate measure. Some want it performed as written, others like the timpanist to play a schlagmanier in this measure. If the second option is chosen, one possible arrangement is written in example 3.15.

3.15. Schlagmanier in the Hallelujah

In the chorus, "Worthy Is the Lamb," pay attention to articulation. The first two phrases should be played on the top of the head and with an articulate stroke—except the final two quarter notes, which can be played with a legato stroke. The chorus holds these notes their full value, and the timpanist should follow suit. The first three measures of rehearsal letter D should be played staccato, but the next three pair of eighth notes should be articulated in a long-short pattern. To do this, the timpanist can play a legato followed by a staccato (bounce stroke) note. The effect of this is to reinforce the additional emphasis the choir places on the first syllable of the words "**bless**-ing," "**hon**-our," and "**pow**-'r" and not stressing the second syllable of those words. Furthermore, the staccato bounce stroke gives a sense of finality to the second syllable of each word that is required by the music. There is no need to write a schlagmanier in the penultimate measure because it is written out—although, one is attempted to play this measure with greater flourish! In the "Amen" section, these notes should be played in a staccato manner, except the quarter notes—measures 6 through 8 after rehearsal letter L. Six measures before the "Adagio" near the end, Handel scores some of the most beautiful notes for timpani. These should be played soloistically, and the sixteenth note needs to be accented slightly to sound like the dotted eighths and quarter notes. The finale can be played without any schlagmanieren.

This ends the discussion of the interpretation of timpani parts in Baroque music. This period is remarkable for many reasons. The timpani evolved into an important instrument of the orchestra. As soon as it entered the concert hall, it was important that the timpani and timpanists adapt to something other than drum corps playing! Composers and timpanists sought a different sound than could be given by small cavalry or huge artillery drums. In response, appropriately sized timpani were used and this allowed timpanists to play the best (or certainly most acceptable) notes on the drums. Timpani heads became marginally thinner and they resonated better than thicker heads. Covered timpani mallets gave timpanists a pallet of color and articulation to satisfy more fully the demands of composers. And, evolving playing styles produced a more full and resonant sound. All in all, timpani tone became an important concern for timpanists.

Baroque music gave timpanists, particularly in the High Baroque, opportunities to use these new technical and artistic developments in playing. Timpanists exercised greater discretion in the use of embellishments and dynamic shaping. The waning of the Baroque and the rise of the Classical era, meant that timpanists would have to adapt to changing compositional demands. This will be the subject of the next chapter.

4

Interpretation of Classical Music

As Donald Van Ess summarized: Classical music sought clarity, balance, simplicity, and refinement. But these characteristics were reflected in the era's art, religion, literature, philosophy, science, and society, too. Classicism was rooted in the eighteenth century rediscovery of the ancient Greeks. Plato used the Socratic method to clarify the meaning of fundamental concepts, such as beauty, and later, eighteenth-century English philosopher, John Locke, believed that we should create clear and distinct ideas. In Classical art, Jacques David's *Death of Socrates* displayed the clarity and crisp lines characteristic of this period. Aristotle believed humans should lead a balanced life: his ethical philosophy was grounded in the "golden mean" (Aristotle 1980, 1106a17–1108a31). In applying this principle to our lives, Aristotle argued that we should avoid excess. Such was a balanced life.

The rationalism of Plato led to certain simplicity in social organization. In the *Republic*, he concluded that a simple, properly ordered, and balanced three-class society was ideal for Greek life (Plato 1961, Books III and IV). John Locke searched for the simplest, least intrusive government grounded in the reasoned discovery of natural rights: rights around which a society should be organized. This society had a limited government: the primary purpose of this government was to protect individual's rights to life, liberty, and property. Regarding liberty, Locke believed that thoughtful, rational individuals would willingly limit the exercise of their freedom. Thus, self-restraint or moderation became a virtue for Locke (Locke 1980, secs. 123–158). Associated with self-restraint was the virtue of refinement. Refinement meant that all things were in their proper place and polished. For the eighteenth-century aristocrat, refinement led to a vision of the proper social order and of impeccable manners.

The preoccupation with clarity, balance, simplicity, and refinement is reflected in musical writing that influenced preclassical and classical composers. J. P. Rameau, in his 1722 book, *Traite de l'harmonie*, claims that the foundation of music is the aural discovery of principles permitting the composer to identify the more specific rules around which music turns. He constructs rules that form the basis of the theory of harmony that is rooted in a harmonic center: the tonic. He concludes, "How marvelous this principle is in its simplicity. So many harmonies, so many beautiful melodies . . . all this arises from two or three intervals arranged in thirds" (Rameau 1950, 569, 564, 567). And J. J. Quantz, writing *On Playing the Flute*, argues that in judging music, it is necessary to apply "dictates of reason." In his discussion of concerti, Quantz identifies the basic principles shaping a composition, and then he discusses the importance of balance. A properly portioned or balanced piece should have four movements of appropriate length (Quantz 1966, 310–315). These rules of composition lead to a certain simplicity. Melodic lines and rhythmic patterns are not cluttered with excessive ornamentation. In orchestral works, this simplicity of line and rhythm enhances clarity or transparency: no instrument dominates another. This results in orchestral balance in which all instruments are clearly heard. Also, the quest for balance shapes the architecture of the composition. The sonata form seeks balance between the exposition, development, and recapitulation sections: (1) a balance of key—tonic, dominant (and modulations); (2) an emotional balance—statement, tension, and resolution; and (3) a thematic balance—a statement of two themes, their elaboration, and restatement. Balance requires restraint: avoiding overindulgence or excess. Classical music is restrained music. Dynamic shading is kept within appropriate limits; and emotions are not provoked as much as they are cultivated. The melodic line represents the ultimate in refinement: it flows up and down in a reasoned or predicable pattern toward the cadence with all notes seemingly in their place. The tempo is appropriate to the emotion the composer wishes to convey: none is too rushed. Such is the nature of classical music (Quantz 1966, 311–315; Bach 1949, 80–81; Van Ess 1970, 202; Kollman 1984, 317–318; Burney 1957, II: 7).

Approaches to Interpreting and Performing Music in the Classical Era (1750–1800)

Daniel Turk, writing in the Classical period, reflects the reasoned, self-restrained approach to playing. He makes it clear that cadenzas should be restrained, but not without sufficient embellishment. The cadenza should reflect the thematic material stated and developed in the music. Identifying this material requires talent, insight, and good judgment. Exercising good judgment involves avoiding the excessive preoccupation with technical virtuosity, limiting cadenzas to an appropriate length, playing within the composed keys, and resolving all dissonances (Turk 1982, 298–302). Turk also counsels restraint in the use of embellishments "That the embellishments . . . used with insight, taste, and selection, can contribute much to making a composition more beautiful cannot be denied. But also even in this regard there can be too much of a good thing. Extempore embellishments must therefore be used sparingly and at the right place" (Turk 1982, 310). In playing variations, the same sense of proportion and self-restraint comes into play. Variations should be appropriate to the character of the piece, ornamented lightly, elaborated with ease, and rhythmically precise (Turk 1982, 311–314).

Turk believes that the primary constituents of good musical execution are clarity, musical expression, appropriate use of ornaments, and a feeling for musical meaning. Mechanical execution, tonal emphasis, and proper phrasing of musical periods define clarity. Every note must be given its proper emphasis and must be heard. Rules guiding the accent of notes include stressing the beginning note of the period and syncopated notes and lingering on appropriate notes, for example. Turk provides guidance in treating the end of periods. This includes rules for properly lifting the fingers from the keyboard and ending a phrase—punctuating it with a comma, period, colon, or semicolon as one would a sentence. Musical expression, the goal of musicianship, is enhanced by shaping the dynamics of a note, articulating tones, and using the appropriate tempo. The dynamic level is dependent upon the character of the music. Ferocious music requires a loud dynamic, whereas tender music requires a softer dynamic. Dissonant chords and deceptive cadences require emphasis, too. Articulation marks effectively shape a musical line or gesture by strengthening some notes, shortening others, or joining others in a slurred manner. Finally, Turk warns against the excessive use of ornaments. Ornaments must suit the music, fit the tempo, and be diverse to avoid boredom. Leonard Ratner rightly notes that the use of ornamentation—so ubiquitous in the Baroque—was confined largely to soloists or an ensemble's leading voice. As the Classical era progressed, composers more carefully indicated how the part should be played. Leopold Mozart expressed this approach best when he wrote:

> To read the musical pieces of good masters rightly according to the instructions . . . not only must one observe exactly all that has been marked and prescribed and not play it otherwise than as written; but one must throw oneself into the affect to be expressed and apply and execute in a certain good style all the ties, slides, accentuation of the notes, the *forte* and *piano*; in a word, whatever belongs to tasteful performance of a piece (L. Mozart 1951, 216).

Thus, the musician in the Classical era was given more direction and asked to exercise less discretion in ornamenting a part than Baroque musicians (Turk 1982, 321–365, 230).

Turk asks musicians to note whether the music requires light or heavy playing. In an extended analysis, he believes that the type of playing is a "matter of the proper application of detached, sustained, slurred, and tied notes" (Turk 1982, 432). In differentiating what constitutes a heavy and light passage, Turk writes:

Compositions of an exalted, serious, solemn, pathetic, and similar character must be given a heavy execution with fullness and force, strongly accented and the like. To these types of compositions belong those that are headed grave, pomposo, patetico, maestoso, sostenuto, and the like. A somewhat lighter and marked softer execution is required by compositions of a pleasant, gentler, agreeable character, consequently those which are customarily marked compiacevole, con dolcezza, glissicato, lusingando, pastorale, piacevole, and the like. Compositions in which lively, humorous, and joyous feelings are predominant, for example allegro scherzando, burlesco, giocoso, con allegrezza, risvegliato, etc., must be played quite lightly whereas melancholy and similar affects particularly call for the slurring of tones and portato. Compositions of the latter type are designated by the words con afflizione, con amarezza, doloroso, lagrimoso, languido, and mesto among others (1982, 348).

Beyond the affective nature of the composition, the tempo and meter often shape whether or not the piece is light or heavy. Quicker tempos should be played lighter and slower tempos more heavily. Similarly, the meter can help determine if music should be played lighter or heavier. A 3/2 meter should be played more heavily than 3/4 or 3/8. Some iambic-type rhythms should be played more heavily than others (Turk 1982, 348–351).

In shifting from the Baroque to Classical periods, musicians must understand the evolving Classical style and the techniques that are necessary to play it. Clarity, balance, simplicity, and refinement epitomize the overall character of the Classical style; however, what these terms mean is more complicated. The timpanist's approach to executing a particular passage or work rests on how well the timpanist interprets and applies these ideas. As Frederick Artz notes, the sonata form is central to the symphony, concerto, chamber music, and keyboard composition (Artz 1962, 267). However, each composer takes this form and manipulates it to suit his or her particular musical needs. Let's examine the orchestral sonata. Carl Czerny (1791–1857) nicely summarizes the sonata principle in his *School of Practical Composition*. The sonata usually consists of four movements (Allegro—often with an Adagio introduction, Adagio or Andante, Scherzo or Minuet, and Finale or Rondo). For example, Mozart's Symphony Nos. 35, 36, 39, 40, and 41; Haydn's Symphony Nos. 92–104; and Beethoven's first and second symphonies follow this model. However, Mozart's Symphony Nos. 34 and 38 use a three-movement form but keep a slow-fast-slow format. Of the four movements, the first is typically the longest—permitting greater thematic development and establishing the home key. The second movement is in a different key and the third and final movements return to the home key. For example, Haydn's Symphony No. 97 begins in C major, the second movement is in F, and the remaining two movements return to C. The first movement of the Classical symphony is often divided into two (and sometimes three) sections. If it is divided into two sections, the first section begins in one key and subsequently moves to a second key.

The second section begins by developing themes in the second key; but the section returns to the home key (Czerny 1979, 241–242). On the one hand, if the first movement is divided into three parts (exposition, development, and recapitulation), the movement starts in the home key and then moves to another key. The thematic material is massaged in the development section and then themes are restated in the recapitulation. In the recapitulation, the music returns to the home key and it gives a sense of finality (Ratner 1980, 220–230). On the other hand, in movements with two sections, new thematic material is introduced and developed in each section. Part A of the first section introduces the first theme in the home key and this is followed by the second theme introduced in a different key in part B. In the second section, the first part's thematic material is developed in the second (and other) keys. This leads to the final section of the movement where the themes are restated in the home key (Kollman 1984, 317–318; Czerny 1979, 242–244). While the sonata form is used in the first movement, composers use alternative forms in subsequent movements. Slower second movements use the sonata, A-B-A, theme and variation, or rondo forms. Minuet movements often use the A-B-A form. The final movement is usually a sonata form, but composers occasionally opt for a rondo or sonatina.

Periodicity is central to the statement and development of themes in Classical music. A period is a musical idea that arrives at a particular point—a cadence. The period is used most often from 1600 to 1900. In the Classical era, periods consist of typically four, eight, twelve, or sixteen measure musical ideas or themes. A longer period might be further subdivided into two phrases (antecedent and consequent) and those phrases might be composed of smaller musical ideas—motives. Since periods give the listener the impression that the music is moving toward some predefined goal, the controlling factor is the cadence. The cadence is a point of repose marking the end of a phrase or period. Two common Classical cadences are the authentic and the half cadence. On the one hand, the half cadence typically marks the end of an antecedent phrase, but ends on a chord other than the tonic. Thus, there was no distinct sense of finality. On the other hand, the authentic cadence typically ends the period on a tonic chord—resulting in a definite sense of arrival and finality. Ratner notes that two other cadences helped composers shape their music: deceptive cadences—cadences in which the tonic is replaced by some other harmony following a dominant note—and inconclusive cadences—cadences based on an inverted tonic or dominant. These two cadences permit the composer to shape the period in different ways. Ratner observes that these four cadences are rhetorically important. A period ending with an authentic cadence is similar to the period at the end of the sentence, while an antecedent phrase ending with a half cadence has the effect of a colon or semicolon (Ratner 1980, 33–35).

Time signatures in Classical symphonies are unsophisticated. Classical symphonies—typically in four movements—often open the first movement with a slow introduction (Adagio), but the remainder of the movement is scored much faster. To accomplish this, composers often wrote in some variation of duple meter. Haydn's Symphony Nos. 99–104 are written in cut time or 8/8. Mozart follows suit in Symphony Nos. 34, 35, 38, and 41. However, Mozart uses 3/4 time in the first movement of his Symphony No. 39. Beethoven's first two symphonies do not differ, in this regard. The Minuet or Scherzo movements of these three composers are in the dancelike 3/4. But their second movements are more diverse. In his last six symphonies, Haydn writes in 3/4 and cut time, and Beethoven uses 3/8 in the first symphony. The spirited last movement of these three composers' symphonies employs some variation of duple meter: 2/4 or 6/8.

Classical composers pay close attention to the rhythmic pulse of the music. Which note gets more emphasis is a function of the composer's preference for where the downbeat of the measure is placed. Ratner rightly notes that to avoid extensive rhythmic repetition, composers displaced the downbeat to add rhythmic variety. Haydn's Finale of Symphony No. 104 provides a good example (see example 4.1). The downbeat appears to be on the second beat of the first, second, fifth and sixth measures and on the first beat in the fourth and eighth measures. Some measures sound like they are in two, while others sound as if they are in three (Ratner 1980, 75).

Ratner argues that classical composers often think in terms of poetic feet. The poetic foot takes a group of syllables and assigns stronger and weaker accents to selected syllables. In referring to Koch's categorization of poetic feet, the trochaic foot emphasizes the first note in a two-beat measure. However, other feet and accented notes were used by Classical composers (see example 4.2). Applying poetic feet to the Haydn passage above (see example 4.1), the first two quarter notes in the first measure are unaccented and the half note that follows is accented. This is an anapestic foot. Bars 2, 5 and 6 are also anapestic. The two whole notes in measure 4 are more legato and this has the effect of accenting them. Accenting these two notes is similar to the spondaic foot cited by Koch. Leaning into the downbeat is sometimes effective in establishing or shaping the melodic line; furthermore, accenting the first beat in the measure helps achieve this goal (Ratner, 1980, 71–72; West 1992, 129–159).

The orchestra grew in size and complexity throughout the 1700s. Adam Carse reports a slight increase in the size of orchestras between the

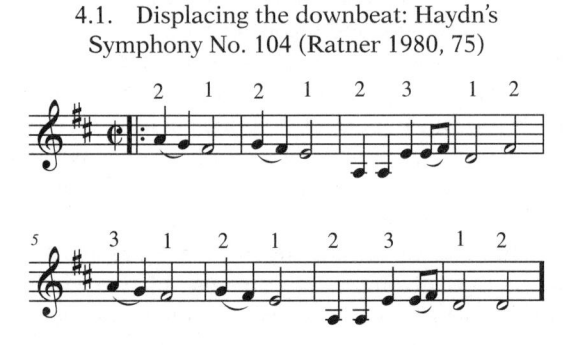

4.1. Displacing the downbeat: Haydn's Symphony No. 104 (Ratner 1980, 75)

4.2. Poetic feet

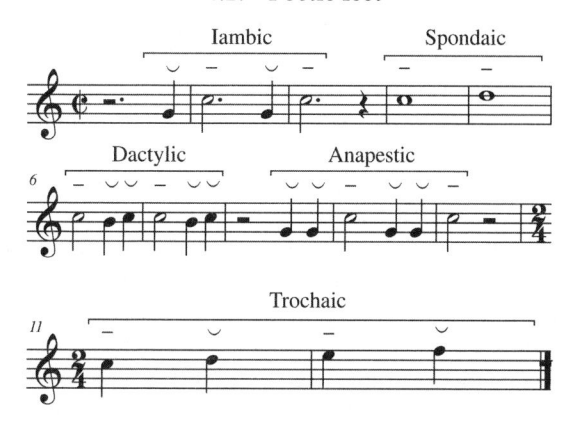

early and late Classical periods. For example, the Dresden Orchestra hired around thirty-five musicians in 1753 and about forty in 1783. The Berlin orchestra grew from approximately thirty-five in 1754 to fifty-eight in 1787. These orchestras were small compared to the Romantic orchestras of the nineteenth century. For example, the London Philharmonic listed around eighty musicians in 1846; although, there were many smaller court orchestras the size of those in the Classical era (Carse 1949, 47–59; 1964, 171). In the Classical orchestra, the strings (violin, viola, cello, and bass) were the foundation of the symphony. In the 1783 Dresden Orchestra, they constituted roughly 63 percent of all musicians. Woodwinds and brass were an integral part of the orchestra—supplemented by percussion. Adding winds and brass to the orchestra progressed slowly during the eighteenth century. In augmenting the strings, the horn and oboe offered harmonic support and the bassoon often reinforced the lower strings. Horns and winds might project their sound in fanfares and marches; and often woodwinds were given preeminence in the trio section of minuets. In the early eighteenth century, trumpets and horns were used in masses, oratorios, and on festive, majestic occasions. According to Carse, they added volume and excitement to the music and they highlighted certain sections of the music. After 1770, trumpets and horns were integrated into the fabric of the music. They added weight and color *throughout* a movement—rather than to just highlight certain phrases or sections in fanfares. Where timpani were employed, they supported the bass line, and they often doubled the bottom trumpet part. Adding additional instruments to the conventional orchestra allowed late Classical composers to paint deeper emotional portraits than in the early part of the eighteenth century. In the orchestral tutti, the availability of more and different instruments meant that composers could intensify the music and deepen its emotional impact (Carse 1949, 10, 134–135, 141; Ratner 1980, 149, 151–152).

Performance practices in the Classical era followed classical ideas of clarity, balance, simplicity, and refinement. Dynamics and articulation provide ways to achieve these goals. The dynamics of Classical music are typically kept within appropriate bounds: typically between *pianissimo* to *fortissimo*. In Haydn and Mozart, *forte* and *piano* are common dynamic markings. To add stress to a note, a *forzando* might be added. Occasionally the crescendo or decrescendo is written in a score; however, this is the exception, not the rule (Ratner 1980, 189). Haydn's Symphony No. 98 is a good example. Most of the symphony is played between the *pianissimo* and *forte*, and the dynamic gestures alternate between *piano* and *forte* phrases or periods. In the last movement, Haydn scores a tutti at *fortissimo* (measure 178). Only in this movement does he score crescendos (see measures 73 and 272). However, these crescendos rarely carry the listener into an emotional catharsis (Haydn 1985a). While the Mannheim orchestra (perhaps the most disciplined in Europe) was noted for employing crescendos and decrescendos, their use in the later Classical period seems quite limited (Burney, 1957, 945). Haydn and Mozart used them sparingly—preferring contrasts between alternating dynamic levels. This trend is particularly evident in the second movement of Haydn's Symphony No. 102 and the first movement of Mozart's Piano Concerto No. 24 (Haydn 1985b; Mozart 1959). As described above, Daniel Turk emphasizes the importance of execution in achieving clarity. In executing Mozart's symphonies, the ascending and descending scalar lines require what Turk would call exquisite "mechanical execution." Allowing each note in a flurry of semiquavers to speak properly requires attention to the attendant articulation. Clarity of line requires a certain balance between instrumental sections. In supporting the thematic line, Mozart gives other instruments an independent voice that needs to be heard. To achieve this, the orchestra must be dynamically and tonally balanced. Finally, the periodic structure of Haydn and Mozart require musicians to clearly begin and end a musical line or theme. Within a theme, the constituent motifs should be clearly stated and properly articulated.[1]

Music and performance practices of the Classical era shape the timpanist's approach to interpreting this music. First, the timpani should project a more transparent or translucent sound. As described in chapter 1, the tonal characteristics of this kind of drum are not so dark that other instruments are obscured by its presence. This permits sections or instruments to be balanced and each instrument heard.[2] Second, the timpanist should carefully punctuate cadences—especially those ending a phrase or period. Pay particular attention to authentic cadences that may clearly denote the end of a phrase. Third, use articulate sticks in movements with quicker tempos and general purpose sticks for other movements. The articulate sticks will permit rhythms, so important to many Classical symphonies, to be articulated and distinctly heard. The general purpose sticks work well in movements with moderate and slow tempos and they effectively execute rolls. Leave softer sticks for special parts that need a dark sound, for example, the opening rolls in Mozart's overture to *Don Juan*.[3] Fourth, play dynamics as written. These typically alternate between *pianissimo* and *fortissimo* (and often between *piano* and *forte*). Crescendo and decrescendos should be used sparingly. The timpani part should be nicely balanced with the orchestra. Fifth, good phrasing often requires making strong contrasts between staccato, nonlegato, and legato notes. Sixth, since the trumpets and timpani often double each other, work out articulation with the trumpet section—especially on when to release quarter and half notes. Seventh, play in a restrained fashion. Eighth, play more toward the top of the drum head—especially in very fluid, quick movements. This will allow all instruments to be heard and the music to feel light. Ninth, muffle often! With *subito* changes in dynamics (between *forte* and *piano*) it in necessary to muffle after the last note of the *forte* gesture to allow the *piano* note to be held. Rhythmic clarity often requires the timpani to be muffled. Muffling is often necessary so that an independent voice in the orchestra is heard—a figure that immediately follows the last timpani note. Be also aware of harmonic changes in a piece that require muffling. Finally, in the mature music of Haydn and Mozart, consider more coloring and dynamic shading to effectively play these parts.

Franz Joseph Haydn

For many, Franz Joseph Haydn represents the epitome of the Classical composer. His symphonies use the sonata form, his melodic lines are simply stated, his periods are gracefully written and flow to the tonic, his dynamics are reserved, his music is restrained emotionally, and his composing reflects an optimism about life that characterized the Classical period. All this is reflected in his writing for the timpani. According to percussionist James Blades, Haydn was trained as a timpanist in Hainburg in his youth, and he played the drums in one of his symphonies in 1791. His writing for the timpani reflects his love for the instrument, and he gives the drums an important voice in his Symphony No. 100 (the "Military"), Symphony 103 (the "Drumroll"), *The Creation,* and the *Mass in Time of War.* Haydn uses the timpani dramatically, rhythmically, and harmonically, and he does much to free the drums from their classical coupling with the trumpets and horns. His knowledge of playing technique was important in shaping the sound of the timpani. In one of Haydn's rehearsals during Salomon's 1794 concert series in London, Sir George Smart relates the following story that gives us a vignette of Haydn's understanding of the instrument.

> At a rehearsal for one of these concerts the kettle drummer was not in attendance. Haydn asked, "Can no one in the orchestra play the drums?" I replied immediately, "I can." "Do so," said he. . . . Haydn came to me at the top of the orchestra, praised my beating in time, but observed upon my bringing the drumstick straight down, instead of giving an oblique stroke, and keep it too long upon the drum, consequently stopping its vibration. "The drummers in Germany," he said, "have a way of using the drumsticks so as not to stop the vibration"— at the same time showing me how this was done. "Oh, very well," I replied, "we can do so in England, if you prefer it" (Smart 1907, 3).

And in Symphony No. 102, he even asks the horns and trumpets to play with mutes, and by extension, the drums could be muted, too (Blades 1970, 159). Thus, Haydn's writing for the timpani is shaped by his classicism and intimate knowledge of the drums.

Haydn's notation of rolls presents problems for the timpanist. In some cases, he uses a tremolo sign and at other times a semiquaver or demisemiquaver note. This raises the question: does he mean something different when he uses tremolo versus a semiquaver roll notation? Generally, no: all these signs denote a roll. The tremolo is often used under a fermata—indicating that the note should be sustained for some time. At other times, Haydn uses the tremolo to clarify that he wants an open roll, not a series of measured notes. The greatest issue concerns whether or not a semiquaver note should be played as measured notes or open (unmeasured) rolls. This was unclear to timpanists in Haydn's time. In measures 78 and 79 of the second movement of Symphony No. 97, Haydn composes a figure that could be played as either sixteenth notes or as an open roll. The London timpanist wrote on the part that playing them as dotted sixteenth notes was "better" (Haydn 1985a, IX: 256). Better than what? I suggest the answer is better than an open roll. If this is so, timpanists in Haydn's time faced the same notational questions that timpanists face today. How does the timpanist determine if a series of sixteenth notes should be played as measured notes or open roll? Several tests can be applied to answer this question. Test 1: does the notation support the rhythmic character of the passage more than the harmonic or melodic character? One the one hand, if the timpani part clearly gives rhythmic emphasis or support to the music, it should be played as measured notes. On the other hand, if the notation is intended to produce a sustained note supporting the melodic or harmonic structure of the music, then the figure should be played as an open roll. As a case in point, Haydn often uses the timpani to double sustained notes in the brass or woodwinds in the London symphonies. Using an open roll would be more appropriate in this context. Test 2: is the passage played at a tempo in which the notes could be executed individually and not as an open roll? Up to a certain point, semiquaver notes could be played individually; but as the tempo increases, there is a point at which individually placed notes sound like an open roll. When that tempo is reached, it is reasonable to think that Haydn intended an open roll. As Haydn knew that the sound of the timpani could be manipulated by the style of playing, it is reasonable to assume that at fast tempos he expected a nice roll and not one whose sound would be stifled by playing faster than one should. What about cases in which the tempo would permit playing either measured notes or unmeasured rolls? Applying the first principle is of some help, but there is a third test. Test 3: is there any marking in the score that suggests that Haydn expected an open roll? For example, a hairpin (crescendo-decrescendo) sign under a note would suggest a roll. In the first measure of Symphony No. 102, Haydn writes a whole note under a fermata with a hairpin dynamic marking. This can only mean that it should be played as an open roll. In other cases, an inspection of critical editions reveals that Haydn wrote in a trill sign that may not have been written into parts (or even conductor's scores). In measure 40 of *The Creation,* Haydn uses a tremolo sign to indicate that the sixteenth notes under the sign should be played as an open roll (Landon 1977, 396). Test 4: does the number of hash marks help determine if a figure should be played as a measured or open roll? In some cases, Haydn will notate a roll with three hash marks that, at the tempo of the passage, would clearly suggest that he intended an open roll (see measure 8 in Symphony No. 99). Test 5: are dots placed over the notes? If so, that would indicate that the notes should be played individually. Measure 38 of *The Creation* has staccato dots placed over the sixteenth notes—clearly suggesting that the notes should be played individually (see example 4.3). However, the following measure has no dots over the sixteenth notes suggesting that this figure should be played as a roll (Brown 1986, 69). Test 6: would playing the passage as an open or measured roll more effectively realize the intention of the composer? Only experience, tradition, and the trained ear can answer this question.

4.3. Test V: discerning rolls in Haydn's *Creation*

Let us look at some commonly played symphonies and masses to explore how Haydn used the timpani and how knowledge of Haydn's symphonic style and the Classical form can help the timpanist interpret his works. Regarding the symphony, Haydn's thirty-one early symphonies (written up to 1765) were thinly scored and without timpani; most were scored for strings, two horns and two oboes. Twelve symphonies were in three movements (fast, slow, and fast) and modern timings suggest that they averaged around fifteen minutes in length: the shortest (No. 1) is five minutes long and the longest (No. 31) is twenty-eight minutes long. From 1765 to 1780, Haydn composed thirty-nine symphonies—sixteen with timpani (and timpani optional/ad lib) parts. By this time, Haydn had settled on the four-movement Classical symphonic form—fast, slow, minuet and fast. The orchestration became more complex and the length of the symphonies increases over the previous period. In addition to strings, it was common for Haydn to score for oboe, bassoon, horns, and occasionally, trumpet. On the average, it took about twenty-two minutes to play these symphonies. The increased duration is in part due to extended elaboration of thematic material and the use of the four-part sonata form. From 1781 to 1790, Haydn wrote twenty-one symphonies—scoring for timpani in six of them. Compared to the previous period, Haydn composes for very similar instruments, and the duration of the symphonies remains about the same. H. C. Robbins Landon and David Jones nicely summarize the Paris symphonies. Haydn now uses a slow introduction to the first (Allegro) movement with more consistency—often this is used to introduce the theme of the Allegro. The first movements are typically filled with energy; melodic, harmonic, and dynamic surprises; and well-developed themes. The second movements are often characterized by thematic repetitions and variations. The third movements, the Minuet/Trio, are typically short and often rich in thematic or harmonic development. The Finales are spirited and dramatic (Landon and Jones 1988, 89–93, 147–156, 215–224).

By 1791, Haydn is reaching the zenith of his symphonic development. He writes thirteen London symphonies—all composed with timpani. The symphonies are in four movements, scored for more instruments, and are longer in duration compared to his earlier symphonies. Haydn continues to compose four movements. The first movement includes a slow introduction (except Symphony No. 95) followed by a lively Allegro, Vivace assai, or Presto. The remaining movements are similar to those of the previous period (slow, minuet/trio, and finale). The symphonies are filled with jokes, surprises (as in the "Surprise" Symphony and the use of timpani and percussion in the "Military" Symphony), energy, balance, changing dynamics, an occasional crescendo, and profound reflections on life. All but the C-minor 95th Symphony are in a major key: D and G constituting seven of the thirteen symphonies. In addition to strings, Haydn regularly scores for flute, oboe, clarinet, bassoon, horn, trumpet and timpani, and the average length of the symphony increases to about twenty-seven minutes. Trumpets and timpani are now employed in most of the slow movements—contrary to the thrust of his earlier orchestration (Landon and Jones 1988, 254–271). Haydn scores the timpani in fourths or fifths in each movement of the thirteen London symphonies. Finally, Haydn's relation to his musicians reflects the growing control composers exercised over the production of their works. By 1791, when Haydn was writing his London symphonies, composers were giving musicians less latitude in interpreting and ornamenting their music. In orchestral pieces, the Baroque convention of permitting player-originated embellishments and writing scores with little direction was going by the wayside. Composers were more explicit in indicating how the musician should approach the music. Leopold Mozart, quoted above, was not unusual in asking performers to pay attention to the part. Haydn felt the same. He composed a work for the Benedictine Abbot, Rainer Kollman, but was unable to attend the ceremony at which his composition, *Applausus Cantata*, was to be premiered. Instead, he sent a letter that reflects his approach to conducting and the expectations he had for the musicians. He directs the conductor to heed strictly the tempos in the arias and recitatives. Haydn writes that "the fortes and pianos are written accurate throughout, and they should be reckoned exactly, for there is a very great difference between piano and pianissimo, forte and fortissimo, between crescendo and forzando and the like." He cautions the violinists to assiduously attend to tied and staccato notes. He concludes, "Finally, I beg everyone, especially the principal musicians, for my sake as well as your own, to use the utmost care possible" (Haydn 1979, 223–225). From this passage and from Sir George Smart's experience with Haydn, it is clear that Haydn had high expectations for his musicians, and in interpreting the part, he expected musicians to cleave faithfully to his notation. All these characteristics shape the way the timpanist can interpret Haydn's last, and particularly the London, symphonies.

The author will analyze Haydn's mature symphonies: Symphony Nos. 94, 100, 102, and 103. Like the other symphonies under consideration, Symphony No. 94 is in four movements. The timpani part is written in d and G for all movements except the second, which is scored for c and G. Asking the timpanist to change the pitch between movements departed from the prevailing style of writing. The second movement of a Classical symphony, often in a different key, would require one or two drums to be retuned. As a result, composers, such as Mozart, usually did not score timpani in the second movement. By the London symphonies, Haydn feels comfortable with writing parts that required pitch changes for one or both timpani. Of the thirteen London symphonies, six require one drum to be retuned between the first and second movements, and two symphonies require two drums to be changed. However, there is a pitch change in the first movement of Symphony No. 94! The G is changed to A. Haydn gives the timpanist twenty-one measures in a quick 6/8 to change the pitch—a short period of time to change a low drum with between seven and twelve tension rods! Then the timpanist was given seventeen measures to tune back to the G. So it is reasonable to suggest that the timpanist had access to an additional large drum or he had ten hands. The former is not out of the question, since London seems to have had a variety of timpani available to timpanists and one could have been borrowed. The latter seems improbable. Also, the Salomon-Haydn concerts were preeminent social affairs that would draw the required orchestral resources for the beloved Haydn. Even if the timpanist attempted to change the pitches, most likely he played with a head that wasn't evenly tuned.

The first movement of this Symphony No. 94 raises several questions about dynamics, articulation, pitch changes, and rolls. The movement opens with an Adagio and then proceeds to a Vivace assai in 6/8; as with quick Classical symphonies, the timpanist must play lightly. Playing more on the top of the drumhead will achieve this goal. There are no technical difficulties in the Vivace assai. Rhythmically, the three eighth notes followed by a quarter note drive this movement (see example 4.4). These four notes should be played evenly throughout the piece with no crescendo or intensification. Bringing out each of these four notes requires concentration; failure to put energy into each note risks playing some notes louder than others. On the low drum, these notes are harder to articulate. Using a mallet with a smaller, harder head and playing the notes hand-to-hand in a staccato fashion will bring out these notes; however, more energy must

4.4. Rhythm in Symphony No. 94

f

be put into the low notes so that they sound at the same dynamic as the higher note. In the twelfth bar of the "Vivace assai" and in the seventeenth and eighteenth bars before letter F, the G should be slightly accented and played into the drum: it gives style to the figure and a sense of finality that is needed at this point. Regarding other articulation, the quarter note thirteen measures after B, at letter C, and three measures before G ends the phrase and should be played as a period—slightly into the drum (see example 4.5). The pitch change in the first movement is not notated in the Kalmus part and timpanist should change the G to an A before letter D. Bars 9 to 12 of rehearsal letter D should be played as an A rather than a d (Landon 1955, 750). After this section, the low drum should be retuned to a G. Muffling should be done at the end of phrases and periods. However, particular attention needs to be paid to two places in this movement. The unmarked quarter notes in measures 4, 6, and 8 after letter D should be played *piano*; since the previous measure is *forte*, the higher drum will need to be muffled immediately before playing the *piano* note. This procedure allows the *piano* notes to be heard. The last three notes of the movement should be muffled or alternatively played short-long-short. Finally, this movement raises the issue of roll notation. The four dotted half notes before letter G are clearly open rolls. To play these notes as measured rolls

4.5. Phrasing Mov. 1, Symphony No. 94

would stifle the sound of the timpani and, as we saw above, Haydn wanted timpanists to produce a more sonorous sound, and an unmeasured roll at this point would achieve this goal.

In the second movement, there are dynamic, articulation, notation, and sticking issues to resolve. Regarding dynamics, the "Surprise" Symphony unleashes its big surprise in this movement. The first two timpani notes at measures 16 and 33 (along with tutti orchestra) were intended to be a surprise, that is, something new to the symphonic world. The timpani help produce this surprise by playing a legato note with some bite and length to it. A small-headed, medium-hard stick, played with some tension between the fingers and the stick, and executed in a manner that gives the note its full value will serve this purpose. Haydn is insistent that the second timpani entrance be played *forte*, one dynamic level under the first note. This itself is a joke more than a surprise: while the musical line leads the listener to expect a loud crack, Haydn instead asks for something less intense—humoring (or surprising?) the audience. In addition, this note comes on the first beat of the measure, when the listener is expecting it to come on the second beat. Making a distinction between the dynamic level of each entrance is important in fulfilling the goals of the composer. The timpani part in the minor key should be played in a staccato manner since the G is played on a large drum and the thirty-second note should be accented. Otherwise, it is apt to get lost. After letter I (see example 4.6), all eighth notes can be played marcato and the quarter notes, legato. At letter K, Haydn notates staccato eighth notes for timpani, horns, and flute. How-

4.6. Playing Mov. 2 Symphony No. 94

ever, in succeeding measures, no such markings follow. It was common for composers to indicate the dynamic level at the beginning of the piece and the remainder of the piece would be played at that level. In this case, Haydn is certainly doing the same thing with articulation. He wants the notes after letter K to be play in a staccato manner. For rhythmic accuracy after letter I, count in four and subdivide the beat as necessary. In some parts, a note is missing in this movement. Three measures after letter I, a quarter note should be placed on the first beat of the measure. Finally, how are the tremolo and the four sixteenth notes played? What kind of roll does Haydn want? The tremolo is clearly an open roll. In the London symphonies, Haydn would notate open rolls as tremolos (if they were played under a fermata). Are the sixteenth notes at the end of the movement rolls? In this case, no. They should be played as measured sixteenth notes because (1) they reflect earlier playing patterns in the bass and celli, and (2) they *can* be played as sixteenth notes. Hashed notes can be played as open rolls when they cannot be played effectively as individually notated rolls. For example, the sixteenth notes before letter G in the first movement could not be played as individual notes and therefore, these notes are open rolls.

The third movement is without difficulty. Dr. Ernst Praetorius places

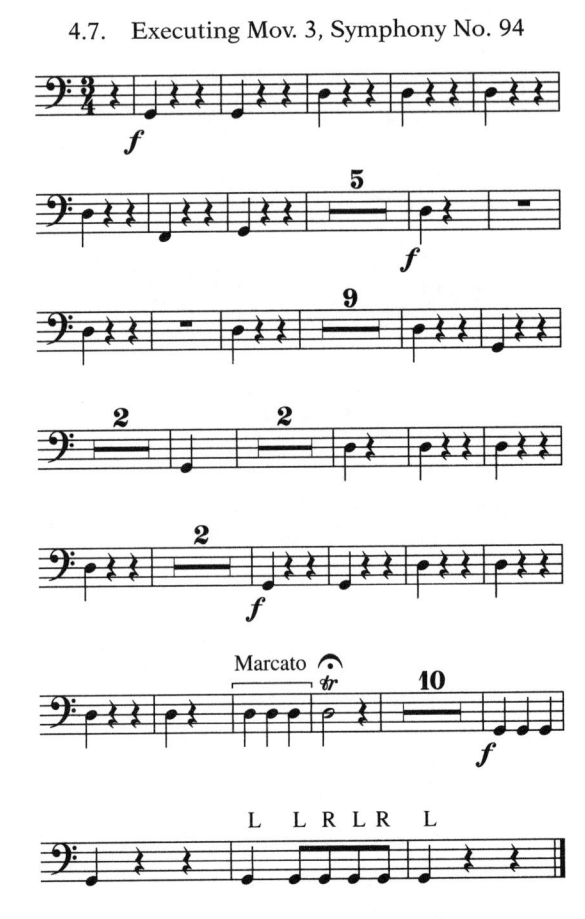

4.7. Executing Mov. 3, Symphony No. 94

110 *Timpani Tone and the Interpretation of Baroque and Classical Music*

a tremolo over the half note in measure 48—clearly to produce a continuous sound that is being sustained by the orchestra (see example 4.7).
The three quarter notes immediately preceding the roll can be played in a more detached, marcato fashion. Finally, the notes two measures before the trio can be sticked L LRLRL (for the left-handed timpanist) for better phrasing. This has the advantage of accenting the first and second beat of the first measure and the first beat of the succeeding measure.

The fourth movement raises three main issues. First, the Allegro di malto tempo and the many eighth and sixteenth notes require a very articulate stick for this movement; otherwise, the rhythm will not come out. These sticks are necessary to bring out the eighth and sixteenth notes when they follow quarter and eighth notes respectively. The timpanist should accent the eighth and sixteenth notes to ensure that they are heard. Adam Carse notes that the timpani were often placed in the rear of Classical orchestras. With larger orchestras today, this means that timpanists need to play on the front edge of the beat so the sound reaches the body of the orchestra and the conductor at the appropriate time (Carse 1949, 45). Second, muffling is an issue throughout this movement. Muffle after the two eighth notes one measure before letter P and two measures before letter Q (see example 4.8). The last two notes of the piece should also be

4.8. Rolls in Mov. 4, Symphony No. 94

Interpretation of Classical Music

muffled and played in a way that gives them their whole value. Third, the eight measures before letter R could be played as either an open roll or measured notes. This should be played as an open roll because (1) the figure does not answer similar notes of another instrument, (2) Haydn scored the timpani to provide the foundation upon which the other parts dance, and (3) it would sound less forced as an open roll. Some scores indicate a diminuendo three measures before letter R, followed by a crescendo one measure before it. However, Landon (Landon 1955, 751) cites a different dynamic marking: a sudden *forte* one measure before letter R (bar 233). Here the timpanist is playing *forte* one full measure before the full orchestral *forte*—a characteristic of Haydn. Additionally, Praetorius and Landon cite the continuation of this roll into the first two measures (bars 234 and 235) of letter R (Haydn 1985c, 60; Landon 1955, 751). What does one do? Haydn was uncomfortable with the use of the crescendo and decrescendo and he used it rarely; rather, Haydn kept to the Classical school's pattern of alternating dynamics (between ***p*** and ***f*** for example). In this case, a sudden *forte* against the *piano* in all the other instruments would be in keeping with the surprise nature of the symphony. What about the roll in the first two measures of letter R? Here it would seem that the Kalmus part makes more sense. A quarter note G on the first beat of letter R would avoid interfering with the melody in the violins and it doubles a single G half note in the trumpet. In summary, play a sudden *forte* one measure before letter R and play a quarter note on the first measure of that letter R. See the companion Web site for a marked timpani part.

Symphony No. 100 (the "Military") is a wonderful piece to play. Each of the four movements have well-written timpani parts. However, the second movement has been reconstructed from parts because no autographed score exists. Particularly moving to eighteenth-century audiences was the second (and the fourth) movement that imported the percussion battery: timpani, bass drum, cymbal, and triangle. After the second performance of the symphony was first played in 1794, the *Morning Chronicle* wrote the following:

> Another new symphony, by Haydn, was performed for the second time; and the middle movement was again received with absolute shouts of applause. Encore! encore! encore! resounded from every seat: the Ladies themselves could not forbear. It is the advancing to battle; and the march of men, the sounding of the charge, the thundering of the onset, the clash of arms, the groans of the wounded, and what may well be called the hellish roar of war increase to a climax of horrid sublimity! which, if other can conceive, he alone can execute; at least he alone hitherto has effected these wonders (Landon 1977, III: 247).

Landon continues by saying that the British audiences cheered for years and as the *Morning Chronicle* reported in 1796, "We cannot describe the agitation excited through the room by the Grand Military Overture of Haydn, nor the universal eagerness with which the second movement was encored" (Landon 1977, III: 247). Why was there such excitement—perhaps no such excitement since the fireworks barge caught fire when Handel's *Royal Fireworks* was played? Clearly, Haydn wrote well for timpani (and percussion) and at appropriate times projected the battery forward in his scores. It is entirely possible that the timpani techniques that Haydn taught to Sir George Smart that same spring (see above) and the use of larger and more sonorous timpani, combined with Haydn's writing to produce a wonderful, new, and exciting sound from the timpani. For the English, at least, the orchestral timpani had come into its own.

The first movement, Adagio; Allegro, raises questions about articulation and rolls. It opens slowly and pastorally but turns rather heavy and dark in color. Like similar introductions in the Classical repertoire, the darker part of this introduction should be played heavier and darker than other parts of the symphony—using a medium-hard stick and allowing the mallet head to play at the bottom of the drumhead. The medium stick is preferable to a softer stick because Haydn asks the timpanist to execute a crescendo roll followed by two well-articulated, heavy notes. There is an issue regarding these two notes. In many parts, these two quarter notes have dots over them. However, the score has two wedges. During the Baroque and Classical eras, some authors differentiate between wedges and the staccato dots. C. P. E. Bach suggests that both dots and wedges indicate staccato phrasing (Bach 1949, 154). Turk adds that dots and wedges (strokes) are staccato notes but wedged notes are even shorter—a point that Leopold Mozart makes (Turk 1982, 432; Mozart 1951, 45). Notes with wedges should be short, but attacked more strongly, Quantz adds (Quantz 1966, 223). Thus, the two quarter notes should be notated with wedges and they should be played in a staccato manner with an accent. A medium, rather than a softer stick, would achieve this articulation. Here we encounter the problem of the roll again. The roll in measures 14 and 15 is notated as sixteenth notes. Should this gesture be played as individual sixteenth notes, as a double stroke roll, or as a single stroke roll? Landon suggests that these should be played as rolls and this interpretation is supported by Haydn's own notation of timpani rolls. However, it is entirely possible that Haydn wanted this figure to be played as sixteenth notes because it would give it an ominous character—what is needed for the music. If Haydn wanted a roll, he could have written them as thirty-second notes (which he uses in the Minuet of Symphony No. 104). This figure is unique for another reason. Haydn is now using a crescendo—one that was rarely used in earlier symphonies. This crescendo was clearly scored to add tension to this phrase, that is, a phrase that is emotionally dark. This analysis suggests that this gesture could be most effectively played as measured semiquavers.

The last measure of the Adagio requires some comment. This is a true open roll: a wavy line marks it in the autograph score and by a trill and line by Haydn's personal copyist, Johan Elssler (Haydn 1985b, LXII). Also, the roll is intended to sustain a note, just as other instruments are doing.

In the remainder of the first movement, there are questions about rolls and dynamics. All the other semiquaver half notes should be played as measured notes. There is no cogent reason to believe that Haydn wanted these figures played as open rolls: he doesn't use the tremolo sign or demisemiquaver notes. Additionally, the measured rolls often support the rhythmic structure of the phrase. The execution of these rolls is straightforward. Given the articulation of most notes in this movement, a medium-hard stick with a small head is sufficient. The rolls are played without any dynamic shading. However, the final rolls five measures from the end can be cross sticked with the stronger hand landing on the first and second beats of the measure. This accents each of the notes slightly and supports the rhythmic line of the phrase. Regarding dynamics, some parts deviate from critical editions. There should be no crescendo ten measures after letter F, two measures before rehearsal H, and nine measures from the end. These phrases need to be played in a more Classical style that admitted few uses of crescendos and decrescendos of this type.

There are no general articulation and tone color questions in the Allegro. It should be played lightly, since it is a fluid, happy, light-hearted movement. Muffling should be done at the end of phrases and periods, as necessary. It is particularly helpful to use a bounce stroke and play a note into the drum to give the sense of finality: the G twelve to fourteen measures after letter A (measures 50–52), the measure of the repeat (measure 124), fifteen measures before F, three and four bars before H (measures 254–255), and fourteen and twenty-one to twenty-three measures after H (beginning at measure 271). Some parts indicate that the three half notes at letter F should be played staccato. While this makes much sense, these notes are not so indicated in the autograph score. However, playing these with some point is necessary in achieving Haydn's intent.

The second movement, which caused such applause in London, has some very fine writing for timpani, but various timpani parts deviate from the traditional score. The problem is that the autograph score has disappeared, and the current score is based upon Johann Elssler's manuscript parts. As Landon notes, there is much inexact copying and there are numerous errors in some parts (Haydn 1985b, iv; Landon 1977, III: 561–562). For example, some parts indicate that the half notes in bars 57–60 (at letter L) should be played staccato—a deviation from the authoritative Elssler part (see example 4.9). Perhaps these were added to the timpani part because wedges were printed above these notes in the basses, celli, violas, trumpets, and horns, for example. Second, there should be no decrescendo three (bar 78) and fourteen (bar 89) measures before letter M. Additionally, Haydn begins the second of these group of eighth notes (measure 89) with a *forzando* (and presumably the first is so accented). Third, the six staccato half notes at letters N (bar 112) and O (bar 134) should not be articulated according to Landon's critical edition. Fourth, there is no diminuendo at the eleventh bar of letter O (measure 144) and nine bars before letter Q (measure 165). There are no other difficulties in any other part of this movement.

The Allegretto raises questions about tone color, articulation, and rolls. This movement calls for a heavy and articulate stick. As a slow move-

4.9. Elssler's timpani part: Mov. 2, Symphony No. 100

ment—heavy, melancholic, and at times frightening—this movement needs to be played in a dark manner. To achieve this, heavier sticks playing toward the bottom of the head of the drum are useful. To articulate the eighth notes on the G drum, use an articulate stick with a hard core. This will help bring out the resonance, color, and articulation. The first ten notes of letter L (bar 57) should be played in a very dark manner: using a heavy stick, German grip, lots of forearm, and letting the mallet head penetrate the head as much as possible (see examples 4.10a and 4.10b). This method will bring out the tone that has a tendency to be swallowed up by the bass drum—the half notes at N and O should be played in the same manner. The four *forzando* notes can be executed with some tension to elicit the startling character of this music. The quavers three and fourteen measures before letter M (bars 78 and 98) should be played staccato, and make sure that all the notes sound the same. Indeed, all eighth notes on the G drum should be played more staccato and with more energy to bring them out. Finally, the two rolls in this movement should be played as open rolls. The c drum should be muffled just before playing the G, seven measures before letter Q (measure 167). This will allow the G to be heard as the orchestra transitions from *fortissimo* to *piano*.

There are no great technical issues in the Menuetto, but some editions require changes. This movement is in a moderate three and should be

4.10a. Color and articulation in Mov. 2
Symphony No. 100

4.10b. Mov. 2, Symphony No. 100 (continued)

played lightly with a medium-hard stick. Pay attention to the eight quarter notes beginning in measure 28. Since the timpani support the trumpets in this phrase and because the trumpets traditionally play a half note, the timpanist can muffle after the second beat of the first seven eighth notes and then muffle the last note after the first beat. In executing this movement, bring out the small notes by slightly accenting them. The sixteenth notes thirteen measures from the end should be brought out, so put more energy into these notes. Some editions of timpani parts do not square with the authoritative Landon score. The staccato dots over the quarter notes in measures 1, 2, 5, 43, and 44 do not occur in Landon's edition of this symphony. Why is this the case when all other instruments have dots over the notes? Perhaps because the timpani sounded dry enough for Haydn and knowing the timpani as he did, he found it unnecessary to score dots. If this interpretation is correct, it makes sense to play these more staccato because modern timpani tend to sing more than period instruments. Also, many conductors ask the orchestra to play the first note stronger than the second note. Finally, Landon does not indicate a crescendo eight bars before the trio. The dynamics move directly from *forte* to *fortissimo*—a characteristic of Haydn and many Classical composers.

The happy music of the Finale Presto has great writing for both timpani and percussion; however, some editions deviate from Landon's authoritative analysis. There are dynamic errors and one note needs to be added. Dynamically, there are no crescendos in Landon's score; therefore, any crescendo should be stricken (see measure 105 or twelve measures before letter T). The figure in this bar should be played *forte*. Some parts have *fortissimo* markings eight bars before letter T (measure 109), at the timpani solo six measures after letter T (bar 122), and at letter X (measure 265): these should be marked *forte*. Haydn, the consummate Classical composer, keeps his forces in balance. In this case, playing *fortissimo* would put the timpani out of balance with other forces in the orchestra. This is particularly true of the timpani solo, which, if played too loudly, destroys the effectiveness of the solo and startles the listener's ear. To make this point even stronger, he marks the beginning of the solo and the concluding beat of this solo in the next measure as *forte*: clearly he didn't want the timpani to flail away. Finally, there is no *forzando* on the semiquaver, dotted half notes nine measures after letter Y (bar 294). This should be played *forte*. Finally, should the timpanist play louder when joined by the percussion? Haydn is very clear here: both percussion and timpani are marked *forte*. Thus, the timpanist and percussionists should adjust their dynamics to achieve a balanced sound. There is one error in some printed timpani parts. Nine measures after R, Haydn scores an additional d quarter note in the second beat of that measure

In executing this movement, there are rolling, sticking, and muffling issues. How should the semiquaver notes be played: as measured notes or as open rolls? These notes, which occur four and five measures from the end of the movement, should be played as measured notes (see example 4.11). The tempo permits them to be played effectively as such, and when

4.11. Rolls and sticking in Mov. 3 Symphony No. 100

these two passages are played as such, it gives the movement forward momentum and drive—which is what is needed in this music. At several points in this movement, the timpanist plays eighth note phrases alternating between two drums. When this occurs, should the timpanist shift or cross stick the passage? Shifting is probably better here because all eighth notes can be played in a similar fashion without fear that cross sticking will produce an accent on the drum that is cross sticked. As is often true with Haydn, muffling should occur at a cadence or in places where letting the drums ring would interfere with the melodic, harmonic, or dynamic line. Muffling at the end of measures 13 and 15 before letter S (measures 94 and 96) allows the woodwinds to answer one another without the interference of the timpani. Muffling after the end of measure 215 prevents any bleeding over into an orchestral rest. Muffling the five quarter notes just before the second beat of the measure at the third bar of letter Y (bar 288ff) supports the articulation of the orchestra and permits the melody in the violins to come through. However, the quarter notes in the first two measures of this phrase can be left to ring throughout the measure since they

Timpani Tone and the Interpretation of Baroque and Classical Music

harmonically and rhythmically support the trumpets and horns. See the companion Web site for a marked timpani part.

The timpani parts for two London symphonies are particularly problematic: Symphony Nos. 96 and 98. The lack of an authoritative score in each symphony has led publishers to print parts that widely vary. Luckily, Landon has provided a timpani part to Symphony No. 98 in his analysis of the symphonies (Landon 1955, 791–794). Because of these difficulties, the author will forego an analysis of these symphonies.

Let's examine some critical passages in Symphony Nos. 102 and 103—two particularly interesting symphonies. In these symphonies, Haydn is composing at the height of his symphonic genius. Haydn uses more articulation marks, open rolls, hairpin rolls, and crescendos and decrescendos. He is also writing timpani into all four movements, which necessitates pitch changes between movements. Similar to other symphonies, he retains the darker *adagio* or *largo* introductions and dynamic contrasts between *forte* and *piano*.

Symphony No. 102 was written in 1794 and the existence of an autograph, revised score provides a clearer road map for an authoritative timpani part (Haydn 1985b, LXXIII; Landon 1977, III: 582–583). There are corrections to the timpani part and technical issues that should be addressed. In the first movement, insert a crescendo at measures 225 and 226 (two measures before H)—the last two measures of that roll. There are no staccato dots over the quarter notes in measures 245, 246, 275–279, and 308–309. In the second movement, there is a decrescendo from *fortissimo* to *piano* throughout measure 25. In measure 54 (three measures after P), mark the eighth note with a wedge. And mark the last note in this movement as a tremolo. In the Menuetto, delete the staccato marks over the quarter notes in measures 50–53. In the last movement, delete the *forzandos* in measures 166–171 (two through six measures after V); although, all other instruments are so marked. Delete the decrescendo in measures 234 and 238 (beginning thirteen measures after X); although, Landon suggests a decrescendo in this measure for all parts except timpani, viola, and bass (Haydn 1985b, 258). Delete the wedges over the quarter notes in measure 282 (four measures before Z).

Technical questions focus on rolls, articulation, and muting. All the semiquaver notes in this part should be played as open rolls—given the tempo of each movement. Particularly interesting is the opening measure of the Largo. Haydn generally steers away from the Mannheim crescendo. Here is one of the exceptions: he scores the whole orchestra with a hairpin dynamic mark. The orchestra crescendos from *piano* to some unknown dynamic level (usually *mezzo forte* or *forte*) and back to *piano* (see example 4.12). To play this effectively, timpanists must start a normal roll and as the sticks are lifted, the speed of the roll must be gradually decreased, and as the decrescendo begins the speed of the roll must be slightly increased until *piano* is reached. The technique effectively starts the roll and allows the sound to blossom as the roll is opened and closed.

4.12. Opening rolls, Haydn's Symphony No. 102

Articulation is somewhat problematic in this symphony. Many times the timpani should play staccato when it is not so marked. Good examples are the first six notes of the first movement's Allegro vivace (see example 4.13). These notes should be played staccato because other instruments are playing staccato at various times and because the tempo is so quick that a staccato stroke is needed to articulate each note. Use a medium-hard or hard mallet with a small head. This same figure occurs again between bars 227 and 232 and is executed in the same manner. The semiquaver notes after rehearsal letter A should be played as an open roll and the following quarter note played with a bounce stroke into the drum. This stroke effectively ends this roll.

4.13. Articulation in Mov. 1 Symphony No. 102

Haydn shows his sophisticated understanding of the timpani in the second movement (see example 4.14). In order to obtain the appropriate articulation, he asks the timpanist to play with a mute (*con sordino*). The problem is that the sextuplets pass by fairly quickly and much of the part is written at *piano*. This means it is very difficult to articulate these notes. First, the notes marked *piano* can be played with one hand—forcing a somewhat more articulate sound. Second, muting the drums and playing staccato with a harder stick effectively articulates these notes. The timpanist should use a heavier mute because some of these muted passages are played *fortissimo* and a heavier mute has the ability to withstand the placement of the stroke and remain in place. The placement of the mute on the drumhead is affected by the amount of muting that drum needs, the degree of articulation the timpanist desires, and the acoustics of the concert hall. Often, the timpanist can play with the mute in the center or just off center of the c drum: timpanists can produce the required articulation and the mute will stay in place. However, the mute may have to be placed

4.14. Executing Mov. 2 Symphony No. 102

more toward the edge of F drum to get the required articulation. In interpreting this part, there is one trap. The *forzando* at letters M and O is really an accent within a *piano* dynamic. One other issue concerns the roll in the last measure—and Haydn wanted a roll! For consistency of sound, the roll can be played with the mute on the drum. Repositioning the mute to the center of the drum (if necessary) after dampening the eighth note five measures from the end, playing the sextuplets a little toward the center, and then playing an open roll produces a sustained sound with the acoustical characteristics of the other notes. This muted roll is effective because the timpanist is playing at the bottom of the timpano's register and, oddly enough, the mysterious sound of this roll fits into the overall ambiance of this movement. Alternatively, a second unmated drum tuned to F could be employed for the final roll. Finally, in the fifth measure from the end, the eighth note is marked with a wedge and followed by an eighth rest. Haydn wants this note to be played staccato, and playing into the head of the drum gives a heaviness and sense of finality that effectively ends this phrase. The drum should then be hand-muffled to avoid colliding with the strings.

The Menuetto can be played effectively by paying particular attention to articulation and the rolls. The grouping of four eighth notes should be played in staccato fashion and the subsequent quarter note should be played legato. In this phrasing, the eighth notes are properly articulated and the legato quarter note supports the rest of the orchestra that typically gives this note greater length and weight. The last two rolls on F should be seamlessly connected to the b-flat, which should be played very legato. Pay attention to muffling so that the timpani does not interfere with the emerging instrumental lines—often played at a lower dynamic level.

Based on the authorized score, several changes should be made in the fourth movement's timpani part. Take out all *forzandos* and decrescendos throughout the part. With these changes made, executing the piece is straightforward. Play all demisemiquaver half notes as open rolls and bring out the two sixteenth notes in the measures after letters U and Z. Pay particular attention to measures 12 and 13 after U. Since the dynamic is *piano* and the part is written in the lower register of the drum, the timpanist should consider playing into the drumhead and executing the figure more toward the center of the timpano. See the companion Web site for a marked timpani part.

Symphony No. 103 ("Drumroll") was composed and premiered in 1795. The symphony consists of four movements: three movements for e-flat and B-flat drums and the second movement composed for c and G drums. Haydn gives the timpanist ample opportunity to retune between the first and second movements, but little time between the second and third. The opening timpani roll solo demonstrates Haydn's knowledge of the instrument and its impact on his English audience; the *Morning Chronicle* reported that the roll "excited the deepest attention" (Landon 1977, III: 595). The symphony shows how well Haydn had mastered writing for the instrument. Like Symphony No. 102, an authoritative score exists. J. P. Salomon later arranged this symphony for piano trio and piano quintet, which attests to the popularity of the piece.

Some timpani parts diverge from Haydn's corrected manuscript score. In the first movement, the opening roll should be a semiquaver, not a demisemiquaver as is sometimes found. The eighth notes from measure 47 to the first two notes of measure 53 should have a staccato dot placed above them—as should all eighth notes in measures 167 to 170. However, the dots above the notes in bar 221 should be stricken. In measures 53 and 54, the *forzando* should be on the fourth and first beat, respectively, and the same is true for measures 172 and 173. The semiquavers in measures 70, 155, and 156 should be rewritten as eighth notes in each measure. Finally, the decrescendo in measures 188, 190, and 192 should be stricken. In the second movement, the eighth note in measure 186 preceding the roll should be deleted. In the Menuetto, the dots over the three quarter notes in measure 7 should be eliminated. In the final movement, the following should be stricken: the crescendo in measures 99 and 100 and the *forzandos* in bars 105, 106, 295, and 297. Dots should be added above the notes in measure 364.

Rolls are the greatest issue in this symphony. The opening roll, repeated in bar 201, gives the timpanist some latitude. Haydn no doubt notated the roll as a semiquaver under a fermata. As we have seen, this is the notation that Haydn uses to write open rolls. Additionally, he writes "Intrada," or short introduction. At what dynamic should it be played? How long should the roll be played? Here there is no consensus because Haydn did not specify this in the manuscript. Concerning the dynamic marking, Landon writes:

But Haydn may have left the dynamic "interpretation" up to the performer. But what did the Viotti Orchestra play? The arrangement for piano trio by Salomon has ⟨hairpin⟩ :, and this "hairpin" has become the traditional way of performance. On the other hand, Salomon's quintet arrangement that also exists in his autograph, has *ff*, presumably followed by a long *decrescendo*. When this reading was first adopted in modern times by the late Hermann Scherchen in 1950, it proved enormously effective (Landon 1977, III: 595).

Unfortunately, the rest of the score provides us with no understanding of how to interpret this part—nor does the introductory movements of his mature symphonies. First, Symphony No. 99 begins *forte* followed by a *piano* section—Haydn could have done the same in the 103rd Symphony because he consistently alternated *forte* and *piano* sections in his movements. Second, Symphony No. 101 begins with an orchestral crescendo and decrescendo over three measures; in No. 102 he reduces this figure to a hairpin dynamic in one measure. Is this gesture a possibility since he had been exploring the use of hairpin rolls during this period of his symphonic writing? Third, in Symphony No. 102, he ends the second movement with a *pianissimo* roll with no dynamic fluctuation; could this be another option? Finally, is a *forzando*, decrescendo roll possible? Of these four possibilities, playing the solo roll as a hairpin roll is best. Executing this gesture as a *forzando*, decrescendo roll is least likely for two reasons. First, this author can think of no evidence in his latter symphonies where he wrote a decrescendo roll—even though the opportunity to do so presented itself (Symphony No. 102 final movement, measures 234 and 238; and the present symphony: first movement, measures 188 and 190). Second, the audience's response to the opening roll is not what one would expect from a *fortissimo* roll. English audiences cheered and applauded the timpani parts (Symphony Nos. 94 and 100), but here the response is more refined: it "excited the deepest attention." Hardly the wording one would use to describe a *fortissimo* entrance—with or without a decrescendo. That leaves us with three other options. A single-measure *fortissimo* roll followed by a *piano* section in the strings and bassoon would not fit into the more reserved introduction. The third and fourth choices are a possibility. A straight *piano* roll with no dynamic fluctuation would suit the music and might elicit the response from the audience that the *Morning Chronicle* noted. However, playing this as a hairpin roll is the author's choice, since Haydn had been effectively experimenting with it in the two previous symphonies, it would fit the character of the introduction, and it would excite "the deepest attention" of the audience. The sweet flavor of this introduction suggests that the crescendo should come out of nowhere, rise to a *mezzo piano* or *mezzo forte*, and disappear into nothingness. The tempo of this solo is around 60 beats per minute and this gives the timpanist time to effectively execute this roll.

Other rolls in the first and second movements deserve attention. In the first movement, measure 90 is notated as six quavers and the following semiquaver figure in bar 91 should be played as an open roll given the tempo of the movement (Allegro con spirito). Measure 157 should be executed as an open roll, reflecting a similar pattern of composition. The other semiquaver notes in this movement should be played as open rolls because (1) the tempo is too fast for a measured roll to sound good, (2) Haydn uses semiquaver notes to indicate a roll, and (3) an open roll doubles a sustained note of another instrument (measures 215–217). The appearance of semiquaver whole notes in the second movement (Andante) suggests that these notes should be played as an open roll; however, the tempo is so slow that these should be played as a measured roll. Indeed, the *forzandos* on the first note of each measure in bars 187 to 191 can be played by individualizing these notes. Furthermore, these five measures of semiquavers repeat the rhythm played by the strings from measures 171–175.

There are articulation and phrasing issues in the second and fourth movements. The second movement is somewhat slow and martial in character; therefore, it should be played more heavily toward the bottom of the head and with a medium-hard mallet (see example 4.15). The sixteenth and thirty-second notes should be articulated, and the dynamic level must be maintained throughout each phrase (bars 109–145). The articulation is necessary because the drums and brass are doubling each other and the brass will play staccato. To dynamically balance the larger and smaller drums, the articulated notes on the G drum should be brought out. The phrasing of this movement is straightforward. The notes should be played hand-to-hand, which gives the rhythmic figures a smooth, progressive flow. In measures 157 and 158, and then in subsequent figures, the c is likely to be drowned out by a resonating G. Therefore, the G should be muffled as

4.15. Rolls and muting in Mov. 2 Symphony No. 102

the timpanist plays the c. This gives the G its full value and allows the c to ring full and resonant.

In the fourth movement, articulation is the main issue. The eighth notes (for example, measures 99–106) should be played as measured notes. In most cases, the timpani support the same articulated, rhythmic figure in the strings and do not double the sustained notes in the bass; therefore, the timpani should not play a roll. Given the tempo (Allegro con spirito), articulating these notes is difficult. Using a hard stick with a small head, pinching the stick, and playing slightly out of the playing spot toward the center of the drum will give greater articulation.

Haydn's *Mass in Time of War (Paukenmesse)* was written in a time of great political upheaval. The French Revolution threatened to overthrow Europe's monarchies and replace them with republican political systems. Napoleon's march through Europe threatened the aristocratic classes with an evolving democratic ethos. As a result, the aristocracies of Europe attempted to halt the military advance of Napoleon and democratic ideas in Europe between 1795 and 1814. Haydn wrote this mass during the early part of this political upheaval and subsequent war (1796). Speculation that it was written as the French were marching into Austria is supported by the rhythmic figure of the timpani in the last movement. As Landon notes, "some scholars have considered the very rhythm of the timpani to be that of the French armies—'the human heart thudding with anxiety'—etc., the anapestic rhythm of which creeps into Haydn's sinister drumbeats of 'uncanny nervousness'" (Landon 1977, IV: 175). The authoritative scores and parts of the reduced and expanded versions of this mass exist. This author will refer to the expanded edition found in *Joseph Haydn Werke*, edited by Jen Peter Larsen (1958).

The Kyrie presents the timpanist with textual, technical, and interpretation issues. On the whole, the timpani parts are fairly accurate. Several dynamic markings should be changed to reflect the authoritative scores. Measure 5 should be marked *fortissimo* and bar 86, *forte* (see example 4.16). The first technical issue concerns the notation of the roll in measure 5. This is an open roll; but should the roll be executed as two rolls or as one sustained roll? It would be best to sustain the roll throughout the measure—doubling the trumpets. However, be prepared to divide this figure into two rolls: this follows the rhythmic pattern in the strings and the choir. Interestingly, the timpani part is written *fortissimo* and the rest of the orchestra and choir at *forte*, and this clearly indicates that Haydn wants this roll to project and to set an ominous tone for this mass. Using a medium stick suffices to bring out all the color of the timpani. Haydn also scores open rolls in measures 9 and 10, and since the drums support the harmonic structure of the music, play the G roll as a single roll. However, be prepared to play two rolls, thereby supporting the rhythmic pattern in the orchestra; making a slight break between the first and second roll supports orchestral phrasing. However, the roll in bar 66, even though it is divided into two semiquaver half notes, should be played as one sustained roll—a roll that would support the sustaining orchestra. In the Lon-

4.16. Opening roll in the Kyrie, *Paukenmesse*

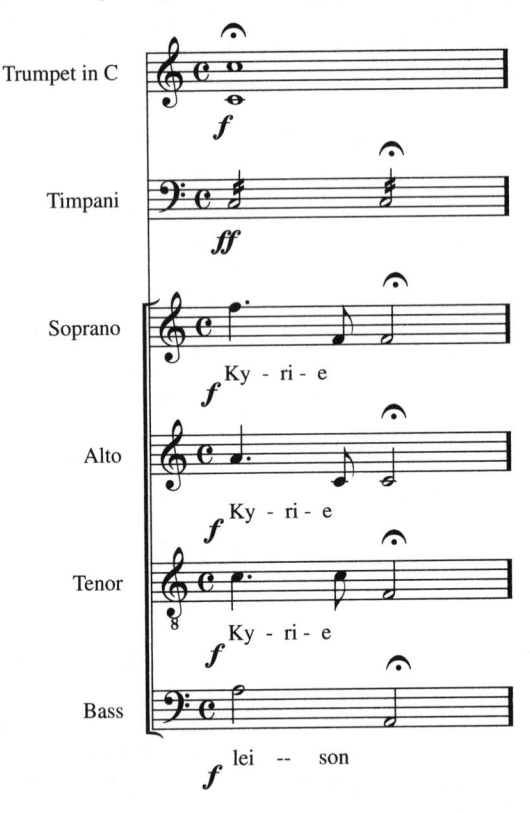

don symphonies, Haydn commonly indicates a sustained roll by semiquaver half notes. This continued into his post-London compositions. Measure 26 is interesting because Haydn marks these three notes with wedges and clearly expects these notes to be played short and a bit heavier—common practice for the time—but reserved for special occasions by Haydn (see Symphony No. 102, fourth movement, measure 283). Using a medium-hard stick is effective in punching out this passage, and since this passage is more fluid and lighter, it suffices for the rest of the Kyrie. Finally, the note at 85 should be dampened immediately after playing it since the orchestra is *subito piano* on the second half of the first beat. In some cases, conductors ask for this note to be played *piano*.

The Gloria contains many textual errors in some timpani parts relating to articulation, and it demonstrates Haydn's evolving understanding of the timpani. In the London symphonies, Haydn rarely uses articulation marks in timpani parts. Dots and wedges first make their appearance in Symphony Nos. 101 and 102. In the Gloria, he asks the timpanist to articulate the notes when they are associated with the first melodic figure; but when the melodic rhythm appears in a different melodic context, he does not call for this articulation. Two sets of corrections should be made to the timpani part. First, the following measures should not have dots above or below the half notes: 4, 40–63, 70–77, 101–124, and 230–235 (though my preference is to play these phrases with dotted notes since these gestures are a restatement of the theme). Second, quarter and eighth notes should be dotted in these measures: 28–39, 63–68, and 225–227. Playing this movement with a medium-hard stick, articulating the dotted notes, and playing lightly on the top of the head is appropriate for this music. This music needs to be punched out and played very evenly so that each note speaks.

It appears that Haydn developed a more sophisticated understanding of the nuances of timpani tone, rolls and articulation after his first visit to England. For example, articulation marks in drum parts make their first appearance in these later symphonies and the number of open rolls in first movements increases significantly after Symphony No. 98. Before Symphony No. 99, there is an average of about one roll per first movement (in movements where rolls occur), but that increases to an average of six rolls for the remaining symphonies. Haydn's first use of muted drums (*con sordini*) occurs in Symphony No. 102. Landon believes that the drums were used in a number of new ways: (1) as solo instruments in *piano* sections (Symphony Nos. 101 and 103), (2) with long, sustained rolls (Symphony Nos. 100 and 104), and (3) as melodic instruments (Symphony No. 99). His use of solo drums in *forte* passages date to Symphony No. 97 (Landon 1955, 588).

There are additional corrections and notational issues in the Gloria. The dynamic marking at measure 76 should be *fortissimo*, not *forte*. The first beat of measure 224 should be a G, not a c. It is apparent that the rolls in measures 259, 289, and 294 should be played as open rolls, and they should be slightly accented. Muffling is self-evident in this piece. Although, the c notes in the last three bars of the movement should not be muffled—allowing the last note of the Kyrie to ring slightly longer.

The Credo also has engraving and dynamic issues. In some parts, measures 100, 113, 171, 173, 175, 283, and 284 have dots over the notes. These dots should be removed. Haydn does place wedges over the notes in bars 308, 309, and 311. Thus, these should be played staccato and somewhat heavily, and the eighth note one measure before the end of the piece should be brought out so it is not lost. The dynamics of the timpani part are *forte* throughout, except for measures 156–159, which are *subito piano*, and measures 160–176, which are marked *fortissimo*. For the timpani, this movement is very tonal and it is best to use a general stick: one that brings out the tone color of the drums, but can articulate as necessary. Thus, the quarter notes should be played legato throughout; but the eighth notes should be played more staccato. Since this movement pitches the timpani in G and c, the G will speak softer than the c. More energy must be put into the G to get the appropriate volume, and those eighth and sixteenth notes played on the G need to be played in a staccato manner so they are brought out. The semiquaver notes in measure 310 should be played as an open roll (see example 4.17). Playing this gesture as measured notes would result in overplaying the head and stifling the sound. Little muffling is necessary in this movement.

4.17. Interpreting the Credo, *Paukenmesse*

The Sanctus is divided into two parts: Adagio and Allegro con spirito. The Adagio is slow and solemn and should be played nobly. Using a medium stick and playing more heavily (toward the bottom of the head) will provide the color and articulation that is needed. The Allegro is much lighter in color and can be played with a medium-hard stick. After playing the quarter note in measures 32 and 34, the timpanist should dampen the head immediately because the strings come in softly immediately after that note.

There are issues of editing and rolls in the Benedictus. In measure 13 a *forzando* should be written in on the first semiquaver of the measure, and from measures 109–111, the part should look like example 4.18.

4.18. Correction to mm. 109–111, Benedictus

Rolls are also a concern in this movement. Play measures 12 and 13 as a sustained, open roll. While the timpani part suggests that this roll should be divided into two rolls with a separate attack on the second roll, all the instruments in the orchestra are sustaining this note and the timpani should do likewise. Haydn also writes in a *forzando* for the timpani and trumpets on the first note of bar 13 (see example 4.19), so the timpanist should begin this roll with a sharp attack (*fz*). Finally, measures 75–78 need to be articulated: played staccato into the head, and more toward the center of the drum.

4.19. Dynamic shaping of Benedictus

The Agnus Dei is well written for timpani and there are few errors in most editions of the timpani parts. Let's begin by looking at the timpani solo at the beginning of this movement. Understanding the choral and historical context of this timpani passage is important to interpreting the part. Juxtaposed to one another are (1) the choir that is singing, "O lamb of God, who takes away the sins of the world" and (2) the timpani—a symbol of war. In the first nine measures, the choir literally pleads God to take way the sins of the world: the sin of war. Oblivious to this cry, the timpani solo follows, and after three measures of solo, the choir enters singing "have mercy upon us"—over the timpani solo. The cry for mercy continues through measure 34. Above the martial sound of the timpani, the choir sings "Grant us peace" as if it is asking for deliverance from war. The timpani must play this part in a way that captures the darkness of war. In the second part of this movement, the Allegro con spirito, Haydn writes more joyous music as the choir sings "Grant us peace." It is as if the scourge of war has been lifted; the timpani and orchestra join in the prayer for peace.

Executing this solo requires the timpanist to draw upon a number of artistic resources. As we have seen, Haydn distinguishes between dots and wedges—the latter played staccato and heavier than the former. All the quarter and eighth notes in measures 10–17 (excluding the first quarter note of bar 10) should be marked with a wedge (see example 4.20). In this solo, Haydn wants to give some weight to these notes. Why play in this fashion? Landon reports that some scholars thought this timpani solo represented the approaching French armies; if so, accenting the first and third beat of the measure would give the passage a martial pulse. To get the necessary articulation, the timpanist can use a hard stick with a small head and play in a staccato fashion. In the *piano* parts of this phrase, the timpanist can move slightly out of the playing spot toward the center of the drum to achieve greater articulation. This is particularly true of the notes on the G drum. To project this solo in the *piano* sections, the timpanist can play the part at a *mezzo piano* dynamic. Haydn does not use wedges over the eighth and quarter notes in solo passages between measures 35 and 39.

4.20. Executing the Agnus Dei Solo

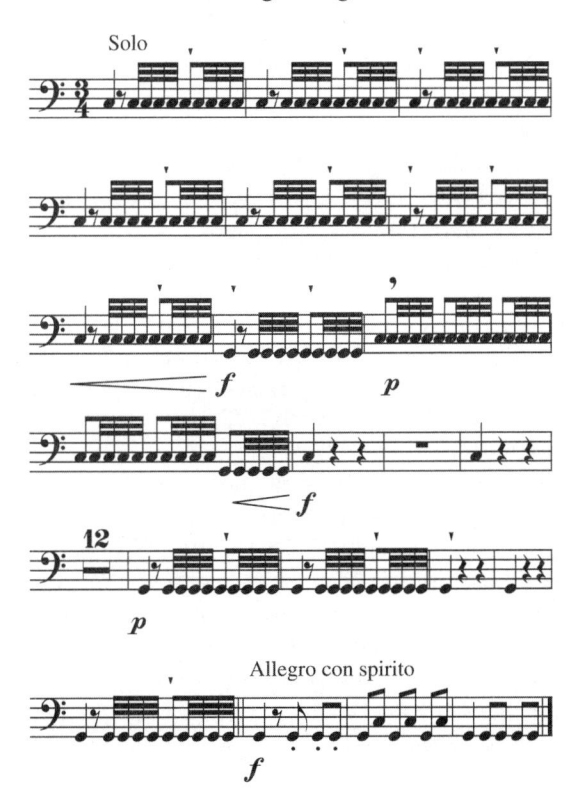

For consistency with the earlier solo figure, these measures can be articulated with wedges in the same manner. In Haydn's earlier works, Haydn typically alternates dynamic markings (*subito forte* and *piano*, for example) and this is the case here—with one exception. In measure 16, he scores a one-bar orchestral crescendo into measure 17, and the orchestra plays *forte* through the first note of measure 18, after which the orchestra plays *subito piano*. Thus, the timpanist should muffle the *forte* eighth note so that the subsequent *piano* section can be heard. To give some emphasis to the phrase "O lamb of God" in measures 20 and 22, Haydn scores a *forte* that should be played heavily.

The Allegro con spirito section is largely without problems. The dots under the notes in measure 52 do not appear in authoritative editions and should be deleted. In other places, for example, measures 56, 76, 83, 85, 87, and 95, the timpanist can end these phrases by playing a staccato note into the drum. For reasons of tonal consistency in this section, the Allegro can be played with the same hard, small-headed stick that was used in the Adagio; or alternatively, after bar 56, the timpanist can switch to a medium-hard stick. Using either stick and playing lightly (more on the top of the head) helps realize the more joyful nature of this music. In measures 73, 76, 83, 85, 87, and 95, the notes can be played slightly into the drum since this gives the kind of punctuation and finality the music needs. The timpanist can crescendo in measures 43 and 44. This adds drama to the moving wind and brass lines. To avoid interfering with the *piano* sections that begin in measures 116 and 120, the timpanist should muffle after playing the first beat of the measure and play into the drum to articulate the *piano* section of this figure. Finally, the timpanist should play an open roll in measure 153. See the companion Web site for a marked timpani part.

Haydn's *Creation* is an oratorio that rivals Handel's *Messiah* in appeal. This oratorio was written in 1798, two years after the *Paukenmesse*. As a mature composition, the timpani part shares much in common with both his symphonies and oratorios, but Haydn uses timpani more creatively. He is more observant of articulation; he uses numerous rolls; crescendos are scored to intensify the drama of the music; the timpani are employed to rhythmically drive the music forward; the timpani are given their own voice (avoiding simply doubling other sections); Haydn uses numerous pitch changes; and the timpani part is well integrated into the harmonic structure of the music. As this is one of the most documented compositions by Haydn, his intentions are well known. For the modern musician and reader, the Eulenburg score most closely duplicates Haydn's final thoughts on the oratorio (Landon 1977, IV: 391–392).

The timpani part for the *Creation* is demanding. Haydn requires numerous pitch changes, scoring movements in c and G, d and A, and b-flat and F—requiring a minimum of three timpani (32-, 29- and 26-inch drums). He scores seven pitch changes throughout the performance; but he gives the timpanist adequate time to retune. Haydn asks the timpanist to pay attention to phrasing, articulation, and crescendos and decrescendos, and he demands strict counting. Finally, he asks the timpanist to make important distinctions between measured notes and open rolls—a subject to which we now turn.

Roll notation in this oratorio require some comment. The opening movement of the *Creation* is the Image of the Chaos and presents several issues. The first whole note under a fermata is marked by a trill and decrescendo. Early drafts and timpani parts indicate that Haydn scored the roll, *con sordino* (muffled); however, in the final version he muted only the strings (Haydn 1925, 1; Brown 1986, 68). This figure can be played with a medium stick. One enduring question concerns measures 38 and 39: should these be played as an open roll or measured notes? (See example 4.21.)

4.21. Phrasing "Chaos" in Haydn's *Creation*

The timpani part helps answer this question. Measure 38 is written with dots under the sixteenth notes, clearly suggesting that these should be played individually. But measure 39 is written without this articulation. Assuming that Haydn or his copyist did not accidentally leave the articulation out, this measure should be played as an open roll. Supporting this interpretation is Landon's analysis. The final sketch of measure 39 is marked with a trill sign. This is the strongest evidence for playing this measure as a roll; although in many modern performances, "this is laboriously performed as sixteen semiquavers" (Landon 1977, IV: 396). To many timpanists, individually playing each note adds drama and strength to this figure. I agree. Measure 47 should be played as individual semiquavers, too. The tempo is slow enough to play them as such, it is in character with the manner in which other semiquaver notes are played, and Haydn could have written a trill sign. There are other places where individual notes should be played: measures 28–30 of Number 2, and measures 159–165 in Number

4.22. Executing No. 28, *Creation*

14. Three other passages present some difficulties. Look at measures 45–47 of Number 28 for Duet and Choir (see example 4.22). Play the first and second measures (and the previous bars not shown here) as individual notes. To ensure that the *pianissimo* notes are articulated, play with a hard stick and place the notes out of the playing spot toward the center of the drum. However, play the last measure (47) as an open roll. (Alternatively, the timpanist can tune two drums to c and muffle G and c, leaving the unmuffled c drum to play the roll.) Playing measured notes in measures 45 and 46 support the rhythmic nature of the music, but the gesture under the fermata should be played as an open roll. It supports the orchestra, which is also holding that note. As we saw earlier, where Haydn writes semiquaver notes under a fermata, he intends a roll. This is true in this case. Play the three bars of semiquavers seven measures from the end of Number 28 as a roll, since the ordinary tempo is so fast that playing these measures as open rolls fits the music quite well; however, at a slower tempo, execute the phrase as measured notes. Play bar 9 of Number 32 as individual notes. The final half note in that bar can be played either as an open roll (although it is not marked as such) or as a single note (see example 4.23). In similar passages in other symphonies, Haydn wrote a tremolo sign for the timpani where both the orchestra and timpani sustained a note. If the conductor holds the fermata for a long time, the timpanist could consider an open roll. If the conductor holds this note for a shorter period of time and the timpanist could play it as a single, sustaining note. Finally, execute the four-measure crescendo in Number 4 as a open roll: the tempo is relatively fast and playing this as measured notes would stifle the resonance of the drum. An open roll produces a full-bodied, blossoming crescendo.

Haydn asks the timpanist to pay particular attention to phrasing in this oratorio (see example 4.24). Look at Number 5 for soprano and choir. Written for c and G drums, timpanists know that they are playing in the low register of the larger drum: this raises both articulation and dynamic problems. Pay special attention to articulating the dotted notes and balancing the dynamics of the G with the c drums by putting more energy into the G timpano. While this movement is not particularly fast (*allegro*), play it with a light flavor, more on the top of the head, and with medium-hard sticks. In measure 16, stick this phrase by beginning with two left-handed

4.23. Interpreting m. 9 of No. 32, *Creation*

4.24. Phrasing No. 5, *Creation*

notes (since the author is left-handed). This permits the pulse to remain in the left hand and allows timpanists to use the stronger hand when they land on the G—the third (and one of the strongest) beat in the measure. In measure 17, the two eighth notes should be played staccato (duplicating the articulation of other instruments of the orchestra); although, Haydn didn't write them as such. Since drums were more percussive in Haydn's day than they are now, perhaps he believed a staccato mark was unnecessary. In measure 19, timpanists have a choice in phrasing this, and subsequent, measures: play the sixteenth notes with one hand, which produces greater articulation, or play the phrase hand-to-hand, which is more fluid. The author prefers the latter since it moves the rhythmic figure forward. Also, play the last quarter note very legato. This note will sustain well, it will strengthen the third beat of the measure, and it will establish a well-phrased measure. Finally, the last sixteenth note in bar 48 should be brought out; otherwise, it is likely to be lost.

In *The Creation*, Haydn pays close attention to articulation. Like other Classical composers, he uses both staccato dots and rests to shorten notes. In measures 25–27 of Number 5, Haydn marks the eighth notes with staccato dots. As we saw earlier, it is uncharacteristic of Haydn to use dots and wedges; however, he does so here and he clearly prefers an articulate passage. However, the next measure, which is written almost identical to the previous bar—excepting the addition of the trombone and contrabassoon—is not so marked. The trombones and timpani double each other, but Haydn does not indicate whether or not these should be played staccato. For musical consistency, the author prefers to articulate each passage in the same manner. The quarter note should be played legato in each of these phrases: permitting it to sound more sustained. In measures 33 and 34, Haydn scores the notes of each instrument with dots, so he obviously intended very short notes. In passing, it should be noted that in some timpani parts, the last timpani note is not dotted—contrary to the score.

Haydn also effectively scores rests to indicate a staccato note. This is clearly the case in measure 34 of Number 5. In the score, the first three eighth notes are played *forte* and the next notes are *piano*. In the timpani part, the rest indicates that this note should be played short (and then dampened to avoid interfering with the violin melody). Similarly, play the two eighth notes in measure 42 staccato because most of the other instruments in the orchestra are playing in the same manner. Playing these notes into the head with a bounce stroke permits the timpanist to effectively articulate them and to give a sense of finality before the timpanist moves to the tonic. See the companion Web site for a marked timpani part.

Wolfgang Amadeus Mozart

Mozart, who was born in 1756 and died in 1791, was a contemporary of Haydn. With Haydn, Mozart shared the Classical style—shaping it with his own imagination. While Haydn was a superb symphonist, Mozart excelled in composing operas and his piano concerti set new stylistic and artistic standards. Mozart's early travel on the continent and to England provided him with a palette of musical ideas from which he drew in shaping his own style. Paul Henry Lang perhaps said it the best when he wrote:

> Mozart never created really new forms but by regarding the existing styles not as unities but as phenomena which contribute toward a general style, he created a universal all-inclusive style which stood above all subspecies. Such a universal style is possible perhaps in music only, because the diversity of languages in literature and the concreteness of the subject in fine arts prevent a final synthesis (Lang1969, 636).

Like Haydn, Mozart's mature symphonic writing developed later in life: after 1785. By this time, he had fully developed his own style, which was very periodic and melodious. His last three symphonies were composed in a little over one year and they expressed a range of passion, the development of sweeping thematic material from smaller motives, and contrapuntal experimentation. His piano concerti reflected his love for the instrument. However, in scoring for piano and orchestra, he placed the orchestra on par with the piano: the orchestra and piano conversed on an equal basis.

In this analysis, the author will analyze Mozart's mature symphonies, Piano Concerto No. 24, and overtures. However, several prior issues should be addressed regarding Mozart's articulation and rolls. Mozart's classical heritage strongly shapes his instrumental writing. Scholar Karol Berger notes that there is a strong interaction between punctuation, voice, key, and theme in Mozart's compositions, but punctuation (the use of the period) integrates the other influences into a powerful compositional style. Mozart uses full and half cadences masterfully in driving the musical phrase to its tonic conclusion (Berger, 1996, 240, 243). The timpanist should be cognizant of these cadences, since they are important in phrasing and articulating the timpani part. In their book, *Interpreting Mozart on the Keyboard*, Eva and Paul Bandura-Skoda discuss the importance of phrasing and articulation in Mozart's works. Mozart uses slurs, dots, and wedges in shaping his music. Mozart scores slurs to indicate (1) a legato phrase and (2) what notes were to be separated from the grouped notes. Legato slurs often extend over several notes and end at the bar line, but occasionally they extend over multimeasure phrases. Articulating slurs are short and rarely extend over more than three notes. Often, the first note is accented—if it is the same value of the following note—and the unslurred notes are played more staccato or more softly. However, in his later works, a slur might tie a note over the bar line and the final note of the slur should be played staccato. Regarding articulation, Mozart uses dots and wedges to shorten notes or to give them special emphasis (Bandura-Skoda 1962, 53–60). Thus, slurs, dots and wedges indicate two forms of playing: legato and staccato. However, there is a third form: the nonlegato. Nonlegato notes are those notes of any value that are neither legato nor staccato. A timpanist may think of this as a pointed legato note.

These analyses are helpful in interpreting timpani parts. In playing Mozart's works, the timpanist needs to consider the kind of articulation Mozart wishes. In particular, should a note or passage be played legato, staccato, or nonlegato? What makes this particularly difficult is Mozart's inconsistency in using articulation markings. Paying close attention to the musical context in which the timpani part is placed, scrutinizing the periodic structure of the piece, examining the score, and studying the timpani part can help the timpanist ferret out Mozart's intentions.

Several types of notation found in timpani parts deserve comment. First, Mozart, like his father, distinguishes between dots and wedges. Dots above notes indicate staccato and wedges indicate a note that is played more heavily and staccato (L. Mozart 1951, 45–47). Even though a timpani note may not have a wedge over it, if another instrument's part is so articulated, timpanists should consider articulating their part in a similar manner. For example, nine and eleven measures after L in the first movement of Symphony No. 39, Mozart concludes a roll with a single quarter note. Mozart uses wedges in the string parts and dots in the wind parts to articulate this note. Clearly, the timpani's quarter note should be treated with greater articulation than what is written in the part. Second, Mozart often does not place dots over notes he wants shortened in timpani parts. The score is a good resource in ascertaining what notes should be played more staccato. Often, he will dot other instruments' notes he wants shortened, and if the timpani is playing, the timpanist's notes should often be shortened. See, for example, the measure before K in the first movement of Symphony No. 39. The timpani's two quarter notes are not dotted, but those of the strings and flute are dotted. It is clear to this timpanist that these notes need to be played in a staccato fashion. Third, Mozart does not indicate when a note should be played legato or nonlegato. Once again, the score is often the best source for determining if a note should be played legato. Two to four bars before K in Symphony No. 39, Mozart write three quarter notes on the first beat of each bar. These notes should be allowed to ring over the bar line. These notes are doubling tied notes in the brass and winds. In other cases, where the timpani are playing a note that doubles a note in another instrument that has a greater value than the timpani's, this might be an indication that the timpani should hold the note the length scored for the other instrument. The first entrance of the timpani in the Overture to *The Marriage of Figaro* is a case in point. Mozart writes quarter notes on the first beat of measures 12 and 13; however, these should be played as legato notes since they are really doubling other instruments. Fourth, Mozart uses dynamic markings in a somewhat different way from Haydn. Haydn often alternated between *forte* and *piano* phrases. Like Haydn, Mozart values orchestral balance, and he does not score the great crescendos or decrescendos—so popular with Stamitz and the Mannheimers. Zaslaw makes a contrary argument. He claims that Mozart left it up to conductors to shape the dynamic line of the Classical pieces they were conducting; unfortunately, Zaslaw doesn't provide evidence to support his position (Zaslaw 1989, 475). Therefore, timpanists should approach their part with a great deal of restraint, playing within the Classical tradition discussed earlier.

Perhaps most interesting was Mozart's use of the tremolo for the timpani. In interpreting whether a semiquaver note should be played as individual notes or an open roll, Haydn presents problems for the timpanist. This is not the case with Mozart. His more mature works clearly indicate that a tremolo sign means an open roll. In other rhythmic figures, the notes are played individually and according to their rhythmic value. It is not surprising that Mozart adopts the tremolo. His father teaches us that a tremolo is a natural, wavelike inundation created by shaking the hand on the violin. A tremolo could close a phrase or a piece. He distinguishes it from the trill (an alternation between two neighboring notes). How are the trill and tremolo notated? Leopold Mozart does not say. For the timpanist, Wolfgang clearly uses the tremolo sign to indicate an open roll (see example 4.25). The tremolo could be written over a single note (A and B), or over notes in multiple bars (C). Furthermore, the tremolo could or could not be tied to a final note (D) (L. Mozart 1951, 186–204).

But there are problems associated with the tremolo. First, should the timpanist roll a note that ends a piece, movement, or phrase but is not notated as a tremolo? Probably not. By the latter part of the eighteenth cen-

4.25. Mozart's use of the tremelo

tury, composers are specifying how they want a part phrased and articulated. Mozart is very clear on his use of rolls and if he wants a roll to end a piece, he would place it there. Indeed, Mozart finds limited use of the tremolo. He believes that the tremolo is a natural part of the human voice, but imitating it on instruments has its limitations.

> "People imitate it [the trembling human voice] not only on wind instruments, but on stringed instruments too and even on the clavichord. But the moment that proper limit is overstepped, it is no longer beautiful—because it is contrary to nature. It reminds me of when, on the organ, the bellows are jolted" (Zaslaw 1989, 480).

Lastly, many final notes stand under a fermata. Fermatas were expected to be neither too long nor too short but the right length and the sound should die out (L. Mozart, 1951, 46; Turk, 1982, 117). A note struck on a timpano is essentially the same thing: an attack that dies out. Therefore, it is best to play these notes as single notes and not as rolls. Second, what is the best way to terminate a roll? Where a final note follows a roll, should this note (1) be rolled, (2) complete the roll as a connected note, or (3) be played as a detached note? On this issue Mozart is unclear. Most of Mozart's rolls are single-measure or multimeasure rolls. There are comparatively few cases where he begins and ends a roll *within* the measure. Therefore, most rolls begin in one measure and end in the next measure—normally on the downbeat. Should rolls carry over into the first beat of the final measure? Here Mozart helps and hinders us (see example 4.26).

4.26. Ending rolls in Mozart

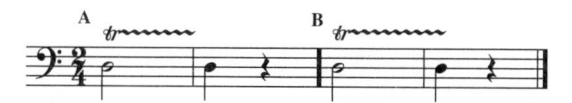

Sometimes the tremolo sign ends at the bar line (A) and other times it extends over it into the single note downbeat of the next measure (B). Reason suggests that timpanists play the concluding note in example B as a tremolo. But in examining the score, it may become apparent that the roll should not cross the bar. How does one decide when to play the final note as a tremolo or as a single note if the tremolo sign crosses the bar line? The timpanist should consider (1) if the rolled note is *tied* to note in the downbeat of the next measure, and (2) if the timpani is doubling another part where the sustained note is tied to the downbeat of the next measure. If either of these conditions applies, the concluding note should be rolled. Even though a tremolo sign may cross the bar, the downbeat may be played as an individual note. This is so for several reasons. In Classical music, the strong beat most often falls on the first measure, and to strengthen the feeling of the rhythm, playing a single beat, rather than tying over a roll, would achieve this effect. Second, the orchestration in the measure in which the roll ends may suggest that a single stroke should be played. Mozart notates rolls in another manner: the tremolo sign ends at the bar line followed by a note on the downbeat of the next measure (rarely does Mozart write a timpani part where the roll is not followed by a note in the downbeat of the next measure). Should the roll extend over into the next measure? Probably not. An inspection of the score may indicate that a legato slur terminates at the end of a measure. This would indicate that the timpani roll should end there too. This is the case with the two timpani rolls eight and ten measures after L in the first movement of Symphony No. 39. There are other clues that a roll should not extend over into the next measure: other instruments are not tied over into the downbeat of the next measure, the rhythm of the next measure distinctly changes to something more pulsating, and any doubling part has a sustained note (or trill sign) that ends at the bar line. These are perhaps the best guidelines on how to conclude a roll in Mozart's later works.

Let's turn to some of the mature symphonies that raise issues for the timpanist. Haydn and Mozart's later symphonies are similar in several ways. All of Mozart's mature symphonies (Symphony Nos. 35 to 41) are in a major key; Haydn wrote only one of his London symphonies in a minor key. This helps explain the rather cheerful first and final movements of Mozart's symphonies. Second, of Mozart's five symphonies that have timpani parts, four have four movements (in the typical fast, slow, minuet, and fast form) and only Symphony No. 38 has three fast-slow-fast movements. Third, four of these symphonies have timpani parts in all but the slow movement. Symphony No. 36 is the only one scored for timpani in all four movements. Fourth, the timpanist need not retune within or between movements—a point of difference with Haydn, who felt freer to change the drum's pitch between movements. Fifth, both Haydn and Mozart experiment with timpani in their earlier symphonic writing (Mozart's Symphony Nos. 7, 8, and 9 have timpani parts) and return to it only later in life—discounting the possibility that timpanists wrote parts ad libitum for Symphony Nos. 20, 22, 23, 26, 28, and 30. Sixth, unlike Haydn, Mozart uses the timpani more traditionally. Trumpets and timpani or horns and timpani typically doubled each other's pitch and quite often their rhythmic gestures. Timpanists should coordinate their parts with the brass—especially in matters related to the release of notes, the conclusion of sustained passages, phrasing, and the length of notes. Mozart's timpani parts, while satisfying to play, are not marked by the bold ingenuity of Haydn, who gives the timpani their own voice in a solo or supportive capacity.

The author will examine Mozart's Symphony No. 32 prior to a more exhaustive analysis of Symphony Nos. 35, 39 and 41. Symphony No. 32 ("Symphony in the Italian Style") is interesting because it is written *in* this style. The Italian style—compared to French and German styles—is lighter, entertaining, singing, homophonic, and charming. This means that the timpani part must not be too heavy. In the autographed score, Mozart wrote neither a timpani nor trumpet part. However, he later composed a trumpet part—an autographed copy of which exists today. This is not the case for the timpani. The timpani part is in someone else's hand (Larsen 1956, 181). Since Mozart did not write a timpani part, should this part be played? Some conductors prefer to leave out the timpani. This symphony is written in the key of G. Since Mozart never wrote a timpani part to a symphony in G, it is reasonable to leave the part out. That said, most conductors use the timpani. Since the symphony was written in G, this presented the composer of the timpani part with the issue of what size drums to use. Today, one can find a part written for d and G drums (26- and 23-inch timpani); however, the critical edition uses larger timpani: d and G drums. Therefore, the timpanist should use the latter arrangement of drums. Regarding errors in the score, the penultimate measure should have only two notes in it: place quarter notes on the first and third beats. The quarter note on the last beat of this measure is an error and has not been corrected in some editions; if played, the timpanist will be playing a solo—the remaining musicians have a rest! Finally, this is a highly periodic work, so look for places to end a phrase by playing the note into the drum—for example, measures 3 and 8 in the first movement.

Symphony No. 35, the "Haffner," was composed in Vienna in 1782 and represents the first of Mozart's mature symphonies discussed here. What size drums should the timpanist use in this piece? The 31- or 32- inch and the 26-inch drums are appropriate. The more exposed rolls on the d drum will sound smooth. However, if the timpanist prefers a more pointed d on the more rhythmical phrases of the symphony, adding a 29-inch timpano pitched to d for these passages serves this function. Medium-hard sticks work well on this piece: they provide the articulation and produce a nice roll.

In the first movement, Allegro con spirito, articulation, rolls, and phrasing are the main issues facing the timpanist. Mozart notates the roll in an interesting way in this movement (see examples 4.27a and 4.27b). The tremolo sign in measure 1 carries over into second measure, but when the theme is repeated in measure 13, the tremolo sign only extends to the end of that bar. In measure 1, Mozart ties neither the doubled parts (horns and trumpets) nor the timpani to a note in the next bar; therefore, the roll should not extend into the first beat of the second bar. The first note of the second bar should be played in a punctuated, nonlegato fashion: the note should be clearly heard. To achieve this, the timpanist must stop rolling a little early in the first measure and clearly attack the quarter note in the

4.27a. Interpreting Mov. 1, "Haffner" Symphony

second measure. Playing this in a nonlegato fashion will allow the note to ring through the first three beats of that measure, doubling the trumpet and horn part. In bar 13, the roll ends in that measure, but the trumpets and horns have notes tied into bar 14. In this case, it is unclear what Mozart intended, using our criteria. The new phrasing of the theme in the horns and trumpets suggests that the timpanist carry over the tremolo into the first beat of bar 14. The author prefers to play this as an individual staccato note that nicely ends the roll. In measure 3 (and in similar measures in this movement), Mozart places staccato marks over the two quarter notes for all instruments in the orchestra. Since Mozart uses staccato marks sparingly—leaving it up to the performer to play staccato in the appropriate places—he is clearly indicating that he wants these and subse-

4.27b. Mov. 1, "Haffner" Symphony (continued)

quent dotted notes to be played staccato. The timpanist then muffles the large drum at the end of the second beat to prevent the sound from carrying over into the third: a rest for the entire orchestra. Most of Mozart's rolls extend over the whole measure; however, in this symphony there are rolls that conclude within the measure. In measure 74 (nine measures after B), he ties a half note roll to an eighth note. This should be played as a single roll with no concluding stroke since this figure doubles the exact rhythm in the trumpets and horns. A similar figure in measure 180 (nine measures after E) should be played in the same manner—the roll encompassing three beats.

Articulation is largely left up to the performer in Mozart's works: a problem shared with the timpani and brass. That said, playing nonlegato is the norm in Mozart, but there are opportunities to shape phrases effectively using legato and staccato strokes. For example, in measures 41 and 42 (nine and ten measures after A), these half notes should be played legato—not primarily because they *are* half notes but because a legato stroke supports the long, whole notes in these sections of the movement. In a similar vein, the first two notes in measures 59 and 61 (five and seven measures before B) should be played legato since they also double other legato-sounding instruments in the orchestra. The three quarter notes of measure 94 (one before C) can be played staccato-legato-staccato. This phrasing nicely compliments and strengthens the bass and celli lines: they play low A, high a, low A. This legato and staccato phrasing can be replicated in the soli passage for timpani and trumpet in measures 173–176 (beginning at the second measure of E). This passage, which restates the rhythm of the theme, should be played out so it is distinctly heard. All notes should be played staccato and into the head, since it is difficult to get good articulation playing *piano* and *pianissimo*. The sole exception is the next-to-last quarter note in this phrase: play it as a legato note. This doubles the tied trumpet note at the beginning of this measure and just sounds nice! The long-short sound nicely ends the phrase with a staccato note. See the companion Web site for a marked timpani part.

The Menuetto is a masterpiece of writing for the timpani. The periodic structure of this movement requires the timpanist to punctuate the line effectively. The two rolls in this movement have tremolo signs ending before the bar line and the rhythmic structure clearly indicates that the quarter note in the second bar should be distinctly heard. Since this quarter note is the final note of this phrase, which should be muffled to prevent it from carrying over into the violin part, play this as a staccato note. The three notes in bars 3 and 4 are normally played staccato; however, if they are not, playing the first two notes nonlegato and the final note staccato gives a sense of finality to this phrase. The timpanist would not use a bounce stroke at this point, reserving it for the final resolution of this eight-measure period. Measures 9–12 sound like a promenade, and the wind and lower string parts have dotted staccato notes. For these reasons, it would be good to use a marcato stroke: this bouncing, legato stroke with some point produces the promenading beat needed in this phrase. A medium or medium-hard stick would suffice for this movement.

The Finale: Presto is played without difficulty. Since it moves quickly, the timpanist should use a medium-hard stick to achieve the needed articulation. Measures 9–12 are normally played staccato, with measures 13–17 played nonlegato. In these latter measures, the timpani provide sustaining support for other instruments and the nonlegato gives some point and a good sustained sound. All the rolls in this movement share the same characteristics: the rolls end before the bar line and the quarter note on the first beat of the next bar should be distinctly heard. When that note is on the lower drum, the timpanist should accent that note to bring it up to the same dynamic level as the notes on the smaller drum. This procedure should be used on similar rhythmic figures on the low drum because their presence can be lost if more effort is not expended on these notes. Finally, the quarter and eighth notes on the low drum need to be clearly articulated.

Symphony No. 39 opens with a wonderful timpani part followed by a quick Allegro, allowing timpanists to exercise their phrasing and articulation skills. Scoring for e-flat and B-flat timpani, Mozart is writing the notes in the best register of the 29- and 26-inch timpani. As a result, the sound of the timpani in the Adagio of the first movement is glorious. Medium-hard sticks with small heads will get the articulation that is needed in both the Adagio and the Allegro (although one could use a medium stick for the roll and subsequent phrases beginning at measure 9). The opening measures in the first movement are, for all intents and purposes, a timpani solo (see example 4.28). There are three traps to avoid. First, this gesture must be strictly counted, subdividing the count to get perfect rhythmic placement of each note. This section is conducted very slowly, other instruments enter unexpectedly on notes the timpanist (and other instruments) are playing, and the timpanist has to establish a solid rhythm for the orchestra.[4] Second, the dynamic level must be maintained throughout this solo; it is easy to take the heat off one note, and if this occurs, it spoils the shape of the line. Third, extra effort should be put into the notes of the larger drum—without doing this, the lower drum will sound off in a distance. The technical execution and phrasing can be accomplished rather easily. All the notes in the Adagio should be played nonlegato except the demisemiquaver notes. The former notes need to be played staccato to

4.28. Opening timpani figure, Symphony No. 39

bring them out. This can best be achieved by playing both notes with the timpanist's stronger hand. This timpanist sticks the notes in the first, third, and fifth measures as marked in figure 4.28. Since my left hand is naturally stronger, I (1) begin the downbeat of the first bar with my left hand; (2) follow this with the two left-handed thirty-second notes; and (3) play the next quarter note with my right hand. The effect of playing LLR is similar to saying "pa-pa-POW" (short-short-long). The author sticks the final three notes of the phrase LLR. The first left stroke on the fourth beat naturally follows the right stroke of the third beat, and playing the sixteenth note with my stronger hand helps ensure that it (the little note) is brought out and is played at the same dynamic level as the other notes. This phrasing now positions the right hand to naturally follow the left in placing the final note of this phrase—of course, at the right dynamic level. Since my right hand is weaker than the left, I make sure this note is dynamically similar to the other notes. To clarify the phrase, muffle both drums after the first quarter note in the second measure. This prevents the timpani from interfering with the *piano* horns, winds, and strings. All other phrases in this section are played in a similar manner. The five-measure roll is relatively exposed and must be started cleanly using a medium stick—one that produces a nice round sound and smooth roll. In starting this soft roll, the timpanist should count strictly and watch the first violins play the final eighth note before the timpani entrance. This will allow the timpanist to cleanly begin the roll. After the playing the roll for five measures, the timpanist plays *forte* with well-pointed notes. Cutting off the roll just short of the measure's end allows the drumhead to settle down and gives the timpanist time to place a *forte* stroke on the downbeat. As in the opening phrase, it is important to maintain the *forte* dynamic level through the rest of the Adagio. Sticking the sixteenth notes (beginning in measure 14) with the stronger hand ensures that they are brought out at the proper dynamic level. Using a medium stick, play these eighth and sixteenth notes somewhat staccato. The remaining measures of this solo are played with a medium-hard stick in the manner described above.

Similar to the "Haffner," there are many opportunities to shape the articulation in ways that support the overall sound. For the Allegro to be played effectively, the timpanist must distinguish between staccato, legato, and nonlegato notes. By so doing, this music will differ in feeling and tone at the appropriate places. In measures 54 and 55 (twenty-nine measures after letter A), the timpanist should play two legato notes—which support the rhythmic and rising melodic line of the music (see example 4.29). The three crotchets in measure 56 should be played nonlegato or even staccato because they phrase this figure better and help push this rhythm toward the tonic. The tonic note should be played legato, which strengthens the downbeat of this measure. Play the next three bars nonlegato. Measure 70 (one measure before letter B) is marked with two staccato dots in some editions, but in the critical edition, no such markings exist. But, wedges are found in all *other* parts. Since the other parts are playing these notes short, heavy, and with some accent, the timpani should do so also. The

4.29. Articulating Mov. 1, Symphony No. 39

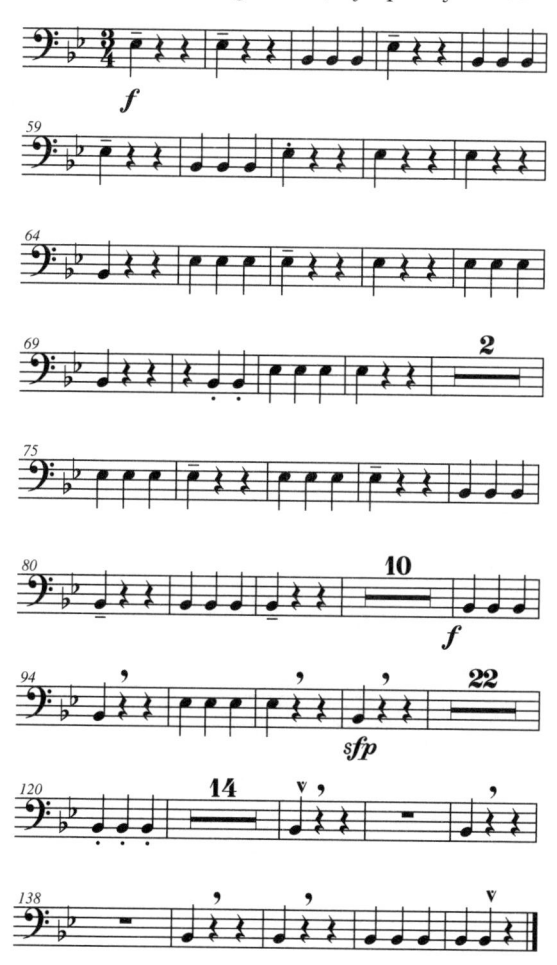

next four notes in measures 71 and 72 can be played nonlegato—which doubles the trumpets and horns. The single quarter note in bars 76, 78, 80, and 82 (beginning six measures after B) should be played legato and the preceding measure nonlegato. The single quarter notes should be legato because they are rhythmically doubling instruments that are sustaining a dotted half note. The cadence points often need some punctuation to give a sense of finality, and this is the case in measure 142 (at the first repeat). On the first beat of that measure, the instruments of the orchestra have an ascending note, and the note on the second beat falls an octave to a G, B-flat, or d. To give the sense of falling and finality, the timpanist can play a bounce stroke into the drum and then muffle it. This technique can be used in similar circumstances in Mozart's works. Three of the movement's most beautiful notes follow at bars 282–284 (four measures before K): these crotchets should be played extremely legato using long, continuous strokes and letting the drumhead sing (see example 4.30). Mozart writes slurred

Interpretation of Classical Music

4.30. Final measures Mov. 1, Symphony No. 39

notes in most of these parts and it is clear that he desired very legato notes. The timpani rolls the ninth and eleventh measures from the end. The tremolo extends to the end of each bar line and this suggests that Mozart wanted the roll to end at that point. Since most of the other parts have dots over the first note in the bar following the roll, it is reasonable to conclude that Mozart wanted the timpanist to play this concluding quarter note in staccato fashion and unconnected to the roll.

There are no great issues in either the Menuetto or Finale: Allegro. The Minuet can be played hand-to-hand, with medium sticks, and nonlegato with no variation in articulation. The Finale can be played in the same manner, but somewhat lighter; however, the note following the only two rolls should be clearly separated from the roll and marked staccato (see example 4.31). In the first case (five measures before B), the crotchet note ends a brass, woodwind, and lower string line and a definite staccato stroke gives the sense of finality. In the second case (seven measures before E), the quarter notes ends a brass and woodwind phrase and the staccato stroke renders a sense of finality, too. See the companion Web site for a marked timpani part.

Symphony No. 41, Mozart's last symphony, was composed in Vienna in 1788—three years prior to Mozart's death and at the height of his symphonic power. He uses the timpani in doubling parts and providing rhyth-

4.31. Ending rolls in Finale, Mov. 1, Symphony No. 39

mic energy to this symphony. Occasionally, he gives the drums their own voice. In the first movement, Allegro vivace, there are no technical difficulties and few interpretive concerns. Mozart composes the timpani part in c and G and the timpanist must bring out the notes and articulation on the lower G drum. Using a medium-hard stick will achieve the articulation that is needed for this quick movement. The opening six notes of the timpani (bars 1–6) should be played fully legato (bringing out the tone of the drum) and then immediately dampening the timpano. Muffling quickly avoids interfering with the ascending string line (see example 4.32).

4.32. Muffling in Mov. 1, Symphony No. 41

The sixteenth note should be brought out in measures 9–14 and the timpano dampened after the third beat of the measure. The whole note should be executed with a single legato stroke. No roll is necessary. There is a roll in measures 83 and 84 (three bars after C) ending with a quarter note in measure 85 (see example 4.33). The tremolo sign extends through the end of the second bar and no doubled part is tied over in the next measure. Thus, the quarter note in measure 85 should be played individually, meaning that the roll must be cut slightly short in order to get good placement on the quarter note. In measure 120 (see example 4.33), the measure of the repeat, the three quarter notes should be played staccato-legato-staccato. This down-up-down phrasing follows the contour of the music and the

4.33. Rolls and phrasing in Mov. 1, Symphony No. 41

final staccato gives a sense of finality—bringing this phrase to an end. Measures 171, 177, and 181 (beginning eight measures before F) should be played staccato since the string and woodwind parts are so marked. The two eighth notes followed by eighth rests in measures 296, 298, and 299 (beginning eight measures after K) should be played staccato. Mozart utilizes rests to indicate a staccato note in this case, and other instruments are marked staccato or pizzicato. Finally, the roll three measures from the end should not be carried over into the penultimate measure. Mozart clearly wants the first beat of that measure to have its own voice.

The Menuetto has some great writing for the timpani, allowing timpanists to demonstrate their understanding of tone production (see example 4.34).

4.34. Phrasing the Mov. 2, Symphony No. 41

Timpani Tone and the Interpretation of Baroque and Classical Music

The *piano* notes in bars 3, 4, 7, and 8 can be played in as either staccato (which seems to be Mozart's intent) or legato (which sounds so beautiful). If played staccato, the notes should be so played and the drum muffled on the second beat of the measure (or whatever is negotiated by the timpanist and the brass). By playing staccato, the beat is clearly defined in the beginning of each measure—a characteristic of Classical music. A medium-hard stick with a small head is appropriate for this movement. The argument for playing the passage in a legato fashion is that it supports the harmony in those measures, takes advantage of the tonal qualities of modern timpani, supports the slurred notes in the strings, and, quite frankly, sounds so good. If played legato, a medium stick played with very long, lifting strokes, placed on the top of the drumhead, and beginning close to the head of the drum will bring out the tone in all its glory. In measures 9–16, Mozart writes a *subito forte* for tutti orchestra and the scoring becomes much darker. The timpanist can play these measures with some weight, arm, and bounce off the head using a nonlegato stroke. The final note ends the period and the timpanist can use a bounce stroke playing into the head to give this a sense of finality. Should measures 17, 19, and 21–24 be played staccato or legato? Here the score is less clear. On the one hand, Mozart scores sweeping phrases in the winds and strings and the timpani can support this with legato strokes. On the other hand, the timpanist can play staccato, which supports similar articulation in the brass and squarely locates the pulse of the music on the downbeat. Whatever approach the timpanist chooses, there should be continuity between how the all these *piano* notes are played. Measures 26–28 should be projected with weight and point. The remainder of this movement can be played in a nonlegato fashion; although, the half notes in measures 30 and 38 should be played legato—doubling the rhythm in the winds and the sweeping nature of this phrase. This recommendation also holds for the quarter notes in bars 57 and 58 that double the rhythm in the violin melody. The final note of this phrase should be played into the drum to give a sense of finality.

The Finale: Molto Allegro is a masterpiece of counterpoint composition and it raises some articulation and phrasing questions. Some editions do not square with the Mozart *Neue Ausgabe sämtlicher Werke* (1930, 260, 261). The dots over the quarter notes in measure 16 are not found in the critical edition; although, they are so dotted in many timpani parts. From a practical standpoint, these should be dotted. A more serious matter concerns the solo written above the timpani part in measures 334, 337, and 347 (see example 4.35). These markings do not exist in the critical edition and it is doubtful that Mozart intended these to be played soloistically, that is, with greater energy and projection. An analysis of the score at these points indicates that this rhythm is being tossed around in the orchestra and when the timpani play this passage, the timpani are doubling other instruments. In so doing, Mozart does not score a louder dynamic marking for the timpani vis-à-vis other instruments. Therefore, there is no evidence Mozart wanted the timpani or any other instrument for that matter to play the passage very strongly.

4.35. Solo figure in Finale, Symphony No. 41

However, there are some places where this rhythmic gesture should be accented. Between measures 264 and 268 (beginning eight bars before F), the timpani echo the rhythmic figure in the trumpets. This figure should be accented (see example 4.36). Measures 319 and 320 (seven measures after G) should be accented in the same manner.

In general, timpanists can follow four norms in playing this movement. First, in cases where Mozart writes three or more quarter notes on the c drum, the notes should be played staccato. Second, the timpanist

4.36. Accenting the solo figure

should play nonlegato with a medium-hard stick and small head. Third, count, count, count—especially in parts where the pulse of the measure is displaced away from the downbeat and where the rhythm is being thrown about the orchestra (measures 172–197, fifteen bars before D). Fourth, the eighth note following a dotted quarter should be brought out to make sure it is distinctly heard. This is important because (1) this figure is the rhythmic component of the fifth and last theme, and (2) the tempo is so fast that the note will be lost if it is not accented.

Finally, this movement raises two issues concerning articulation and rolls. The strongly periodic nature of this music means that the cadence note should be played more into the drum to give a sense of finality (see measures 35, 151, 271, 356, 360, and 408). The half notes written at the *piano* dynamic level should normally be played very legato (measures 227–230, 284–290, and 354–355). In these measures, the timpanist is doubling sustained notes in the brass. The roll beginning at measure 223 should be carried through the beginning of the downbeat to measure 225, and this note should be played staccato (see example 4.37).

4-37. Articulation in the Finale, Symphony No. 41

Interpretation of Classical Music

As this music transitions to the tonic and the violins introduce the next theme, this phrasing supports the sweeping nature of this music. Finally, the last five measures are traditionally played in a soloistic, military manner. Only the brass and timpani have this rhythmic figure and it drives the music to its successful conclusion. Projecting the timpani with the brass is warranted.

Mozart's overtures are a staple of symphonic programming, and several deserve comment in greater detail. The *Impresario* or *Schauspieldirektor* is a relatively short, high-energy overture where articulation is the main concern. Written in G and c, this overture presents the perennial problem of articulation and dynamic projection on the lower drum; therefore, the G notes should be brought out. With the exception of staccato and a few legato passages, the thrust of this overture should be played nonlegato with a medium-hard stick. This gives the articulation that is needed throughout this quick-tempo piece and on the lower drum. The third measure (and subsequent figures) should be played staccato. In measures 13–22, the timpanist plays quarter notes that are notated with wedges and are scored *forte* for other instruments; so it is clear that Mozart wanted a heavier note (see example 4.38). These notes should be played heavily

4.38. Phrasing the *Impresario Overture*

(more toward the bottom of the head) with a lot of lift, and immediately dampened. When this melody is repeated at measure 127 (seven measures after D), the timpani have two notes. The first note should be played heavily and with lift, but the second one should be played with a bounce stroke and slightly into the drum—effectively finalizing this rhythmic figure. Muffling notes is important in this overture. In measures 13–22 the timpanist should dampen quickly, allowing the note on beat 2—played by the rest of the orchestra—to come through clearly. At a quick tempo, the rolls in measures 107 and 109 (after letter C) could be eliminated and replaced with a half note. First, the function of rolls is to sustain a note and at a fast tempo a half note will satisfy this need. Second, playing a tremolo makes this measure sound forced, and this music must be free and move agilely from one note and one measure to the next. Finally, the six quarter notes beginning in measure 173 (twenty-five measures after E) can be played very legato and on the top of the head. See the companion Web site for a marked timpani part.

The Overture to the opera *Don Giovanni* (or *Don Juan*) is another composition that tests the technique of the timpanist. The overture consists of two parts: a slower Andante that is dark and heavy, and a freer Allegro molto, which is lighter and more fluid. The timpanist must adjust stick choice and touch to accommodate these differing styles. The timpani part, written in d and A, means that the bottom note will be played on a tighter head; thus, articulation is less problematic than a G or lower note. The A on this large drum gives a much more voluminous sound—which is needed for the Andante. In terms of stick selection, the Andante can be played with a medium soft mallet, providing color and body to these notes. The rest of the overture can be played with medium-hard sticks.

The Andante is tragic and dark and this should shape the approach timpanists take to interpreting and playing this section of the overture. In terms of tone, the notes in the Andante should be played heavily and darkly. Regarding rolls, this heavy, dark color can be achieved by rolling palms down and in a very relaxed manner so that the sticks reach down to the bottom of the head. All other quarter and half notes can be played very legato, palms down, and deep into the head. How should the rolls be executed? The rolls in measures 1, 3, 15, 18, and 30 are followed by a quarter note on the downbeat of the next measure (see example 4.39). The tremolo sign extends into the downbeat of the quarter note measure, and, although some editions tie these two notes, the tremolo should not be tied to the concluding note. Should the concluding note be played as a roll or placed as an individual note? Further examination of the score indicates that the brass (in all measures other than measures 9 and 10) have their sustained note tied to the quarter note in the subsequent bar. Thus, applying the rules developed above, the timpani should extend the roll into the first beat of the quarter note bar (refer to page XXI of Mozart, *Neue Ausgabe sämtlicher Werke*, Serie II, Werkgruppe 5, Band 17 for a copy of the first page of the autograph score). Measures 9 and 10 should be played as a continuous roll, and the timpanist should shift seamlessly from the d to the A at bar 11—as if the roll in bars 10 and 11 were tied. Measure 18 should be treated different. The *forte* roll leading into the *piano* quarter note in the next bar means that the roll must be dampened at the last minute so the *piano* c note can be distinctly heard. The same technique must be used in measure 28. The roll in measure 11 should encompass three beats, supporting the same sustained brass notes. Finally, the last roll in the Andante ends before

4.39. Interpreting *Overture to Don Juan*

the final bar. The quarter note on the downbeat in the next bar signals the end of the Andante and the beginning of the Allegro molto. This quarter note should not be rolled, but played as a distinct, staccato note: clearly defining the end of the Andante. Finishing with the discussion of rolls, the rolls in measures 157, 161, 165, 169, 193, and 197 (beginning nine measures after rehearsal letter E) should be continued through the first beat of the next measure, since the wind and brass parts are so tied.

In the Allegro molto, there are two places where some timpani parts differ from the critical edition. The *forte* notation in measures 56, 58, and 60 (after letter A) of some timpani parts does not exist in the critical edition, so the timpanist should not emphasize these notes. Measures 238 and 242 (at letter H) have a *forte* noted in some timpani editions; although, all other parts are marked *forzando*; thus, these two notes should be played *forzando*—with a sharp attack. Also, Mozart wrote two endings for *Don Giovanni*. The second ending is most commonly played; if the timpanist has the less common ending, it can be found in the *Neue Ausgabe sämtlicher Werke*, Serie 2, Werkgruppe 5, Band 17, page 227. Concerning articulation, the medium-hard stick creates the articulation that is needed for nonlegato playing. While the tempo is not overly quick in this section, the timpanist should bring out the eighth notes, for example, measures 51–53, and any eighth note on the low drum (see example 4.40). Punctuating notes and phrasing the cadence is important in this section. Measures 111–114 (thirteen to sixteen measures after C) should be played with a bounce stroke into the drum. This gives a sense of finality to this phrase, immediately before the strings and flute enter with a thinner scored mel-

4.40. Articulating and phrasing *Don Juan*

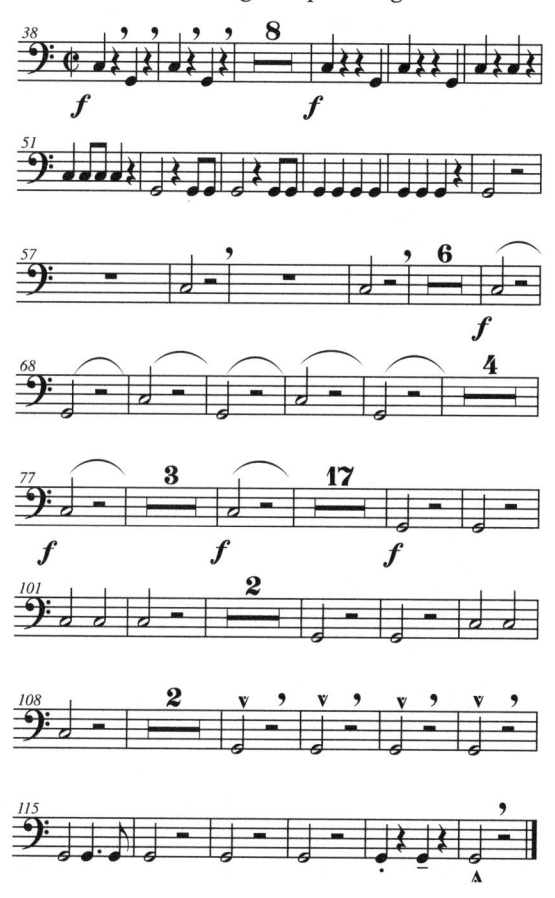

ody. Each quarter note in measures 147 and 148 (two measures before D) should be muffled: this permits the subsequent eighth notes of this rhythmic motive to be distinctly heard. The legato notes in measures 67–72, 77 and 81 (beginning ten measures before B) should be allowed to ring, since the timpani is doubling the brass and the brass is playing whole notes. Finally, playing the figure in measures 119 and 120 (two measures before D) short-long-short (staccato-legato-staccato) supports ascending (second) and descending (third) notes, and this method effectively punctuates the end of this phrase. And to nicely punctuate the bar at rehearsal F, the timpanist can play a bounce stroke into the head. See the companion Web site for a marked timpani part.

The timpani part in *The Magic Flute* overture is masterfully written because it explores nuances of tone shading and articulation encountered in Mozart. The scoring, written for e-flat and B-flat drums, means the timpani will sound more brilliant—the notes played in the upper register of each drum. By playing on tighter heads, it will be easier to articulate the notes in the Allegro sections of this overture. Mozart specifically writes dots over many eighth notes, and because this music moves relatively quickly, greater articulation is needed to bring out the smaller, sixteenth notes. In the opening Adagio, Mozart notates a sixteenth note followed by a half note on the downbeat (see example 4.41). This should be played with two things in mind. First, the sixteenth note should speak as loudly as the half note. Second, this figure should be phrased so that the sixteenth and half note sound like the following: pa-pow. To achieve this effect, the sixteenth should be played staccato and the half note legato with some arm. The notes in measures 5 and 7 may be marked *forzando*. In the Breitkopf and Hartel critical edition, the notes are marked *sfp*. In performance practice of the time, this means an attack followed by a diminuendo—something the timpani does quite naturally. These notes should be played in this manner and allowed to ring.

4.41. Interpreting the entrance to *The Magic Flute*

Articulation is important in the relatively quick Allegro. Beginning with measure 39 (rehearsal letter A), the four half notes can be played legato and the following quarter note with a bounce stroke into the drum (see example 4.42). This phrasing effectively punctuates the ending of this phrase. Measure 45 (seven bars after A) can be played staccato, which seems to be Mozart's intent, but bars 46 and 47 can be played legato—largely doubling the winds and giving the phrase a sweeping quality. Mozart wants staccato eighth notes in measure 51; in fact, all the instruments with a similar rhythmic figure are so notated. A staccato stroke produces the required articulation and still provides the fluidity this part needs. The notes in measures 54 and 56 (before B) are written as half notes and not rolls; although, some timpanists prefer to roll these notes throughout the measure. Should these notes be rolled? One the one hand, the timpani is doubling the trumpets, which are sustaining the note the entire measure; therefore, it stands to reason that the timpani should sustain this note as a roll. On the other hand, Mozart could have notated this as a roll and didn't, and therefore, the note should be played as written. It is best to play the part as written and allow the note to ring through the measure—which is possible with the modern timpani. This is the best solution. Next, the quarter notes on counts 1 and 3 (if the timpanist is counting this in four) in measures 72 and 73 should be played staccato and muffled quickly. This allows the string part, which is playing on counts 2 and 4, to come through clearly.

4.42. Phrasing in *The Magic Flute*

The second Allegro replicates the phrasing discussed above; however, there are some interesting phrasing issues that deserve elaboration. The timpanist can treat the B-flat rolls and subsequent quarter note differently in measures 175 and 177 (see example 4.43). Both rolls end at the bar line, but other instruments are tied to the concluding quarter note in the next measure. The rolling guidelines developed above would suggest that the timpani hold the roll over into the next measure. This timpanist prefers to end this roll at the bar line and to play the quarter note legato, lifting the stick up very high. The effect of this is to provide the violins, which begin the melody with a series of B-flat semiquavers, with a point of departure—a send-off. But the second roll should be treated differently. The quarter

4.43. Articulation in mm. 175–192, *The Magic Flute*

Interpretation of Classical Music   157

note is the last note in the phrase, so the timpanist should play the roll to the end of measure 177 (one bar before letter D) and then play the quarter note with a bounce stroke into the drumhead. Measures 186–190 (and replicated in bars 195–199) can be elegantly phrased. In measure 186, the three quarter notes on the low drum can be played staccato and with the same hand—which gives a consistency of sound. The quarter note on the downbeat of the following measure should be played legato. Playing this note legato gives a send-off to the melody in the oboe. Finally, should the semiquaver quarter notes in bars 219–221 (beginning eight measures from the end) be played individually or as a short roll? This measure is interesting because Mozart is apparently reserving the rhythm for the timpani. If so, he wanted the timpani to clearly articulate these notes. Unfortunately, the tempo is normally taken so fast that this effect cannot be realized and trying to play all four semiquavers may interfere with playing the following two eighth notes. What is the solution? As a compromise, the timpanist can play the semiquaver notes as a three-note trill. This gives the timpanist the time to attack the subsequent eighth notes and it will mimic the rhythmic effect that Mozart desires. See the companion Web site for a marked timpani part.

Brief remarks should be made about two other Mozart overtures: *Cosi fan Tutte* and *The Marriage of Figaro*. *Cosi fan Tutte* begins like *The Magic Flute*. The quarter note of the first bar should be played legato and the subsequent sixteenth and quarter notes staccato and legato, respectively. This produces the "pa-pow" effect described above. The sixteenth notes in measures 4 and 5, because they are in the low register of the larger drum, can be easily lost. The timpanist should bring out these notes at the same dynamic as the other notes. The quarter note in measure 45 following the roll can be played as a legato note since it gives a send-off to the melody in the violins. The quarter note in measure 175 can be played as a bounce stroke into the drum since it ends this phrase. Bar 241 should be marked *piano*, so the timpanist should make sure that the G drum is muffled prior to placing the *piano* note on the c.

The Marriage of Figaro is written in d and A for the timpani. Articulation, muffling, and phrasing are particularly important in this piece because the tempo is so quick. Regarding articulation, generally play all quarter and eighth notes staccato or nonlegato, and half and dotted eighth notes legato. The first phrase in measures 12–18 should be played in a more staccato manner—with the exception of the first two quarter notes, which should be played legato. These two notes double tied whole notes in the winds and the brass. The last quarter note in bar 17 should be dampened because the first beat in measure 18 is normally played *piano* or perhaps *mezzo forte*. The single quarter notes in measures 35, 37, and 39 present an interesting problem. The first half of this measure in the violin part is marked *forte* and the second half is marked *piano* in the critical edition (1973, 8). Wind and horn parts, which are sustaining their notes, are marked *fp*. However, the timpani are unmarked in the critical edition. It would appear that the timpani should play the part with a distinct attack and then let the sound die out—as a *fp*. This accords with how *fortepiano* notes were played at the time, but also supports the dynamic gesture in the violin part. The timpanist should be attentive to cadence points where a bounce stroke into the drum properly brings the phrase to a close (see measures 95, 135, and 171—one measure before A, B, and E). The notes in measures 250–283 should be played with a staccato stick and some notes should be accented, played legato or played staccato (see example 4.44). In most cases, these legato notes support longer notes held by instruments playing the melody or harmony. The eighth notes in bars 284, 286, and 288 (beginning eleven measures from the end) should be brought out so they can be heard. Finally, the only roll in the piece occurs two measures before letter C. The tremolo extends over the two bars before C and the quarter note that ends the roll at letter C should be treated as a single note. Furthermore, this quarter note at letter C ends the phrase; consequently, treating it as a single note effectively terminates this phrase. See the companion Web site for a marked timpani part.

4.44. Articulation and accents in *Overture to Figaro*

Mozart's Piano Concerto No. 24 (K. 491) contains masterful and nuanced writing for the timpani. Written in c and G, the timpani part does not present any technical problems in the first movement, Allegro, but the final movement, Allegretto, has rhythms on the lower drum that must be cleanly articulated if they are to be heard as written. Proper phrasing and articulation are the greatest challenges to the timpanist in this concerto. Unless otherwise noted, the norm is to play nonlegato with a medium or general stick, except where the need for different articulation and phrasing makes it necessary to use legato or staccato mallets. Measures 13–15 can be played nonlegato; however, the quarter notes in measures 16 and 18 need to be articulated differently (see example 4.45). The two quarter notes in these bars can be phrased short-long: staccato and then legato. In the critical edition, the violin has two crotchets too, and Mozart places wedges over the violins' notes. In measure 16, the first violin note is an F-sharp and the second note

4.45. Phrasing mm. 13–99 in Piano Concerto No. 24

160 *Timpani Tone and the Interpretation of Baroque and Classical Music*

ascends to an E-flat. By playing the first note staccato and the second note legato, the timpanist not only differentiates these two notes from the previous ones, but phrases the timpani line similar to the violin line. Use this same phrasing in measures 66 and 68 (four and six measures after B), and in measures 475 and 477 (four and six measures after letter I). The phrasing after bar 501 (twenty-nine measures after I) is the reverse of what was just described. In this case, the second violin note descends from the first. Therefore, play the two quarter notes in measures 501, 503, 505, and 506 long-short: either nonlegato or legato and followed by a bounce stroke into the drum that ends this part of the phrase. The sweeping phrases in measures 48–51 (fifteen measures after A) suggest that the timpanist play these three notes very legato. There are numerous legato slurs and notes tied over into the next bar that suggest these notes should be played legato and sustained. This is true of the notes in bars 81–85 and 491–495 and for the same reasons (beginning ten measures before C and nineteen measures after I). Finally, there are three rolls in this movement that should be treated differently. The first roll, beginning at bars 97 (starting seven measures after letter C) and 507 (seventeen bars before the end), should extend almost up to the placement of the quarter note in measures 99 and 509, respectively. This quarter note on the c drum should be played very legato with lots of lift to bring the tone out. To further define the c, the timpanist could muffle the G when the stroke is placed on the c. This provides a point of departure for the melody that begins on c, too. Mozart made the final roll absolutely clear. The four-measure roll should be extended through the first beat quarter note of the next measure. Not only is the sustaining, doubling trumpet parts tied over, but Mozart also ties the last rolled dotted half note to the concluding quarter note in the next bar.

The Allegretto of this piano concerto should be carefully counted and well articulated. The first six notes should be very tonal, but must be punctuated: using a medium-hard mallet and playing marcato suits this purpose. The rest of the movement should be played with a hard stick (excepting the last four bars, which can be played with a medium-hard mallet). In measure 89 (letter A) and subsequent measures, it is relatively easy to bring out the sixteenth note on the c (29-inch) drum because the timpanist is playing on a tight head. The difficulty rests in the G drum that speaks in its lower register. More energy and articulation must be invested in these sixteenth notes to bring them out. See the companion Web site for a marked timpani part.

An analysis of Mozart's timpani parts would not be complete without reference to his (and Franz Xavier Sussmayr's) Requiem. Mozart wrote the timpani part in the first movement; the remaining movements were written by Franz Xavier Sussmayr, Franz J. Freystädtler, or Joseph Eybler based on Mozart's sketches.[5] In playing the Requiem, one is struck by the lyricism of the music, its grand sweeping lines, and the lack of periodicity (that otherwise characterizes his symphonic work). The timpani part is written in d and A; 31- and 29-inch drums can be used. These are good choices because the timpanist can depend on these drums to provide the color and articulation that this music requires. How much this movement reaches back to the Baroque, forward to the Romantic period, or is rooted thoroughly in classicism will determine the kind of interpretation one gives to the notes. This timpanist sees the Requiem as an evolving Romantic piece. The Adagio of the first movement, Requiem, is dark and somber and the fugal treatment of the Kyrie is plaintive. The timpanist should use a medium-soft stick in the Adagio. This stick produces a dark color; although, it articulates well. The opening timpani statement in measures 7 and 8 should be dark, played with a nonlegato stroke, in a heavy manner, palms down, and with a little arm (see example 4.46).

4.46. Interpreting the Requiem in Mozart's Requiem

Measures 13 and 14 should be played nonlegato and the thirty-second note should be brought out. In measures 43 (letter E), 44, 59 (two measures before G), and 87 (one bar before M), a slight crescendo can be made on the three eighth notes leading to the placement of a legato stroke on the third beat. This phrasing supports the rising line in the soprano and woodwinds. In measure 48 (one measure before the Allegro), the first half of the timpani figure must be projected and played slightly toward the center of the drum, increasing its articulation. The subsequent half note should be played as a single note because a modern, well-tuned timpano has the ability to sustain this note. As the tempo quickens in the Allegro, the timpanist can use a medium stick that will give good tone quality and better articulation. The last two measures of this movement should be played with a medium mallet, but approached in a dark manner. The last four sixteenth notes can be progressively intensified—increasing the tension prior to its resolution to the tonic. Depending on how long the final note is held, the timpanist may need to roll this note—although it is not so noted in the score.

The Dies Irae is stern, rhythmic music that benefits from a medium-hard stick that will articulate well in a quicker movement. Following the much slower Requiem, the timpanist should be ready to play this fast movement and it requires a quick stick change. The opening statement by the timpani presents no challenges. With ascending musical lines in the choir and in parts of the orchestra, slightly crescendo the four eighth notes in bar 12 and play the following quarter note legato (see example 4.47). The note in measure 19 (three measure before P) ends the phrase and it can be played with a bounce stroke into the drum. Measures 52–55 (beginning four bars before T) should be played staccato—supporting similar articulation in the orchestra. The rest of the movement can be played in strict time to the end.

The timpanist's parts in the Rex Tremendae, Confutatis, and Lacrimosa are not difficult parts. In Rex Tremendae, the timpanist should play the sixteenth notes at the same dynamic level and ensure that each note is rhythmically placed. Regarding the latter, this requires strict counting and subdividing the count (see example 4.48). A medium-hard stick will produce the required sound and articulation. The final two eighth notes should be executed as staccato notes and both should be dampened immediately. This rhythmic gesture is doubled in the brass, winds, and voices. The Confutatis and Lacrimosa should be played with a soft stick. In the Lacrimosa, a soft stick will bring out the singing and sad quality to the words of this movement: "Mournful that day, when from the dust shall rise guilty man to be judged. Therefore spare him, O God. Merciful Jesus, Lord grant them rest." Bars 21–24 require special comment (see example 4.49). The fourth beat of measure 21 (an A) can be played with a nonlegato stroke, followed by an accented stroke played with arm and plenty of bounce on the first beat (the tonic) of the next measure. This d should be given plenty of length—supporting the very long downbeat in the horns, bassoons, and choir. The following two measures should be played in the same manner. This sticking produces the tension and release that Mozart writes into the score. To conclude this movement in all its glory, the four quarter notes in measures 26 and 27 can be played *mezzo piano*, the next four quarter notes should crescendo to a *mezzo forte*, the first half of the roll should crescendo

4.47. Executing the Dies Irae

to *forte*, and the last measure should maintain that dynamic. The crescendos—which support the rising line in the horns, bassoons, and trumpets—add needed tension prior to the resolution to the tonic in the last measure.

The Sanctus and Agnus Dei are fine parts for the timpani. In the Sanctus, the tempo and the sixty-fourth notes in the first three bars require a hard stick through the first measure of the Allegro, at which point a medium-hard stick should be used. All notes in the first three bars should

4.48. Articulating the Rex Tremendae

164   *Timpani Tone and the Interpretation of Baroque and Classical Music*

4.49. Interpreting the Lacrimosa

be played at the same dynamic level and each of the sixty-fourth notes should be clearly articulated and projected (see example 4.50). As these notes are not grace notes, they should be played as individual notes. In measure 6, the four demisemiquaver notes should be played individually and projected. A diminuendo over the last three notes in measure 5 nicely supports the strings line, which is playing a descending octave.

Finally, the Agnus Dei can be tonally and dynamically colored. In example 4.51, the semiquaver and demisemiquaver notes in measures 8 and 9 of the Agnus Dei require a medium-hard stick to bring out the articulation of these notes, yet the quarter notes leading up to this figure should be played very legato and tonally. This can be executed in one of two ways: (1) use the medium-hard stick throughout these nine measures, but play very legato, or (2) play the first five notes with a medium stick and then switch to medium-hard mallets. This timpanist favors the former method.

4.50. Executing the Sanctus

4.51. Shaping the entrance to the Agnus Dei

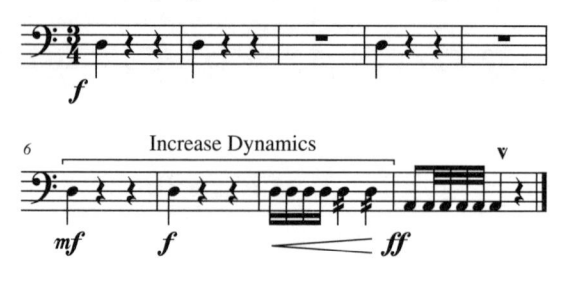

This leaves time to execute the next two measures effectively: executing a crescendo throughout the eighth measure and then punching out the notes in measure 9. To execute this effectively, the timpanist must strictly count these measures to keep an even tempo—especially in the crescendo measure (see Ex. 4.51). Finish this phrase with a bounce stroke into the head—ending the phrase for the entire orchestra. The timpanist has a brief respite before coming in after the Adagio. In measures 76 and 77 (letter Q), execute a slight crescendo on the three eighth notes leading to the placement of a legato stroke on the third beat. This phrasing supports the rising line in the soprano and woodwinds, and is duplicated in measures 92 and 120 (four measures after R and one before X). The measure before the Allegro (bar 81) should be played as it was in the first movement: project the first half of the timpani figure and play slightly toward the center of the drum, thereby increasing its articulation. Play the subsequent half note as a single note because a modern, well-tuned timpano sustains this note. To wrap up the Requiem, play the last four sixteenth notes in the penultimate measure with increasing intensity leading to a final roll—without a stinger. Amen. See the companion Web site for a marked timpani part.

Conclusion

This concludes these thoughts on timpani tone and the interpretation of Baroque and Classical music. The author hopes that readers found a few ideas to help them interpret and execute the music of these two periods. These two musical eras provide performance practice norms for the timpanist. Indeed, the Baroque and Classical periods shaped each composer's own compositional style but was in turn shaped by the idiosyncrasies of the composers of that period. These two eras witnessed the introduction and integration of the timpani in orchestral music. Changes in the size of timpani, quality of timpani heads, playing styles, and mallets gave composers in the High Baroque and Classical eras a new sound with which to work. Timpanists of this time period pioneered the development of mallets and playing styles that improved timpani tone. Today, we will probably never know the degree to which timpanists, timpani manufacturers, calfskin head fabricators, composers, and conductors were responsible for the achievements in timpani tone during the latter half of the eighteenth century. One thing is certain: Haydn fully experimented with the timpani in an orchestral context, and for that reason, his writing shaped the choices later composers made in scoring for that instrument. Haydn liberated the timpani from its military roots and its dependence on trumpet and horn lines. In so doing, he gave the timpani their own voice and position in the orchestra—no small accomplishment at that. By all accounts, English audiences in the 1790s responded with amazement and wonder. At the same time, composers struggled to find the best way to notate timpani parts. While evolving timpani notation was composer-dependent, articulation and rolling notation was fairly similar among composers. An examination of autographed scores reveals some general rules that composers applied in writing their timpani parts. These rules, described throughout this book, can help timpanists interpret their parts—especially when there is some doubt on how a part should be played.

Consequently, the evolution of the timpanist's art in the later half of the eighteenth century laid the groundwork for the Romantic composer, conductor, and timpanist. They became familiar with how the timpani could be effectively employed in an orchestral context; but they became increasingly aware of its limitations. The more freewheeling Romantic composers expected more from their timpani than what the drums permitted. These limitations spurred future developments in timpani construction, rapid tuning mechanisms, new mallets, thinner heads, superior pitch, and better sound projection. But that is another story.

Appendix

Discography

There seems to be a nearly unlimited number of performances of the works discussed in this text. The CDs cited below are intended to give the listener a deeper appreciation of the artistry of the timpanists performing these works. I used several criteria in selecting these CDs. First and foremost, I selected works in which the timpanist had something to say. This is simply a matter of interpretation and, if you spend time with these CDs, you will discover that the timpanists come from different schools of timpani—the so-called Duff, Hinger, Goodman, or Viennese schools, for example. So while the sound of the timpanists may be different, you will find that each made a statement about how the part should be interpreted and executed. Second, I selected CDs that remained faithful to the Baroque and Classical style. In making these selections, I tried to avoid imposing my own view of what it means to be faithful to the Baroque and Classical style. Therefore, you will find some CDs that include period instruments and others that use contemporary instruments. You will find performances in which the conductors have differing interpretations of the Baroque or Classical style. However, the overarching point is that the performances represent genuine attempts to recapture the musical *Zeitgeist*, the spirit of the age, in these recordings. Third, the recordings are selected from conductors and orchestras or ensembles with an international reputation. Some of the recordings are considered among the top recordings of a particular work, while others may not. Whether or not they represent seminal recordings, I have selected performances marked by fine drumming and interpretive insight.

I have often selected two or more CDs of a single work. I have done this because no one timpanist or conductor can lay the claim to the only interpretation of the piece. So you can enjoy different approaches to playing these great Baroque and Classical masterpieces. In the process, I invite you to suspend judgment on the relative merits of authentic versus contemporary performances. Each have their strengths and I think we can all appreciate approaches that both bring to rendering persuasive performances of these works. In so doing, I believe you will appreciate even more the quality of drumming on these CDs.

Johann Sebastian Bach

Mass in B Minor

Johann Sebastian Bach. 1985. *Mass In B Minor*. The English Baroque Soloists. John Eliot Gardiner. Archiv Produktion. 415514-2.

———. 1990. *Bach Mass in B Minor*. Atlanta Symphony Orchestra. Robert Shaw. Telarc. CD-80233.

———. 2006. *Messe in H-Moll*. Akademie für Alte Musik Berlin. Berlin Classics. 0184012BC.

George Frideric Handel

Royal Fireworks Music

George Frideric Handel. 1985. *Royal Fireworks Music*. The English Consort. Trevor Pinnock. Archiv Produktion. 447279-2.

The Messiah

George Frideric Handel. 1995. *Messiah*. Academy of St. Martin-in-the-Fields. Neville Marriner. London. 44824-2.

———. 2002. *The Messiah*. The London Philharmonic Orchestra. John Alldis. Sparrow. SPD1560.

———. 2006. *Messiah*. Freiburger Barockorchester. Harmonia Mundi France. 901796.98.

Franz Joseph Haydn

Symphonies

Franz Joseph Haydn. 1976. *Haydn The London Symphonies Nos. 93, 94, 97, 99, 100, and 101*. Royal Concertgebouw Orchestra. Sir Colin Davis. Philips. 442 614-2.

———. 1977. *Haydn The London Symphonies Nos. 95, 96, 98, 99, 102, 103, and 104*. Royal Concertgebouw Orchestra. Sir Colin Davis. Philips. 442-611-2.

———. 1990. *Haydn Symphonies No. 92 "Oxford," No. 94 "Surprise," and No. 96 "Miracle."* Cleveland Orchestra. George Szell. Sony Essential Classics. SBK 46332.

———. 1994. *London Symphonies 99 and 100*. London Classical Players. Roger Norrington. EMI Classics. 5551922.

———. 1994. *London Symphonies 101 "Clock" and 102*. London Classical Players. Roger Norrington. EMI Classics. 5551112.

———. 2008. *Symphony No. 94 "Surprise" and Symphony No. 96 "Miracle."* Academy of Ancient Music. Christopher Hogwood. L'Oiseau-Lyre. 414330-2.

The Creation

Franz Joseph Haydn. 1983. *Die Schöpfung*. Wiener Philharmoniker. Herbert von Karajan. Deutsche Grammophon. 410 718-2.

———.1991. *The Creation*. City of Birmingham Symphony Orchestra. EMI Classics. CDS 754159-2.

———.2002. *Die Schöpfung*. Balthasar-Neumann Chor und Ensemble. Thomas Hengelbrock. Deutsche Harmonia Mundi. 0547277537-2.

Mass in Time of War "Paukenmesse"

Haydn, Franz Joseph. 1992. *Missa in Tempore belli and Missa Angustiis*. New York Philharmonic. Leonard Bernstein. Sony Classical. SM2K 47563.

———. 2003. *Heiligmesse und Paukenmesse*. The English Baroque Soloists. John Eliot Gardiner. Philips. B0000032-02.

Wolfgang Amadeus Mozart

Symphonies

Mozart, Wolfgang Amadeus. 1960. *Mozart Symphonien Nos. 35–41*. Karl Böhm. Deutsche Grammophon. D 212241.

———. 1983. *Mozart Symphonies Nos. 35 "Haffner" and 39*. Cleveland Orchestra. George Szell. CBS Records. MYK 38472.

———. 1987. *Mozart Symphonies Nos. 40 & 41 and Eine Kleine Nachtmusik*. Cleveland Orchestra. George Szell. MK 42418.

———. 1988. *Symphony No. 35 and Symphony No. 36*. Academy of Ancient Music. Jaap Schroder. London Records. 417 760-2.

———. 1990. *Symphony No. 38 and No. 39*. The English Baroque Soloists. John Eliot Gardiner. Philips. 426 283-2.

———. 1997. *Mozart: The Symphonies*. No. 32, CD 11; No. 41, CD 16. Academy of Ancient Music. Christopher Hogwood. L'Oiseau-Lyre. 452 496-2.

Requiem

Mozart, Wolfgang Amadeus. 1983. *Requiem*. Staatskapelle Dresden. Peter Schreier. Philips. 411 420-2.

Notes

Preface

1. Cloyd Duff writes about this in his article, "Timpanist, Musician or Technician?" *Percussionist* 6:2–9 (1968)—it remains an article well worth reading.

Chapter 1

1. There is speculation on how the bowl shape influences its sound. Timpanist Henry Taylor, one-time timpanist with the London Symphony Orchestra, observed that the American spherical, shallow spherical, normal English (parabolic), and German machine bowls differ in tonal quality (Taylor 1964, 22–32). One might differ with his description of the tonal characteristics of the bowl shapes he describes; however, there is little doubt that different bowl shapes produce different timpani tone color.

2. Amelie Kruse-Regnard conducted interviews with three contemporary European timpanists who use the German (or Viennese) and French methods. In his interview published as "Die Wiener and die französische Paukenschule in Vergleich" (2003), Kruse provides pictures of how Richard Hochrainer (former timpanist with the Vienna Philharmonic), Gerald Fromme (Vienna Radio Symphony Orchestra), Michael Vladar (Vienna Symphony), and Didier Benetti (National Orchestra of France) hold their sticks.

3. In discussing the timbre of instruments, Robert Lundin in *An Objective Psychology of Music* notes that the number of partials or overtones, intensity of the fundamental and partials, and the distribution of energy

among partials account for differences in instrument timbre. He reports "the greater the intensity, the more partials will be present" (1953, 49). For timpanists, this means that a note played with greater intensity (more energy and point) will have more upper partials. This gives the tone a brighter sound.

4. For surveys about the development and nature of mallets, see Nancy Benvenga, *Timpani and the Timpanist's Art* (1979, chap. 2); Edmund Bowles, "On Using the Proper Timpani in the Performance of Baroque Music" (1976); Percival Kirby, *The Kettle-Drums* (1930, chap. 4); Henry Taylor, *The Art and Science of the Timpani* (1964, chap. 4); and Jeremy Montagu, *Timpani and Percussion* (2002, chaps. 5–7).

5. The sound of larger drums and smaller drums differ. One difference concerns the diffuseness of the sound. Robert Lundin, in *An Objective Psychology of Music*, says that lower organ tones sound more voluminous (I would say "diffuse") than higher organ tones (1953, 53–57), and G. J. Rich in his article, "A Preliminary Study of Tonal Attributes," reports "The larger (lower) tones seem to have a greater diffuseness. It seems as if the smaller (higher) fill space more compactly" (Rich 1919, 15). Thus, higher notes sound more compact or dense. S. S. Stevens in his 1934 article, "Tonal Density," concludes that higher tones are denser than lower tones and higher tones sound louder than lower tones. The relatively "diffuseness or tightness" of the sound has implications for timpanists. Since lower tones sound more diffuse and are not as loud as higher tones, playing a high and a low note with equal amounts of energy will result in the "dense," high note sounding louder than the "diffuse," low note. If a timpani part requires an A and d, it would stand to reason that the timpanist should put slightly more energy into the A; the two notes will then sound at the same dynamic level. Of course, if timpanists want the upper note to sound louder than the lower note, they simply have to put a similar amount of energy into each note and the listener will notice the difference.

6. This point is eloquently made by Fred Hinger, one-time timpanist with the Philadelphia Orchestra (Hinger 1981, 3–4).

Chapter 2

1. For a more thorough analysis of *Finlandia*, see John Tafoya's article, "The Finer Points of 'Finlandia'" (2009, 18–19).

2. For a very interesting and, in my estimation, good use of very open grace notes, listen to Essa Pekka Salonen's recording of Sibelius's Symphony No. 5. The timpani's last two notes of the piece are played very open and this gives a certain finality to the piece (Sibelius 1987).

Chapter 3

1. Opinion is divided on how to play this figure. Nicholas Ormrod and Jeremy Montagu argue that the timpani part should not be played as written. For Ormrod (1997, 55–56), Bach's use of the Gallant compositional style leads the timpanist to play the part within the trumpet's triplet figure: a quaver and four semiquavers. Montagu suggests this and another alternative: playing the four semiquavers in the last beat of the trumpet's triplet figure (2002, 89–90). Finally, Frederick Neumann in *Performance Practices*

of the Seventeenth and Eighteenth Centuries (1993, 98, 154) suggests that the two against three figure was not uncommon in Renaissance and Baroque compositions; therefore, consideration should be given to playing these figures as written. In deciding whether or not to assimilate duple (or binary) into triple (or ternary) meter phrases, the performer should consider whether the tempo allows it to be played as written, whether the binary figure is part of the rhythmic motif of the music, and whether the duple-triple meter phrase clarifies contrapuntal, rhythmic, and thematic material.

2. Helmuth Rilling argues that the Sanctus has five different rhythms. The timpani part should be interpreted in the context of a triplet, one of these rhythms. In this case, the timpani's four thirty-second notes should begin on the last note of the triplet. This rhythmic arrangement pushes the rhythm forward into the next beat (Rilling, 1984, 118).

3. For a complete, more detailed secondary analysis of what notes are eligible for being treated equally or unequally, see Robert Donington's *The Interpretation of Early Music* (1974, 386–387).

4. For a helpful discussion of the use of dots and strokes in Bach, see John Butt's *Bach Interpretation* (1990, 25–34).

5. Frederick Neumann, in *Ornamentation in Baroque and Post-Baroque Music*, concludes that composers differentiated between the trill and the tremolo—the latter being a vibrato or fast, regular fluctuation of pitch, timbre, loudness, or a combination of these (1978, 366, 511). The tremolo differed from the trill—a rapid alternation of notes. Since a roll on a timpano is typically executed on one drum and on a single pitch, the sustained sound would be best described as a tremolo.

6. Roland Kohloff, one-time timpanist with the New York Philharmonic and author of *Beethoven Symphony No. 5: Timpani Master Class with Roland Kohloff* plays the final bar with a "gorgeous *fff*" single stroke roll. He reaches this conclusion after considering the possibility of playing "a very rapid movement with the sticks for the first half note and then play[ing] the second note, under the fermata, with slower strokes" (2007, 19).

7. Gerald Carlyss prefers to play the thirty-second notes individually and not as a roll (Carlyss, 2006, 77); although, at the typical tempo this phrase could be effectively played as a roll.

8. For insightful interpretations of the Mass, see Rilling's *Johann Sebastian Bach's B-Minor Mass* (1984), George Stauffer's *Bach: Mass in B Minor* (1997), and John Butt's *Bach: Mass in B-Minor* (1991).

9. Percussionist James Cooper persuasively demonstrates the manner in which Bach limited the liberty of the timpanist to use schlagmanieren. In his article "Timpani Parts in German Baroque Music" (1999, 252–253), Cooper demonstrates that Bach's revisions of the opening ten measures of *Tönet, ihr Pauken! Erschallet, Trompeten* effectively established the composer's control of the timpanist's interpretation of the timpani part. By substituting a tremolo for quavers in measures 5 through 8, he limited the timpanist's ability to use schlagmanieren in these measures. For a fuller treatment of the schlagmanieren, see Johann Ernst Altenburg, *Trumpeter's and Kettledrummer's Art* (1974); Gerassimos Avgerinos, *Lexicon der Pauke* (1964); Edmund Bowles, "The Double, Double, Double Beat of the Thundering Drum: The Timpani in Early Music" (1991); and Harrison Powley, "Some Observations on Jean Georges Kastner's *Methode complete et raisonnee de timbales*" (1980).

10. I am inclined to believe that this roll is misplaced and I do not play it. Charles Cudsworth, who viewed the score, writes that "It is a particularly cramped manuscript, not easy to decipher and Handel, in changing his mind over the instrumentation, made numerous additional directions and cancellations, scribbled on the score in a polyglot mixture of English, French, and Italian" (Cudsworth n.d., iv). The condition of the score suggests that the tremolo is misplaced. Furthermore, there seems to be no ornamental or musical reason to roll this note—especially since similar notes are not so rolled.

11. Pfundt, in *Die Pauke*, makes a similar observation. He gives the timpanist some latitude in when to roll a note. At a slow tempo, a half or whole note might be rolled—something that would not be necessary at a fast tempo (Pfundt 1849, 22–23).

12. Johann Eisel makes a similar suggestion. While he does not include a roll in his hypothesized manner of ending a final cadence, he does recommend that timpanists use a "Zungen-Schlag"—a broad category of rhythmic gestures—and complete the cadence with a single note (Eisel 1738, 68). In short, the suggestions of Eisel and Speer can be employed effectively in this three-measure Adagio. Johann Ernst Altenburg believes that timpanists could improvise cadences to effectively conclude a piece (Altenburg 1974, 108). Finally, Mary Cyr, in *Performing Baroque Music*, notes that the Baroque Adagio was more than a slower tempo; it was a concluding cadence that a soloist could embellish (1992, 38–40). Given performance practices of that day, it is reasonable for a timpanist to employ schlagmanieren in the second measure of this cadence.

Chapter 4

1. Mozart's Symphony No. 35 (1930) makes this point well. The first movement's five-measure rhythmic figure and associated theme defines the material that will be subsequently developed in this movement. Constituent motifs of this figure are developed in various parts of the movement with the theme giving it overall unity.

2. Cloyd Duff, timpanist with the Cleveland Orchestra during the Szell and Maazel years, used timpani that had this kind of sound and translucence: the Dresdner Apparatebau timpani and Anheier cable drums. Listen to any of the recordings by George Szell and the Cleveland Orchestra and you will notice how the timpani do not overpower any particular instrument and how they permit other instruments to project through the timpani. A good recording is *Mozart Symphonies Nos. 35 "Haffner" & 39* (Mozart 1983). Jim Atwood, timpanist with the Louisiana Philharmonic Orchestra, has a good discussion of these timpani in his article, "Dresdner Apparatebau Timpani: The Original Dresden Drum" (2009).

3. Cloyd Duff crafted his Number 5 stick for use in Classical symphonies. The mallet, made with a bamboo handle and cork core, produces a translucent, articulate sound, and it allows instruments to project through the timpani. The mallet is limited to passages that are no louder than *mezzo forte*.

4. John Tafoya, in *The Working Timpanist's Survival Guide* (2004, 6–7) offers similar advice: play the part at the same dynamic level, use a sixteenth note subdivision, and slightly accent the thirty-second notes to

bring them out. Other timpanists have suggested counting the first measure's rhythm in the second, mostly empty, measure as a way of accurately counting this measure and connecting it to the timpani entrance in the third measure.

5. Julian Rushton in *Mozart* (2006, 228) and Piero Melograni in his *Wolfgang Amadeus Mozart: A Biography* (2007, 244) agree that Mozart composed the first movement. Mozart sketched the score from the Dies Irae through the first eight bars of Lacrimosa and the Amen figure. The Sanctus, Benedictus, and Agnus Dei were completely composed by Sussmayr, Freystädtler, and Eybler.

References and Resources

Albrecht, Theodore. 2000. Beethoven's Timpanist, Ignaz Manker. *Percussive Notes* 38 (4):54–61.

Altenburg, Johann Ernst. 1974. *Trumpeter's and Kettledrummer's Art*. Trans. Edward H. Tarr. Nashville: Brass Press.

American Drum Company. 2009. General Information [on bowls]. http://www.americandrum-w-light.com/home.html.

Arbeau, Thoinot. 1972. *Orchesographie*. Geneva: Minkoff Reprint.

Aristotle. 1980. *Nichomachian Ethics*. Trans. David Ross. Oxford: Oxford University Press.

Artz, Frederick B. 1962. *From the Renaissance to Romanticism*. Chicago: University of Chicago Press.

Atwood, Jim. 2009. Dresdner Apparatebau Timpani: the Original Dresden Drum. *Percussive Notes* 47 (1):11–15.

Avgerinos, Gerassimos. 1964. *Lexicon der Pauke*. Frankfurt am Main: Verlag Das Musikinstrument.

Bach, Carl Philipp Emanuel. 1949. *Essay on the True Art of Playing Keyboard Instruments*. Trans. William J. Mitchell. New York: W. W. Norton and Co.

Bandura-Skoda, Eva and Paul. 1962. *Interpreting Mozart on the Keyboard*. Trans. Leo Black. London: Barrie and Rockliff.

Barra, Donald. 1983. *The Dynamic Performance*. Englewood Cliffs: Prentice-Hall, Inc.

Beck, John, ed. 1995. *Encyclopedia of Percussion*. New York: Garland Publishing, Inc.

Benvenga, Nancy. 1979. *Timpani and the Timpanist's Art*. Goteborg: Gothenburg University.

Berger, Karol. 1996. The First Movement Punctuation Form in Mozart's Piano Concertos. In *Mozart's Piano Concertos*, ed. Neal Zaslaw. Ann Arbor: University of Michigan Press.

Berlioz, Hector. 1970. *Traite d'Instrumentation et d'Orchestration*. Farnborough: Gregg International Publishers.

Berlioz, Hector and Richard Strauss. 1948. *Treatise on Instrumentation*. Trans. Theodore Front. New York: Edwin F. Kalmus.

Bertsch, Matthias. 2001. Vibration Patterns and Sound Analysis of the Viennese Timpani. http://iwk.mdw.ac.at/Forschung/pdf_dateien/2001e_MB_ISMA_timpani.pdf.

Bessaraboff, Nicholas. 1941. *Ancient European Musical Instruments*. New York: October House, Inc.

Blades, James. 1961. *Orchestral Percussion Technique*. London: Oxford University Press.

———. 1970. *Percussion Instruments and Their History*. London: Faber and Farber Ltd.

Blades, James and J. Montagu. 1976. *Early Percussion Instruments from the Middle Ages to the Baroque*. London: Oxford University Press.

Bloom, Allen D. 1988. *The Closing of the American Mind*. New York: Simon and Schuster, Inc.

Blume, Fredrich. 1967. *Renaissance and Baroque Music*. New York: W. W. Norton and Co., Inc.

———.1970. *Classic and Romantic Music*. Trans. M. D. Herter Norton. New York: W. W. Norton and Co., Inc.

Boatwright, Howard. 1956. *Introduction to the Theory of Music*. New York: W. W. Norton.

Bowles, Edmund A. 1972. Eastern Influences on the Use of Trumpets and Drums During the Middle Ages. *Anuario Musical* 26:1–26.

———. 1976. On Using the Proper Timpani in the Performance of Baroque Music. *Journal of the Musical Instrument Society* 2:56–68.

———. 1979. Nineteenth-Century Innovations in the Use and Construction of the Timpani. *Journal of the American Musical Instrument Society* 5–6:74–143.

———. 1991. The Double, Double, Double Beat of the Thundering Drum: The Timpani in Early Music. *Early Music* 19 (3):419–435.

———. 1997. The Timpani and Their Performance (Fifteenth Through Twentieth Centuries): An Overview. *Performance Practice Review* 10:192–211.

———. 1998. Mendelssohn, Schumann, and Ernst Pfundt: A Pivotal Relationship between Two Composers and a Timpanist. *Journal of the American Instrument Society* 24:5–26.

———. 2002. *The Timpani: A History in Pictures and Documents*. Hillsdale: Pendragon Press.

Brown, Harold. 1971. Orchestral Timpani Parts: To Change or Not to Change? *NACWPI Journal* 20:27–33.

Brown, A. Peter. 1986. *Performing Haydn's "The Creation."* Bloomington: Indiana University Press.

Bukofzer, Manfred. 1947. *Music in the Baroque Era*. New York: W. W. Norton.

Burney, Charles. 1957. *A General History of Music*. New York: Dover Publications, Inc.

———. 1979. *An Account of the Musical Performances in Westminster Abbey and the Pantheon*. New York: Da Capo.

Butt, John. 1990. *Bach Interpretation*. Cambridge: Cambridge University Press.

———. 1991. *Bach: Mass in B Minor*. Cambridge: Cambridge University Press.

Carlyss, Gerald. 2005. *Symphonic Repertoire for Timpani: The Nine Beethoven Symphonies*. Maryland: Meredith Music Publications.

———. 2006. *Symphonic Repertoire for Timpani: The Brahms and Tchaikovsky Symphonies*. Maryland: Meredith Music Publications.

Carse, Adam. 1940. *The Orchestra in the XVIIIth Century*. Cambridge: W. Heffer and Sons, Ltd.

———. 1949. *The Orchestra from Beethoven to Berlioz*. New York: Broude Brothers.

———. 1964. *The History of Orchestration*. New York: Dover Publications, Inc.

Charlton, David. 1971. Salieri's Timpani. *Musical Times* 112 (1544):961–962.

Cherry, Kalman. 1980. Sound-Color-Form. *Percussive Notes* 19:71–72.

Cone, Edward T. 1968. *Musical Form and Musical Performance*. New York: W. W. Norton and Co., Inc.

Cook, Gary. 1988. *Teaching Percussion*. New York: Schirmer.

Cooper, John M. 1999. Timpani Parts in German Baroque Music: The Schlagmanieren Revisited. *Early Music* 27 (2):249–266.

Copland, Aaron. 1957. *What to Listen For in Music*. New York: McGraw Hill.

Couperin, Francois. 1974. *L'Art de Toucher le Chavecin*. Trans. Mary Halford. Van Nuys, CA: Alfred Publishing Co., Inc.

Cudsworth, Charles. n.d. Introduction. *The Musick for the Royall Fireworks*. London: Ernst Eulenburg, Ltd.

Cyr, Mary. 1992. *Performing Baroque Music*. Portland: Amadeus Press.

Czerny, Carl. 1979. The Sonata as a Whole. In *Music Through Sources and Documents*, ed. Ruth Halle Rowen. Englewood Cliffs: Prentice-Hall: 241–247.

Dart, Thurston. 1954. *Interpretation of Music*. London: Hutchinson's.

Davenport, David. 1983. The Art of Tempering the Kettledrum. *Percussive Notes* 21:50–59.

———. 1995. Carl Nielsen, Symphony No. 4: The Timpani Parts. *Percussive Notes* 33 (2):53.

Dean, Winton. 1959. *Handel's Dramatic Oratorios and Masques*. London: Oxford University Press.

Dearling, Robert. 1982. *The Music of Wolfgang Amadeus Mozart: The Symphonies*. London: Fairleigh Dickinson University Press.

Dobney, Jayson. 2007. Historic Timpani at the National Music Museum. *Percussive Notes* 45 (2):13–17.

Donington, Robert. 1974. *The Interpretation of Early Music*. New York: St. Martin's Press.

Duff, Cloyd E. 1968. Timpanist, Musician or Technician? *Percussionist* 6:2–9.

———. n.d.a. Changing Plastic Timpani Heads. *Yamaha Drum Lines: Education Series* 9.

———. n.d.b. Mounting Remo Plastic Heads the Cloyd Duff Way. *Remo Percussion Topics* 6.

Einstein, Alfred. 1945. *Mozart: His Character and Work*. Trans. Arthur Mendel and Nathan Broder. New York: W. W. Norton and Co., Inc.

Eisel, Johann Phillip. 1738. *Musicus autodidaktos*. Erfurt: Hohann Michael Funcken.

Farmer, Henry George. 1960. *Handel's Kettledrums*. London: Hinrischen.

———. 1962. Monster Kettledrums. *Music and Letters* 43 (2):129–130.

Firth, Vic. 1963. *The Solo Timpanist*. New York: Carl Fischer.

———. 1976. Tips on Timpani. *Instrumentalist* 30:49–51.

Fastl, H. and H. Fleischer. 1992. Über die Ausgepragtheit der Tonhöhe von Paukenklangen. *Fortschritte der Akustik*, 237–240.

Fletcher, Neville H. and Thomas D. Rossing. 2000. *Science of Percussion Instruments*. New Jersey: World Scientific.

Forsyth, Cecil. 1935. *Orchestration*. 2nd Ed. London: Macmillan and Stainer and Bell.

Frazeur, Ted C. 1969. Some Thoughts on Timpani and Intonation. *Percussionist* 6:113–118.

Friese, Alfred and A. Lepak. 1954. *The Friese-Lepak Timpani Method*. New York: Henry Adler, Inc.

Galpin, Francis W. 1910. *Old English Instruments of Music*. London: Methuen and Co., Ltd.

Goodman, Saul. 1948. *Modern Method for Timpani*. New York: Belwin-Mills.

Green, Barry and W. T. Gallwey. 1986. *The Inner Game of Music*. New York: Doubleday.

Harding, Rosamund. 1938. *Origins of Musical Time and Expression*. London: Oxford University Press.

Hardy, Howard and J. Ancell. 1961. Comparison of the Acoustical Performance of Calfskin and Plastic Drum Heads. *Journal of the Acoustical Society of America* 33:1391–1395.

Haydn, Joseph. n.d. *Twelve London Symphonies*. 2 Vols. London: Ernst Eulenburg, Ltd.

———. 1925. *Die Schöpfung*. London: Ernst Eulenburg, Ltd.

———. 1958. Missa in tempore belli. In *Joseph Haydn Werke*. Herausgegeben vom Jens Peter Larsen. Munchen: G. Henle Verlag.

———. 1979. Letter Concerning the Performance of the Applausus Cantata. In *Music Through Sources and Documents*, ed. Ruth Halle Rowen. Englewood Cliffs: Prentice-Hall: 223–226.

———. 1983. *Symphonies 89–92 in Full Score*. Ed. H. C. Robbins Landon. New York: Dover Publications, Inc.

———. 1985a. *Critical Edition of the Complete Symphonies: 93–98*. Ed. H. C. Robbins Landon. New York: Dover Publications, Inc.

———. 1985b. *Critical Edition of the Complete Symphonies: 99–104*. Ed. H. C. Robbins Landon. New York: Dover Publications, Inc.

———. 1985c. *Complete London Symphonies*. Ed. Ernst Praetorius and H. C. Robbins Landon. New York: Dover Publications, Inc.

———. 1994. *"Nelson" Mass and Mass in the Time of War*. New York: Dover Publications, Inc.

Heise, Birgit. 2001. Wooden Timpani. *The Galpin Society Journal* 54:339–351.

Hinger, Fred. 1981. *Technique for the Virtuoso Tympanist*. Hackensack, New Jersey: Jerona Music Corp.

———. 1982a. *The Timpani Player's Orchestral Repertoire: Beethoven Symphonies*. Vol. 1. Hackensack, New Jersey: Jerona Music Corp.

———. 1982b. *The Timpani Player"s Orchestral Repertoire: Brahms Symphonies*. Vol. 2. Hackensack, New Jersey: Jerona Music Corp.

———. 1983a. *The Timpani Player's Orchestral Repertoire: Tchaikovsky*. Vol. 3. Hackensack, New Jersey: Jerona Music Corp.

———. 1983b. *The Timpani Player's Orchestral Repertoire: Sibelius*. Vol. 4. Hackensack, New Jersey: Jerona Music Corp.

———. 1984. An Interview with Fred Hinger. *Percussive Notes* 22:69–72.

———. 1985. *The Timpani Player's Orchestral Repertoire: Richard Strauss*. Vol. 5. Hackensack, New Jersey: Jerona Music Corp.

———. 1986. *The Timpani Player's Orchestral Repertoire: Igor Stravinsky*. Vol. 6. Hackensack, New Jersey: Jerona Music Corp.

———. 2000. Interpreting Timpani Parts. *Percussive Notes* 38 (1):43–46.

Hochrainer, Richard. 1968. The Timpanist. *Percussionist* 5:299–300.

———. 1977. Beethoven's Use of the Timpani. *Percussionist* 14:66–71.

———. 1980. The Viennese Timpani and Percussion School. *Percussionist* 17 (2):88–102.

Hochreither, Karl. 2002. *Performance Practice of the Instrumental-Vocal Works of Johann Sebastian Bach*. London: Scarecrow Press, Inc.

Jimenez, A. 2003. The Verdi Timpani Parts: The Case for Historically-Informed Emendations Part II: Why and How to Emend. *Percussive Notes* 41:44–53.

Kastner, Georges. 1845. *Methode complete et raisonnee de Timbales*. Paris: Schlesinger.

Keller, Hermann. 1965. *Phrasing and Articulation*. Trans. Leigh Gerdine. New York: W. W. Norton and Co., Inc.

Kirby, Percival. 1930. *The Kettle-Drums*. London: Oxford University Press.

Knauer, Heinrich. n.d. *Paukenschule*. Leipzig: Friedrich Hofmeister.

Kohloff, Roland. 2007. *Timpani Master Class with Roland Kohloff: Beethoven Symphony No. 5*. Maryland: Meredith Music.

Kollman, Augustus F. C. 1984. An Essay on Practical Musical Composition. In *Music in the Western World*, ed. Piero Weiss and Richard Taruskin. New York: Schirmer Books.

Kruse-Regnard, Amelie. 2003. "Die Wiener und die franzosische Paukenschule im Vergleich." http://iwk.mdw.ac.at/instrumentenkunde/dokumente/2003d_Kruse_Regnard_Pauke.pdf.

Lampl, Hans. 1996. *Turning Notes into Music*. Lanham: The Scarecrow Press.

Landon, H. C. Robbins. 1977. *Haydn: Chronicle and Works*. Vols. III and IV. Bloomington: Indiana University Press.

———. 1955. *The Symphonies of Joseph Haydn*. London: Universal Edition and Rockliff.

Landon, H. C. Robbins and D. W. Jones. 1988. *Haydn: His Life and Music*. Bloomington: Indiana University Press.

Lang, Paul Henry. 1966. *George Frederic Handel*. New York: W. W. Norton and Co., Inc.

———. 1969. *Music in Western Civilization*. New York: W. W. Norton and Co, Inc.

Larson, Jens Peter. 1956. The Symphonies. In *The Mozart Companion*. Ed. H. C. Robbins Landon and Donald Mitchell, 156–199. London: Faber and Faber, Inc.

Levine, David. 1977. Percussion Instrument and Performance Practices in Beethoven's Music. *Percussionist* 15:1–6.

Locke, John. 1980. *Second Treatise of Government*. Indianapolis: Hackett Publishing Co., Inc.

Ludwig, William F., Sr. 1957. *Ludwig Timpani Instructor*. Chicago: Ludwig Drum Co.

Lundin, Robert W. 1953. *An Objective Psychology of Music*. New York: The Ronald Press Co.

Maier, Joseph F. B. C. 1954. *Museum Musicum Theoretico Practicum*. Kassel: Bärenreiter-Verlag.

Maxey, Linda. 1998. On Stage: The Art of Performing. *Percussive Notes* 38 (2): 41–42.

MacIntyre, Bruce C. 1998. *Haydn "The Creation."* New York: Schirmer Books.

McCausland, Lloyd. 1995. The Plastic Drumhead: Its History and Development. In *Encyclopedia of Percussion*, ed. John Beck. New York: Garland Press.

Melograni, Piero. 2007. *Wolfgang Amadeus Mozart: A Biography*. Trans. Lydia G. Cochrane. Chicago: University of Chicago Press.

Mersenne, Marin. 1957. *Harmonie universelle*. Trans. Roger E. Chapman. The Hague: Martinus Nijhoff.

Meyer, Leonard B. 1956. *Emotion and Meaning in Music*. Chicago: University of Chicago Press.

Meyer, Ramon. 1975. Timpani: The Creation of Silence. *Percussionist* 12: 43–49.

Montagu, Jeremy. 1976. *Making Early Percussion Instruments*. London: Oxford University Press.

———. 2002. *Timpani and Percussion*. New Haven: Yale University Press.

Mozart, Leopold. 1951. *A Treatise on the Fundamental Principles of Violin Playing*. Trans. Edith Knocker. London: Oxford University Press.

Mozart, Wolfgang Amadeus. 1930a. *Symphony in D Major (No. 35)*. Ed. Theodor Kyoyer. London: Ernst Eulenburg, Ltd.

———.1930b. *Symphony in C Major (No. 41)*. Ed. Theodor Kroyer. London: Ernst Eulenburg, Ltd.

———. 1933. *Symphony in E-flat Major (No. 39)*. Ed. Theodor Kroyer. London: Ernst Eulenburg, Ltd.

———. 1955. Die Zauberflote. *Mozart's Werke*. Serie V, No. 20:1–26.

———. 1957. Sinphonie in C. *Neue Ausgabe sämtlicher Werke*. Serie IV: Werkgruppe 11, Band 9: 187–266, Kessel: Bärenreiter Verlag.

———. 1958. Die Schauspieldirektor. *Neue Ausgabe sämtlicher Werke*. Serie II: Werkgruppe 5, Band 15, Kessel: Bärenreiter Verlag.

———. 1959a. Konzerte für Klaviere und Orchester 24. *Neue Ausgabe sämtlicher Werke*. Serie II: Werkgruppe 55, Band 7:85–162, Kessel: Bärenreiter Verlag.

———. 1959b. Sinphonie in Es Dur. *Neue Ausgabe sämtlicher Werke*. Serie IV: Werkgruppe11, Band 9:1–62, Kessel: Bärenreiter Verlag.

———. 1968. Don Giovanni. *Neue Ausgabe sämtlicher Werke*. Serie II: Werkgruppe 5, Band 17:1–27, Kessel: Bärenreiter Verlag.

———. 1973. *Le Nozze di Figaro. Neue Ausgabe sämtlicher Werke.* Serie II: Werkgruppe 5, Band 16 (1): 5–28, Kessel: Bärenreiter Verlag.

———. 1983. *Symphonies Nos. 35 "Haffner" & 39.* Cleveland Orchestra. George Szell. CBS Records. MYK 38472.

———. 1987. *Requiem.* New York: Dover Publications, Inc.

———. 1990. *Requiem.* Kassel: Bärenreiter Verlag.

———. 1991. Cosi fan tutte. *Neue Ausgabe sämtlicher Werke.* Serie II: Werkgruppe 5, Band 18 (1).

Mueller, Erwin C. 1976. *A Timpani Method Based on the Performance Practices of Edward M. Metzenger with an Application of These Practices to the Symphonies of Beethoven and Brahms.* Dissertation. Muncie, IN: Ball State University.

Neumann, Frederick. 1978. *Ornamentation in Baroque and Post-Baroque Music.* Princeton: Princeton University Press.

———. 1993. *Performance Practices of the Seventeenth and Eighteenth Centuries.* New York: Schirmer Books.

Ormrod, Nicholas. 1997. Stylistic Interpretation in Eighteenth Century Timpani Parts. *Percussive Notes* 35 (1):54–58.

Papastefan, John L. 1978. *Timpani Scoring Techniques in the Twentieth Century.* Ph.D. Dissertation. Walden University.

———. Timpani Roll Notation: Observations and Clarifications. *Percussive Notes* 20 (1):69–71.

Patton, Duncan. 1996. Timpani: Basic Sound Production. *Percussive Notes* 34 (1):54–56.

———. 1998. Timpani Articulation and Tone Color. *Percussive Notes* 36 (6): 46.

Payson, Al. 1971. The Timpani Mute. *Percussionist* 9 (2):46–47.

Peinkofer, Karl and F. Tannigel. 1981. *Handbuch des Schlagzeugs.* Mainz: Schott.

Pfundt, Ernst G. B. 1849. *Die Pauken.* Leipzig: Breitkopf und Hartel.

Plato. 1961. The Republic. In *The Collected Dialogues of Plato,* ed. Edith Hamilton and Huntington Cairns. Princeton: Princeton University Press.

Pollart, Gene J. 1976. The Uses and Innovations of Percussion in the Works of J. S. Bach and Handel. *Percussionist* 13 (3):75–80.

Power, Andrew. 1983. Sound Production of the Timpani. *Percussive Notes* 21 (Part I) 62–64; (Part II) 65–67.

Powley, Harrison. 1980. Some Observations on Jean Georges Kastner's *Methode complete et raisonnee de timbales (c.a. 1845). Percussionist* 17: 63–73.

Praetorius, Michael. 1986. *Syntagma Musicum II: De Organographia.* Trans. David Z. Crookes. Oxford: Clarendon Press.

Quantz, Johann Joachim. 1966. *On Playing the Flute.* Trans. Edward R. Reilly. New York: The Free Press.

Rack, John E. 1990. A Closer Look at the Timpani Parts in the Symphonic Use of the Early 19th Century. *Percussive Notes* 28 (6):51–54.

Rameau, J. P. 1950. Traite de l'harmonie. In *Source Readings in Music History,* ed. Oliver Struck. New York: W. W. Norton and Co.

Ratner, Leonard G. 1980. *Classic Music: Expression, Form, and Style.* New York: Schirmer Books.

Rayleigh, Lord. 1929. *The Theory of Sound.* New York: McMillan and Co.

Remsen, Eric. 1981. Editing the Timpani Parts of the Orchestral Music of the 18th and 19th Centuries. *Percussive Notes* 19:50–59.

Remy, Jacques, ed. n.d. *Ludwig van Beethoven Symphonies*. 2 Vols. Paris: Editions Musicales Alphonsi Leduc.

———. n.d. *Franz Schubert Symphonies*. Paris: Editions Musicales Alphonsi Leduc.

———. n.d. *Robert Schumann Symphonies*. Paris: Editions Musicales Alphonsi Leduc.

Rich, G. J. 1919. A Study of Tonal Attributes. *American Journal of Psychology* 30 (2):121–164.

Rilling, Helmuth. 1984. *Johann Sebastian Bach's B-Minor Mass*. Trans. Gordon Paine. Princeton: Prestige Publications, Inc.

Rimsky-Korsakov, Nikolay. 1964. *Principles of Orchestration*. New York: Dover Publications, Inc.

Rosen, Charles. 1972. *The Classical Style: Haydn, Mozart, Beethoven*. New York: W. W. Norton and Co.

Rosen, Michael. 1998. How to Clear Timpani Heads. *Percussive Notes* 36 (3):47–50.

———. 1997. Mounting Plastic Heads on Timpani with a Mainscrew. *Percussive Notes* 37(1):59–62.

———. 1996. Mounting Calf Heads on Timpani. *Percussive Notes* 34 (2): 57–61.

Rosenberg, Donald. 2000. *The Cleveland Orchestra Story: "Second to None."* Cleveland: Gray and Co.

Rossing, Thomas D. 1982. The physics of kettledrums. *Scientific American* 247:172–178.

———. 1998. *The Physics of Musical Instruments*. New York: Springer.

———. 2000. *Science of Percussion Instruments*. New Jersey: World Scientific Publishing Company.

Rossing, Thomas D. and G. Kvistad. 1976. Acoustics of the Timpani: Preliminary Studies. *Percussionist* 13:90–98.

Rothschild, Fritz. 1961. *Musical Performance in the Times of Mozart and Beethoven: The Lost Tradition in Music*. London: A. and C. Black.

Rushton, Julian. 2006. *Mozart*. New York: Oxford University Press.

Sachs, Curt. 1940. *The History of Musical Instruments*. New York: W. W. Norton.

Sadie, Julie Anne, ed. 1998. *Companion to Baroque Music*. Oxford: Oxford University Press.

Schweitzer, Albert. 1966. *J. S. Bach*. Trans. Ernest Newman. 2 Vols. New York: Dover Publications, Inc.

Seele, Otto. 1895. *Pauken-Schule zum Selbstunterricht*. Leipzig: Breitkopf und Hartel.

———. n.d. *Schule für Pauke*. Zimmermann-Schule, Nr. 120.

Sexton, Peggy. 1998. Secrets of the Timpani. *Percussive Notes* 36 (1):46–49.

Shivas, Andrew. 1957. *The Art of Timpanist and Drummer*. London: Dennis Dobson.

Sibelius, Jean. 1987. *Symphony No. 5*. Philharmonia Orchestra. Esa Pekka Salonen. CBS Records. MK 42366.

Sietz, Frederick. n.d. *Modern School of Tympani Playing*. Indianapolis: Leedy Manufacturing Co.

Simco, Andrew P. 1998. Performing the Timpani Parts to "Symphonie Fantastique." *Percussive Notes* 36 (2):62–65.

———. 1999. The Timpani Parts to Mahler's Symphony No. 2, "Resurrection." *Percussive Notes* 37(3):46–54.

Smart, Sir George. 1907. *Leafs from the Journals of Sir George Smart*. Ed. H. Bertram Cox and C. L. E. Cox. London: Longmans, Green and Co.

Snider, Larry D. 1976. Concert Preparations for the Timpanist. *The Instrumentalist* 31 (5):68–71.

Speer, Daniel. 1974. *Grundrichter Unterricht der musikalische Kunst oder Vierfaches musikaisches Kleeblatt*. Leipzig: Peters.

Spitta, Phillip. 1951. *Johann Sebastian Bach*. Trans. Clara Bell and J. A. Fuller-Maitland. 2 Vols. New York: Dover Publications, Inc.

Stauffer, George B. 1997. *Bach: The Mass in B Minor*. New York: Schirmer Books.

St. Foix, Georges de. 1947. *The Symphonies of Mozart*. Trans. Leslie Orrey. London: Dennis Dobson.

Stevens, S. S. 1934. Tonal Density. *Journal of Experimental Psychology* 17: 585–592.

Stowell, Robin, ed. 1994. *Performing Beethoven*. New York: Cambridge University Press.

Stuart, Robert B. 1977. Rhythmic Clarity for Timpanists. *WW-BP* 16:38–42.

Sullivan, Donald. 1997. Accurate Frequency Tracking of Timpani Spectral Lines. *Journal of the Acoustical Society of America*: 101:530–538.

Sullivan, J. W. N. 1960. *Beethoven: His Spiritual Development*. New York: Vintage.

Tafoya, John. 2004. *The Working Timpanist's Survival Guide*. New York: Carl Fischer.

———. 2006. Unusual Techniques for the Orchestral Timpanist to Accommodate Extraordinary Requests form the Podium. *Percussive Notes* 44 (5):72.

———. 2009. The Finer Points of "Finlandia." *Percussive Notes*: 47(2):18–19.

Taylor, Henry W. 1964. *The Art and Science of the Timpani*. London: John Baker.

Terry, Charles Sanford. 1932. *Bach's Orchestra*. London: Oxford University Press.

———. 1963. *The Music of Bach*. New York: Dover Publications, Inc.

Titcomb, Caldwell. 1956. Baroque Court and Military Trumpets and Kettledrums: Technique and Music. *Galpin Society Journal* 9:56–81.

Tobischek, Herbert. 1997. *Die Pauke*. Tutzing: Hans Schneider.

Tourte, Robert. n.d. *Methode de Timbale*. Paris: Salabert.

Turk, Daniel Gottlob. 1982. *The School of Clavier Playing*. Trans. Raymond H. Haggh. Lincoln: University of Nebraska Press.

Vanderbrock, Othon. 1794. *Traite General de Tous les Instruments a vent a l'usage des Compositeurs*. Paris: Chez Boyer.

Van Ess, Donald H. 1970. *The Heritage of Musical Style*. New York: Holt, Rinehart, and Winston, Inc.

Virdung, Sebastian. 1993. *Musica Getutscht: A Treatise on Musical Instruments*. Trans. Beth Bullard. Cambridge: Cambridge University Press.

West, M. L. 1992. *Ancient Greek Music*. Oxford: Clarendon Press.

White, Charles L. 1963. What Sticks to Use. *Percussionist* 1:1–2.

Zaslaw, Neil, ed. 1989. *Mozart's Symphonies*. Oxford: Oxford University Press.

Zhang, Qican and X. Su. 2005. High-speed Optical Measurement for the Drumhead Vibration. *Optics Express* 13 (8):3110–3115.

Index

Altenburg, Johann Ernst, 61, 64, 73
Arbeau, Thoinot, 61, 63
accent(s)
  cross sticking and, 118
  roll, first note of, 36
  short notes, 48, 90, 92, 111, 117, 151
  stingers, 53
accents, kinds
  agogic, 42–43
  dynamic, 42
  melodic, 42
  metric, 44–45
  tonal, 44
acoustics
  of heads, 7–8
  of mallets, 7–8
  of mutes, 8–9
  of timpani, 3–6, 173 n. 1, 174 n. 5
American style, 14–16
articulation
  acoustics and, 7–8
  Bach's use of, 83–84, 175 n. 4
  Baroque markings and, 74
  Baroque music and, 71–72
  Classical music and, 101–103
  drum heads and, 25–26
  drums and, 4
  drum size and, 64, 91, 92, 143–144, 147, 152
  grip and, 22–23, 29, 68, 115
  Handel's use of, 86
  Haydn's use of, 120–122, 127
  intensifying notes and, 20, 22, 24
  mallets and, 5, 10, 12–13, 66–67
  marcato strokes, 41–42
  methods, 51
  Mozart's use of, 135–136, 142, 143, 144–146, 155–156, 157–159, 160, 161, 163–165
  phrasing and, 40, 45, 56, 92
  playing spots and, 19, 27–28, 52
  playing style and, 16
  tone color and, 25
  using arm and, 23, 24, 25, 115
  using one hand and, 48, 49

Bach, Carl Philipp Emanuel, 73, 74, 75

Bach, Johann Sebastian
    articulation, 71–72, 73, 74–75, 83–84
    B-Minor Mass, 80–84, 175 nn. 2, 8
    Cantata No. 130, 72
    dynamic markings, 67, 70, 73–74, 81–82
    inequality, 70–71, 175 n. 3
    mallets, 83
    phrasing, 71–73
    rhythmic interpretation, 70, 82–83, 174–175 nn. 1–2
    rolls in music of, 75–76, 82
    sacred cantatas, 63
    timpani, use of, 63–64
Baroque era, 61–62
    accents, 75
    articulation markings, 74–75
    doctrine of affections, 62
    double dotting, 69
    dynamic changes, 73–74
    inequality, 70–71
    phrasing, 71–72
    rhythmic patterns, 70, 174–175 nn. 1–2
    subito dynamic markings, 74
    timpani (*see* timpani, Baroque)
Baroque timpani. *See* timpani, Baroque
Beck, John, 31
Beethoven, Ludwig van
    Coriolanus Overture, 37–38
    Egmont Overture, 37, 53–54
    psychology of, 36–37
    rolls, 78–79
    Symphony No. 3, 57
    Symphony No. 5, 57, 78, 175 n. 6
    Symphony No. 7, 31, 40, 41, 43, 48–49, 56
    Symphony No. 9, 31, 42
    Violin Concerto, 49
Berlioz, Hector, 12, 23
Bowles, Edmund, 63–68
Brahms, Johannes
    Symphony No. 1, 19, 22, 23, 24, 25, 29, 46, 47, 49
    Symphony No. 4, 53
    Tragic Overture, 36, 37, 42
    Variations on a Theme of Haydn, 37

Bruch, Max
    Violin Concerto No. 1, 39, 46, 48
Brahm's stick, 37

Classical era, 95–96
    accents, 97–98, 100
    articulation markings, 101, 102, 142
    classical ideal, 95–97
    interpreting timpani parts, 102–103
    orchestra size, 100–101
    poetic feet, 100, 101
    performance practices, 101–103
    periodicity, 99–100
    phrasing, 97, 103, 135, 138
    sonata form, 98–99
    subito dynamic markings, 50, 103, 126, 127, 130, 149
Copland, Aaron, 35
cores. *See* mallet(s)
crescendo. *See also* decrescendo
    Bach's use of, 81
    Baroque music and, 73–74
    building excitement and, 36, 47, 130
    building tension and, 46
    Classical music and, 35, 45–46, 101–102
    Handel's use of, 87–89, 91
    Haydn's use of, 112, 113, 114, 119, 123, 130, 132
    Mannheim Orchestra's use of, 46, 102, 119, 136
    Mozart's use of, 136, 162–163, 166
    notation of, 74
    rising musical lines and, 38–39
    tonal coloring and, 36
    weighting notes, to, 45
cross sticking, 114, 118

decrescendo. *See also* crescendo
    Bach's use of, 73–74, 81
    Baroque music and, 73, 74
    Classical music and, 35, 45–46, 102–103, 114, 136
    drum size and, 26
    falling musical lines and, 38–39, 91

Haydn's use of, 112, 114, 119, 122, 123
"inaudible," 39
Mannheim Orchestra's use of, 102, 136
Mozart's use of, 136
natural, 89
releasing tension and, 46–47
Romantic music and, 35–36
Donington, Robert, 69, 71, 73–74, 75
Duff, Cloyd, v, 5, 15, 17, 21, 40, 47, 53, 169, 176 n. 3
"Duff style," 15
Dvořák, Antonin
"New World" Symphony, 19–20, 39, 49–50
dynamic shading, 45, 74, 81, 88–89, 96, 103

Eisel, Johann, 61, 66–68
embellishments
grace notes, 44, 47–48, 70
Enesco, Georges
Rumanian Rhapsody No. 1, 30

felt
American, 12, 13, 23
covers (*see* mallets)
German, 12, 13, 23
voicing, 13
Firth, Vic, 17
French style, 14–16, 21, 29, 30

German style, 14–16, 21, 30, 33
Goodman, Saul, 30

Handel, George Frideric
articulation, 86–87
double dotting, 85
dynamic markings, 87–90
London timpani, 64–65
mallets, 86
Messiah, 75, 90–92, 130
Royal Fireworks, 39, 85–90
schlagmanieren, 85–85
timpani, use of, 84
Haydn, Franz Joseph
Creation, The, 130–134
George Smart and, 68, 103–104, 106–107, 113

Mass in Time of War, 125–130
rolls, 103–105
Symphony No. 94, 107–112
Symphony No. 100, 112–119
Symphony No. 102, 119–122
Symphony No. 103, 122–125
Hinger, Fred, 11, 20, 51, 169, 174 n. 6

intensifying notes and rolls, 22, 33, 37, 39, 42, 46, 53–54, 55, 91, 166

Knauer, Heinrich, 30

Lalo, Eduard
Symphonie Espagnole, 44–45
legato mallet. *See* mallet(s)

Maier, Joseph, 66
mallet(s), 9–14
balance, 12, 21
Baroque, 67, 174 n. 4
cores, 12
coverings, 12–13, 14, 51, 67, 76
legato, 7, 10, 11, 32–33
sponge, 12, 23
staccato, 7, 8, 12, 13, 14, 18, 28
marcato, 28–29, 41–42, 57, 83, 86–87, 111, 142, 161
Mendelssohn, Felix
Fingal's Cave, 19
Symphony No. 5, 41
Mersenne, Marin, 61, 73
Metzenger, Edward, 27–28
Mozart, Leopold, 71–72, 75, 97, 106, 113, 135, 136, 137
Mozart, Wolfgang Amadeus
accents, 135
articulation, 135, 136–137
Cosi fan Tutte Overture, 158
Don Juan Overture, 102, 153–155
dynamic markings, 45, 102, 136
Impresario Overture, 152–153
Magic Flute Overture, The, 155–158
mallets to use with, 35
Marriage of Figaro Overture, The, 136, 158–159

Mozart, Wolfgang Amadeus
    (continued)
  nonlegato as a norm, 142
  Piano Concerto No. 24, 102,
    160–161
  punctuating cadences, 135
  Requiem, 161–166, 177 n. 5
  rolls, 78, 135, 136–138
  sonata form, 98, 138
  style, 19, 23, 35, 134
  symphonic development, 138–139
  Symphony No. 32, 139
  Symphony No. 35 "Haffner,"
    139–143
  Symphony No. 39, 143–146
  Symphony No. 41, 146–152
Mozart mallet, 11
muffling
  articulating notes and, 29, 51–52
  Baroque music and, 87
  clarifying notes and, 50, 103
  avoiding dissonance and, 50,
    119
  Haydn's use of, 111, 114, 127
  Mozart's use of, 147, 152–153, 158
  ending phrases and,, 50, 108,
    114, 118
mutes
  acoustics of, 8–9, 10
  articulating passages and, 51, 91
  kinds of, 40–41, 52
  Haydn's *The Creation* and, 131
  Haydn's Symphony No. 102 and,
    104, 120, 121, 127

nonlegato, 41–42, 103, 135–136,
    139–140, 142, 143–145, 149,
    151, 158, 160–161, 162

Pfundt, Ernst, 30, 44, 80, 176 n. 11
portato, 41, 98
Poulenc, Francis, 38, 58
Purcell, Henry, 80

Quantz, Johann Joachim, 69, 71,
    73, 75, 96, 113

Rachmaninov, Sergei
  Piano Concerto No. 2, 42
rolls
  Bach's use of, 82, 83, 85, 86

Baroque notation problems, 69,
    75–80
Beethoven's use of, 78, 79
beginning, 18, 36
darkening or lightening, 19, 20,
    24, 32, 33, 36, 49
double stroke, 75–80
drum choice and, 25
hairpin (*messa di voce*), 19, 47, 120
Handel's use of, 85–86, 90, 91
Haydn's use of, 104, 108–109,
    110, 111, 112, 113, 114,
    117–118, 119, 121, 122–124,
    125–126, 127, 131–132
intensify/relax, 55
"inaudible decrescendo," 39
measured, 27
Mozart's use of, 102, 136–138,
    139–141, 142, 144, 153–154,
    157–158, 161, 166
single stroke, 77–80, 82, 83, 86,
    113, 138
stinger, ending with, 25, 53
tense, 22
tests for rolling
  Haydn, 104–105
  Mozart, 136–138
  Pfundt, 176 n. 11

schlagmanieren, 73, 82, 85, 86, 90,
    92, 175 n. 9, 176 n. 12
Schubert, Franz
  Unfinished Symphony, 79
Schweitzer, Albert, 62, 70, 73, 81
Seele, Otto, 30
Sibelius, Jean
  Finlandia, 31, 36, 37, 53, 174 n. 1
  Symphony No. 5, 174 n. 2
Smetana, Bedrich
  Moldau, The, 37
Speer, Daniel, 61, 67–68, 85–86
staccato mallet. *See* mallet(s)
stingers, 53
Strauss, Richard
  Burlesque, 42–43

Tafoya, John, 174 n. 1, 176 n. 4
Tchaikovsky, Peter I.
  Nutcracker, 79
  Overture to Romeo and Juliet, 22,
    33, 52, 55

Swan Lake, 79
Symphony No. 4, 53
Symphony No. 5, 51
Symphony No. 6, 31, 56
timpani, Baroque
  bowl shape, 65–66, 173
  grip, 68
  heads, 66
  mallets, cartwheel and ball, 67–68
  mallets, covered, 66–67
  playing style, 68
  size, 62–65
timpani, professional
  Adams, 3, 4
  Clevelander, 3
  Goodman, 4
  Hinger, 4
  Ringer, 3, 4, 10
  Schnellar, 3
  Walter Light, 3, 4, 6, 7, 8, 10, 17

timpani heads
  calfskin, 16–18, 28, 78, 166
  insert rings, 17
  Remo and Evans, 16–18, 28
tonal shading, 21, 30, 49–50, 59, 67, 90
tremolo. *See* rolls
Turk, Daniel Gottlob, 40, 72, 75, 96–98, 102, 113, 137

Virdung, Sebastian, 61, 63, 66

Wagner, Richard, 36
  Die Meistersinger zur Nürenberg, 44
  "Funeral Music," 45

Yancich, Mark, 32
Yancich, Paul, 16, 29, 47